SureTrak Project Manager® 2.0

User Manual

Please send your comments about SureTrak to:

Primavera Systems, Inc.
Two Bala Plaza
Bala Cynwyd, PA 19004
Telephone: 1-610-667-7100
FAX: 1-610-667-0652
Internet: sttech@primavera.com
World Wide Web site: www.primavera.com

Expedition, Primavera Project Planner, P3, TimeSheet Professional for Primavera, and SureTrak Project Manager are registered trademarks; Monte Carlo, Parade, DataStore for Primavera, ReportSmith for Primavera, and Concentric Project Management are trademarks of Primavera Systems, Inc.

All other brands and product names are trademarks or registered trademarks of their respective companies.

 This manual is printed on recycled paper.

Table of Contents

Part 4: Updating and Managing the Schedule

Part 6: Creating and Printing Layouts and Reports

Preface

This manual is designed to help you work with SureTrak Project Manager. SureTrak helps you plan and control your project schedule, from planning the activities needed to complete the project to tracking project progress and determining how quickly it can be completed.

Read this chapter to understand how to use this manual and how to access customer support.

Using SureTrak Documentation, Help, and Tutorial

If you haven't used SureTrak, are new to formal project scheduling techniques or Critical Path Method (CPM) scheduling, start with the *Getting Started in SureTrak* part to learn the details.

Organization This manual is organized into six parts:

Part 1: Getting Started in SureTrak This part explains formal project management techniques, including establishing types of work and workperiods, developing a network of activities, identifying resources necessary to complete the project, and updating progress on your work. This part also contains setup instructions for network and standalone versions of SureTrak and information on upgrading from Microsoft Project to SureTrak.

Part 2: Developing Projects SureTrak enables you to create new projects by adding and modifying activities, creating relationships between these activities, and developing calendars for a project. This part includes instructions for assigning resources, costs, and revenue, building a schedule, and defining the critical path for your project.

Part 3: Organizing Project Information This part concentrates on setting up the coding structure (Work Breakdown Structure and Activity Codes), grouping and sorting activities, selecting activities by filter, and summarizing project data.

Part 4: Updating and Managing the Schedule This part explains how to create target dates for your project, update your activities' progress and resources and costs, analyze resource use with profiles and tables, and level resources to resolve overallocation problems. It also contains information on sending projects and activities to other users using E-mail.

Part 5: Customizing Project Information This part discusses how you can customize the appearance of your project. It includes instructions for controlling the activity columns, Bar chart, and PERT view; and explains SureTrak's configuration options, toolbars, and other display characteristics.

Part 6: Creating and Printing Layouts and Reports SureTrak includes reports and graphics that communicate information about projects. This part discusses how to use SureTrak layouts and reports to create the view you want. It also discusses how to customize and print the project.

SureTrak Help System SureTrak provides an extensive Help system to supplement the documentation. Use SureTrak Help to access information about commands and dialog boxes. SureTrak Help also includes context-sensitive step-by-step procedures for performing each SureTrak function. To access Help, start SureTrak and choose Help.

Tutorial SureTrak provides several online lessons that teach the basic skills required to use SureTrak. To access the tutorials, start SureTrak and choose Help, Tutorial.

Documentation Conventions

The SureTrak manual generally tells you how to perform functions using the mouse to perform menu commands such as *choose File, Save*. In most cases, step-by-step procedures are presented as numbered lists.

For information about customizing the toolbars, see the *Customizing SureTrak's Default Options* chapter.

A picture of an icon often is shown to the left of steps. Icons help you quickly access dialog boxes or perform an action. Many icons are available from the default toolbar. Other icons appear on the editing toolbar and print preview toolbar. You can customize each toolbar to contain the icons you want by adding or removing icons.

In procedural steps, a plus sign (+) between two keys indicates that you should press and hold down the first key while pressing the second key, for example, Ctrl+F12. A comma between two or more keys indicates that you should press and release each key in order, for example, Alt,F,O.

This manual uses the following terms; you should become familiar with them so that the concepts and steps are easier to understand.

Term	Meaning
Arrow keys	Press one of the four directional keys: the up, down, right, and left arrow keys.
Choose	Use the mouse or key combination to choose a specific command or option and initiate an action.
Click	Press the left mouse button once.
Double-click	Press the left mouse button twice, in quick succession.
Right-click	Press the right mouse button once.
Drag	Press the left mouse button and hold it down while you move the mouse pointer to the desired location; then release the button.
Point	Move the mouse pointer so that it rests on an item.
Select	Highlight an item by clicking it with the mouse or using the arrow keys.
Icon	A graphic representation (on any SureTrak toolbar) of a SureTrak command that provides quick access to a dialog box or carries out a command instantly. For example, a graphic representation of a clock represents the Schedule Now command.

Obtaining Technical Support

If you have a question about using SureTrak that you cannot resolve with information in the SureTrak documentation, online Help, or your network administrator, call SureTrak Technical Support at the times and locations listed below.

If your question involves output, you may want to fax an example to Technical Support before calling.

Before you call Technical Support, try running SureTrak alone to see if the problem or issue continues when no other programs are in memory. If the problem persists, call from a phone near your computer in case the SureTrak Technical Support representative has questions about your computer or system. Also, have SureTrak running on your computer and have the documentation with you. Be prepared to give specific details about the problem and any notes about the problem, for example, if you received an error message.

Have your serial number and company information ready; to display your serial number, choose Help, About SureTrak.

Office	Time Zone	Hours	Telephone	FAX	Internet Address*
Bala Cynwyd, Pennsylvania, U.S.A.	EST	8:00-7:00 (Mon-Fri) 9:00-2:00 (Sat)	1-610-667-7100	1-610-667-0652	sttech@primavera.com
London, England, U.K.	GMT	8:30 - 5:30 (Mon-Fri)	44-181-748-7751	44-181-748-2846	uksttech@primavera.com
Toorak, Victoria, Australia	EAT	8:30 - 5:00 (Mon-Fri)	61-03-9888-4644	61-03-9888-4744	austech@p3aus.com.au

*You can also address Primavera's World Wide Web site at http://www.primavera.com

 In the United States, we periodically and randomly monitor technical support calls to ensure that we are providing the highest quality of support to you.

Primavera maintains a bulletin board so you can dial in and ask questions, download files, or start a dialogue with other users of Primavera products. The telephone number for the bulletin board is 1-610-660-5833. Use your communication software (such as CrossTalk, Procomm, or Carbon Copy in "terminal mode") to access the bulletin board. You are prompted for your name and serial number when logging on (there is no connect charge, but telephone toll charges are billed). When you register, you'll receive information about how to use the board.

If you have a CompuServe account, you can ask questions through the TCMVEN forum. You can also download and upload files using the Primavera Library. Ask your questions in the Primavera section of the TCMVEN forum. The Primavera system operator responds to your questions; other CompuServe subscribers can also read your message and enter a response. Address private messages (to be read by the Primavera system operator only) to user 76004,2245; via the Internet, the CompuServe address is 76004.2245.

All Primavera products are backed by comprehensive support and training. To request product literature, contact your local dealer, call Primavera at 1-610-667-8600 or send your request via E-mail to **sales@primavera.com** in the United States. In the United Kingdom, call 44-181-748-7300 or E-mail your request to **intlsale@primavera.com**.

Getting Started in SureTrak

In this part: *Installing SureTrak*

Upgrading from Microsoft Project

Project Management Basics

Part 1 explains how to install SureTrak Version 2.0 on your computer, whether it is a standalone PC or part of a network, and whether you are installing from the CD-ROM or from diskettes. Part 1 also discusses upgrading from Microsoft Project to SureTrak and how to make the transition smoothly.

If you are new to SureTrak, read this part to understand the fundamentals of project management — planning, controlling, and managing. You will learn about the process of how to think carefully about what you want to accomplish, laying out all the steps, and obtaining the resources necessary to carry out those steps in order to accomplish your project goals.

Installing SureTrak

Getting started with SureTrak is easy. Install it, acquaint yourself with the SureTrak window, and you're ready to work.

You can set up SureTrak for different types of working environments and run SureTrak on different kinds of computers. You can also experiment with sample projects or run the tutorial to familiarize yourself with SureTrak.

Read this chapter to learn how to install SureTrak on a server, workstation, or standalone computer and to become familiar with SureTrak directories and files.

Before You Begin Setup

Before installing SureTrak, make sure you have the appropriate hardware, software, and operating environment:

Hardware and software requirements

- 486/66 or better computer

- Approximately 38 MB of hard disk space, depending on installation options selected

- 8 MB RAM required, 16 MB recommended

- Graphics card compatible with Microsoft Windows 3.1, such as VGA

- Microsoft Windows 3.1, Windows for Workgroups 3.11, Windows NT 3.51 or higher, Windows 95, OS/2 3.0 or higher

- VGA or SuperVGA monitor

- Mouse

Choosing a method of installation SureTrak Setup provides five installation options: Typical, Custom, Minimal, Server, or Workstation.

A *typical installation* requires 38 MB of disk space and includes all SureTrak program files, tutorials, online help, clip art, sample scripts, and sample projects. Choose Typical Installation to install all SureTrak files to your computer's hard drive, or to a network drive. If your computer does not have sufficient available space, Setup informs you that you need to remove unnecessary files from your hard drive. If you do a Typical Installation to your hard drive, you will only be able to run SureTrak on that computer. If you do a Typical Installation to a network drive, SureTrak can be run on the network only from the computer on which the Typical Installation was made.

A *custom installation* enables you to select the SureTrak components you want to install. Choose this option if you do not have enough space on your hard drive to install all SureTrak components, or if you do not plan to use some components, such as the sample projects or clip art. The optional SureTrak components are the tutorial, online help, sample projects, sample SoftBridge scripts, and Open DataBase Connectivity (ODBC) drivers.

A *minimal installation* requires 16 MB of disk space and enables you to perform a quick install of SureTrak. Choose this option to install only those files necessary to run SureTrak.

A *server installation* installs a shared copy of SureTrak on a network file server. Like a custom installation, the server installation enables you to choose the SureTrak components you want to install. Choose Server Installation to install SureTrak on a network file server where several users can share access to it. After completing a Server Installation, you will need to do a Workstation Installation from each computer that will share access to this network copy of SureTrak. This option enables a network administrator to install SureTrak with all the necessary files for setting up workstations without installing SureTrak on his or her own computer or drive.

A *workstation installation* sets up the icons for the workstation from a previously installed server version. The workstation installation includes all SureTrak 2.0 programs included with a typical installation but does not set up SureTrak on the computer from which you are running Setup.

Directories created during installation Whichever option you choose, when you install SureTrak, the Setup program creates the following directories.

Directory	Files in Directory	Can Directories Be Made Read Only?
\STWIN	Program files	Yes
\STWIN\PROJECTS	Sample projects	No; each file in the directory can be made Read Only
\STWIN\LAYOUTS	Shared layouts	No; each file in the directory can be made Read Only
\STWIN\CLIPART	Windows metafiles	Yes
\STWIN\SCRIPTS	Sample Basic scripts	No; each file in the directory can be made Read Only
\STWIN\TEMPLATE	Template projects	Yes
\STWIN\HTMFILES	HTML sample files	No
\STWIN\ODBC	Files required by ODBC	Yes, on server installations only
\STWIN\SYSTEM	Files required for Object Linking and Embedding (OLE) 2.0	Yes, on server installations only

For more information about making a file Read Only, see *Multiuser Considerations* later in this chapter.

Sample projects When you perform an installation, SureTrak copies the following sample projects to the \PROJECTS directory in the SureTrak program directory.

Project Name	Project Description
APEX	The design, engineering, expansion, and modernization of a manufacturing plant. This sample project is an example of a P3 project group with member projects.
SWDV	The machine enhancement, reporting systems enhancements, and routine maintenance of a financial institution. This is an example of a project group with member projects.
BILLING	The development and implementation of a customized billing system. This is an example of a standalone SureTrak project.
ENGR	The design, engineering, submittal tracking, installing, construction, testing, and start-up for a new automobile plant. This is an example of a project group with member projects.
RADIO	The licensing, purchasing, staffing, marketing, engineering, testing, and launch of a new radio station. This is an example of a standalone SureTrak project.
VIDEO	The creative development, client approvals, audio and video production, and manufacturing ramp-up of a marketing video. This is an example of a standalone SureTrak project.

 If you are installing SureTrak from a disk, SureTrak copies a subset of the sample projects to the \PROJECTS directory.

Reinstalling SureTrak

After you have initially installed SureTrak, you may need to update existing files, reconfigure SureTrak, or add or remove serial numbers from a server installation. When you run the Setup program again, Setup displays the SureTrak Project Manager Setup dialog box, indicating that it detects a previously installed copy of SureTrak. The dialog box provides information about each reinstallation option. Choose the option then click OK to continue.

Installing SureTrak on a Standalone Computer

The SureTrak Setup program makes installation easy and provides help if you have a question or experience a problem.

To install SureTrak

1 Start Windows and close any open applications. Insert the SureTrak CD in the CD-ROM drive.

   If installing using diskettes, place Disk 1 in the floppy drive.

2 From Windows 95, click Start then click Run. From Windows 3.1, choose File, Run from Program Manager.

3 Type **d:\setup** (where **d:** is the letter of the CD-ROM drive you are using). Or, type **a:\setup** (where **a:** is the letter of the floppy drive you are using). Click OK.

4 The SureTrak Setup program then loads the InstallShield Wizard.

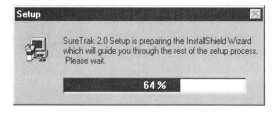

To verify that SureTrak Setup is the only open program, press Alt+Tab.

5 SureTrak Setup recommends that you close all other open programs before you continue. If necessary, close any open programs, then click Next to continue.

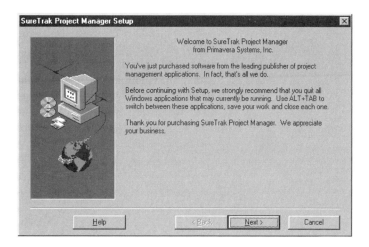

6 SureTrak Setup displays the Primavera License Agreement that describes the terms for using SureTrak. Click Accept to continue the installation. SureTrak Setup then analyzes your system before continuing the installation.

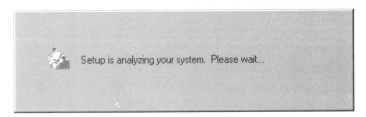

7 SureTrak Setup prompts you for the SureTrak 2.0 Key Disk, which contains the serial number for your licensed copy of SureTrak. Insert the Key Disk in the floppy disk drive, removing Disk 1 if you are installing by diskette. Click OK.

8 Enter your name and company name, and then verify them. To view this information later, choose Help, About SureTrak. Click Yes to continue.

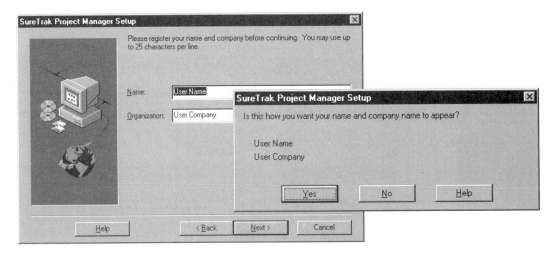

9 Specify the path to install SureTrak. To accept the default path, click Next. To search for a path, click Browse. If you specify a path that does not currently exist, SureTrak prompts to create the new directory.

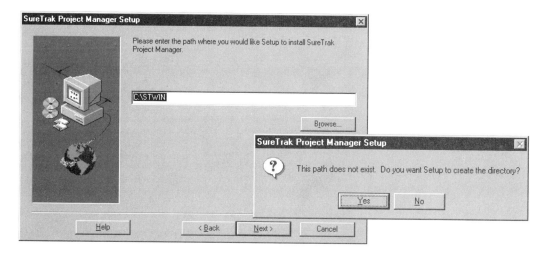

For a description of each option, see *Before You Begin Setup* earlier in this chapter.

10 SureTrak Setup offers several types of installation. Choose an installation type depending on the disk space available on your computer and the options you want to install.

SureTrak detects if you are running Setup from the server installation and displays the workstation installation option.

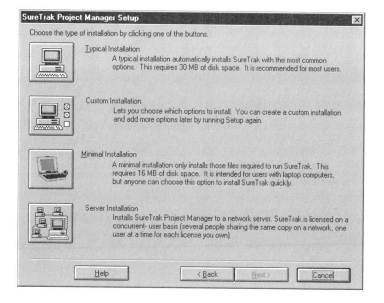

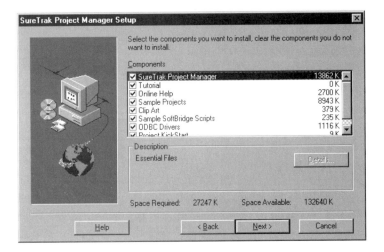

If you are upgrading from Microsoft Project to SureTrak, be sure to load the Help files, then read the For Microsoft Project Users *topic.*

11 After you choose an installation option, specify whether to configure SureTrak for Project Groups capabilities.

If you choose Project Groups, SureTrak uses Project Groups as the default project type. Project names must be exactly four characters. You can open projects interchangeably in Primavera Project Planner (P3) or SureTrak without changing the project type; you will be able to use SureTrak's ODBC capabilities.

For more information about project types, see the *Working with Project Groups* chapter.

If you choose SureTrak, it will be the default project type; SureTrak runs faster with SureTrak project types. Project names can contain up to eight characters. To open a SureTrak project in P3, you must first save the project as a Concentric (P3) project type in SureTrak; to use SureTrak's ODBC capabilities, you must first save the project as a Project Groups, Concentric (P3), or Finest Hour project type.

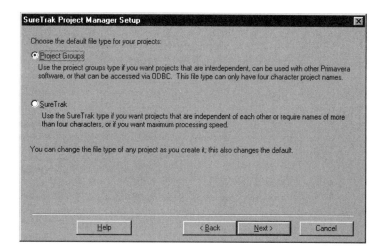

12 SureTrak prompts you to choose whether to overwrite project templates, layouts, and sample projects. Click Yes to overwrite all existing files with new files. Click No if you do not want SureTrak Setup to modify those files.

13 SureTrak Setup also prompts you to choose whether to restore the settings in the existing STWIN.INI file to the default settings. Click Yes to overwrite any custom settings you have created.

14 Choose a program group name. SureTrak Setup creates a Primavera program group by default. SureTrak adds the following programs to the Primavera group.

Program Name	Description
SureTrak Project Manager 2.0	The SureTrak application, version 2.0.
SureTrak Uninstall	Enables you to remove SureTrak and its associated applications from your computer.
SureTrak Online Manuals	Opens the online version of the SureTrak documentation. (CD-ROM version only.)
SureTrak 2.0 Readme.txt	Contains information about SureTrak, changes to the documentation, and details about new features in SureTrak 2.0.
SureTrak 2.0 Tutorial	The SureTrak 2.0 tutorial.

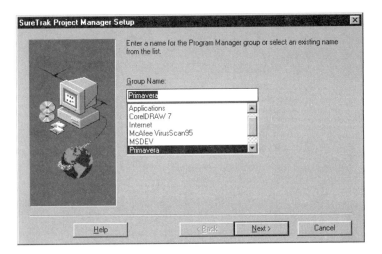

15 SureTrak informs you whether SureTrak was successfully installed. Mark the Install Adobe Acrobat Reader 3.0 checkbox to use Adobe Acrobat to view SureTrak online manuals and information. Then, choose to register SureTrak either online or offline.

If you choose online registration, SureTrak opens the World Wide Web browser and places you on a Web page that contains an online registration form to fill out.

If you choose offline registration, SureTrak opens a Help file that contains a registration document you copy to Microsoft Word and fill out.

16 Click Finish to complete Setup.

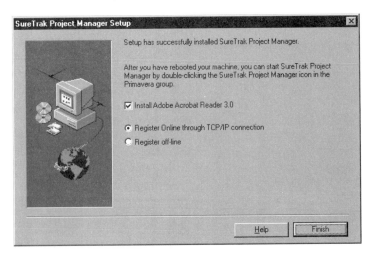

17 If you marked the Install Adobe Acrobat Reader 3.0 checkbox, SureTrak prompts you whether to install Adobe Acrobat at this time.

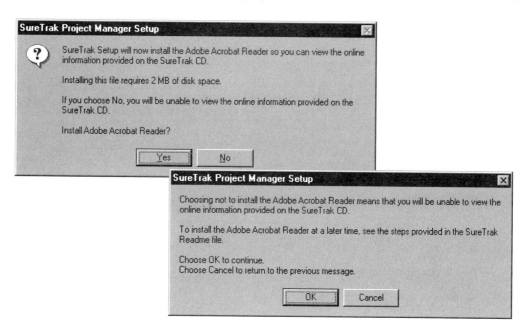

Installing SureTrak on a Network Server

If you purchase a LAN Pack or more than one copy of SureTrak, you can install it once on a network fileserver and have several users access the software from their workstations at the same time. More than one user can then open and share projects stored on the fileserver. The number of users who can use SureTrak at the same time depends on the number of serial numbers your installation has. Each copy of SureTrak has one serial number. There must be one purchased SureTrak license for each user.

To enable Setup to display the Server Installation option, make sure you specify a network drive when prompted.

 You cannot remove serial numbers from LAN Packs.

After you create a directory structure for your network and operating environment, use the SureTrak Setup program to install SureTrak, as described earlier in this chapter.

Once you install SureTrak on a network server, you may want to make some of the directories Read Only to protect the files from being overwritten.

Network software SureTrak successfully runs with the following network software:

- Artisoft Lantastic 5.0 or greater

- Banyan Vines 5.53 revision 6 or greater

- Microsoft NT Server 3.5 or greater

- Microsoft Peer to Peer Networks

- Novell Btrieve NLM (Brequest) 6.10B or greater

- Novell NetWare 3.11 or greater

For more information about network server installations, see *Multiuser Considerations* later in this chapter.

- PC-NFS 5.1

Setting Up User Workstations

After SureTrak has been installed on a network server, perform a Workstation Installation for each computer on the network that will use SureTrak. Make sure the computer on which you want to perform the workstation installation has Read Write access to the following files and their drives and directories:

- AUTOEXEC.BAT
- CONFIG.SYS
- WINDOWS directory
- WINDOWS\SYSTEM directory
- SSCDB.STW file in the \STWIN directory (or in the directory pointed to in the STWIN.INI file).

To set up user workstations

1 From Windows 95, click Start then click Run. From Windows 3.1, choose File, Run from Program Manager.

2 Click Browse and select SETUP.EXE from the network drive and directory where SureTrak is installed so that Setup displays the Workstation Installation option. For example, if SureTrak was installed in F:\STWIN, run F:\STWIN\SETUP.EXE on each workstation to install the necessary programs on the workstation.

3 Follow the steps for *Installing SureTrak on a Standalone Computer*, presented earlier in this chapter.

4 During Setup, specify the location of SureTrak on your network for the project files.

When you install SureTrak on a network, SureTrak adds a default STWIN.INI file to the program directory with the filename STWININI.DEF. Network administrators can customize this file using Notepad. Then, when an individual user runs the Workstation Setup option in the SureTrak Setup program, SureTrak uses this file as the starting STWIN.INI file.

 Individual users can make changes to their workstation copies of SureTrak that may affect their STWIN.INI files. The workstation STWIN.INI files will then differ from the STWININI.DEF file on the server.

Multiuser Considerations

SureTrak can be installed on a network and files can be shared. SureTrak provides project-locking; only one user can work in the same project at the same time in Read Write mode. When you open a project in SureTrak with Read Write access, other SureTrak users can open the project in Read Only mode only, which means that they can make changes, but can only save them to another project name.

 When working with project groups and member projects, initial users can access different member projects of the same project group in Read Write mode.

Making the STWIN directory Read Only In a multiuser environment, you may want to make some directories Read Only to protect specific program files from accidental deletion.

To make the \STWIN directory Read Only, perform these steps:

1 Create a directory on the network and assign it read, create, write, erase, file-scan, and modify rights. For example, create a directory called \STWORK.

2 Move the SSCDB.STW file from the \STWIN directory to the new directory.

3 Edit the STWIN.INI file by adding a WORK setting to the Directories section that points to the new directory. For example, [Directories] WORK=F:\STWORK.

4 Through your network security program, assign the \STWIN directory Read Only rights.

5 Restart SureTrak to apply this change.

Adding and removing serial numbers If you install SureTrak on a network server, you will probably need to give additional users access to SureTrak from time to time. Choose the Add or Remove Serial Numbers option to add serial numbers so other users can use SureTrak; this requires purchasing additional copies of SureTrak.

After you install multiple SureTrak serial numbers on the network server, several users can access the same network copy of SureTrak simultaneously—one user per installed serial number. However, once you install those serial numbers on the network drive, you cannot use those licenses on standalone computers.

To add serial numbers to an existing SureTrak installation

1 Insert the CD-ROM or Disk 1 in the appropriate drive and run the Setup program from any computer already set up as a SureTrak workstation.

2 When Setup displays the first SureTrak Project Manager Setup dialog box, click Continue.

3 When Setup displays the next dialog box, choose Add or Remove Serial Numbers, then click OK. Setup lists the serial number(s) currently installed for the network version of SureTrak. The bottom of the dialog box displays the serial number(s) you can add from the diskette.

4 Click Add. SureTrak adds the new serial number to the Installed Serial Numbers table. If the table now lists two serial numbers, two users can access SureTrak simultaneously on a first-come, first-served basis.

Starting SureTrak

After installing SureTrak, follow this procedure to start SureTrak:

1 From Windows 95, click Start, Programs, SureTrak, and then select SureTrak Project Manager 2.0.

From Windows 3.1, double-click the SureTrak 2.0 icon in the Primavera group.

2 If you selected password protection during Setup, enter your user name and password.

3 SureTrak displays a welcome window. Choose to run the tutorial, start a new project using the Project KickStart Wizard, start a project using a SureTrak template, open an existing project, or open the last edited project.

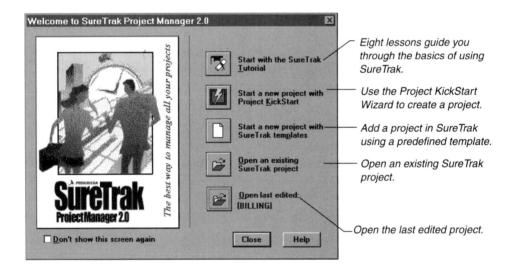

Upgrading from Microsoft Project

If you're upgrading from Microsoft Project, SureTrak makes the transition smooth and easy. SureTrak has many features similar to those of Microsoft Project, as well as features unique to SureTrak.

Read this chapter to gain an understanding of how to switch to SureTrak after using Microsoft Project.

Converting Data from Microsoft Project to SureTrak

SureTrak enables you to open a file created in Microsoft Project 3.0 or 4.0 in SureTrak and to save it either as an .MPX file or a SureTrak project. Using the .MPX file for opening Microsoft Project files in SureTrak enables you to use SureTrak with project data you have already entered in Microsoft Project.

To open a Microsoft Project file in SureTrak

1 In Microsoft Project, save the file in .MPX 3.0 format.

2 In SureTrak, open the file, or project, as an .MPX file.

SureTrak and Microsoft Project features You can compare SureTrak's versatile Activity form, Activity columns, and Bar chart with Microsoft Project's task sheet, task form, and Gantt chart. Also, with SureTrak's Activity form, which corresponds to Project's task form, you can quickly input and review an activity's codes, constraints, costs, dates, predecessors, resource assignments, revenue, successors, and update information.

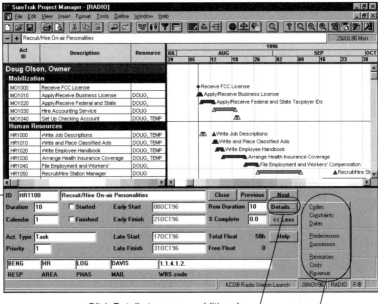

SureTrak's Activity form corresponds to Project's task form; use it to add information about each activity.

Click Details to access additional information about activities.

For more information about using scripts, see the *Customizing SureTrak's Default Options* chapter.

Using SureTrak scripts To convert all zero-duration activities to start milestones simultaneously, use the ZER2MIL script. This is especially useful if you are pasting activities from another application, like Microsoft Project.

Comparing Features

Compare SureTrak's Resource profile with Microsoft Project's resource graph. In SureTrak, you can display quantity, costs, revenue, net, budget, earned value, and BCWS (budgeted cost for work scheduled). The profile can also display totals per time interval, peak (the highest amount during each time interval), or average (the average amount during each time interval) values.

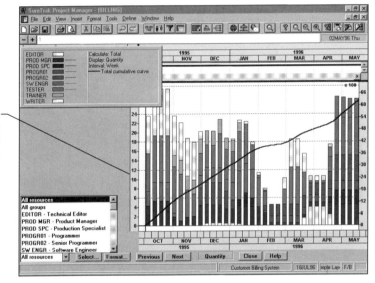

Choose View, Resource Profile to display information for a single resource, several resources, or a defined group of resources, as well as for one or more activities.

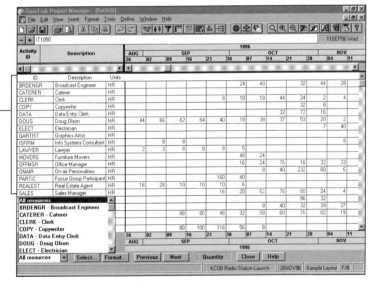

View resource information in tabular form by displaying the Resource table (choose View, Resource Table).

For more information about printing, see the *Printing Project Information* chapter.

Printing a project If you are upgrading from Microsoft Project to SureTrak, you'll enjoy total control over printing. You can print any element in the SureTrak window singly or in combination with other elements. For example, you can print a report that contains only the Resource table, or you can print the Resource profile in combination with the Bar chart, omitting or including the Activity columns.

You can choose to view all pages of a project in Print Preview.

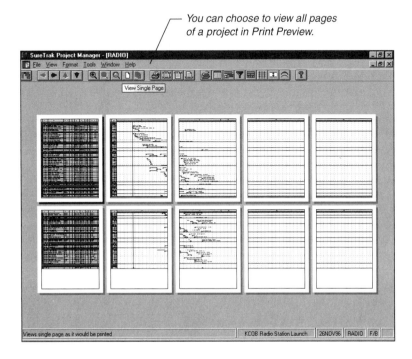

SureTrak's interactive Print Preview enables you to look at multiple pages, a single page, or details of a page. Moreover, you can change the appearance of your project—screen colors, which activities are displayed and how they are organized, the timespan and time interval of the timescale, row height, sight lines, and more—right in Print Preview.

Performing Familiar Tasks

Use the following table to find the SureTrak features that correspond to specific Microsoft Project features, and to take advantage of SureTrak's proven project management approach as well.

Microsoft Project Feature	SureTrak Command(s)	SureTrak User Manual Chapter
View	View, Layouts	Using SureTrak Layouts
Task Sheet	Format, Columns	Customizing the Bar Chart View
Task Form	View, Activity Form	Adding Activities
Task Detail Form	View, Activity Detail, any menu item	Adding Activities
Preferences	Tools, Options	Customizing SureTrak's Default Options
Link tasks	Edit, Link Activities	Linking Activities with Relationships
Unlink tasks	Edit, Unlink Activities	Linking Activities with Relationships
WBS codes	Define, WBS Codes	Creating a Work Breakdown Structure
Outlining	Format, Organize Insert, Indent Insert, Outdent	Adding Activities; Organizing and Summarizing Activities
Print preview	File, Print Preview	Printing Project Information
Filters	Format, Filter	Selecting Activities by Filter
Reports	Tools, Reports	Creating SureTrak Reports
Leveling	Tools, Level	Leveling Resources
Updating	Tools, Schedule	Updating Activities
Gridlines	Format, Sight Lines	Customizing the Bar Chart View
Customizable Toolbar	Tools, Customize, Toolbar	Customizing SureTrak's Default Options
Resource, Base, Standard, and Project Calendars	Define, Calendars	Defining Project Calendars
Resource Sheet	Define, Resources	Building a Resource Plan
Resource Usage View	View, Resource Table	Analyzing Resource Use with Profiles and Tables
Resource Form	View, Activity Detail, Resources	Building a Resource Plan

Microsoft Project Feature	SureTrak Command(s)	SureTrak User Manual Chapter
Resource Graph	View, Resource Profile	Analyzing Resource Use with Profiles and Tables
Fixed-duration and Effort-driven Tasks	View, Activity Form	Adding Activities
Macros	Tools, Basic Scripts	Online help

In addition, enjoy these features found exclusively in SureTrak:

- Publishing reports on the World Wide Web

- Project KickStart Wizard that helps you create new projects easily

- Activity codes for organizing your project

- Combined Gantt and resource charts

- Progress Spotlight that highlights activities that should have progressed

- Discrete base calendars for activity scheduling

- Suspend and resume dates for interrupted activities

- Varying resource availability

- "Before and after" resource leveling comparison

- Resource leveling priority, compare preleveled and leveled dates, and establish up to six different limits for a resource for different timeperiods.

- Resource and Bar chart legend onscreen

- Flexible organization: you can change the way you group activities instantly, just by switching your organizational method to a different activity code or other data item. You are no longer stuck to a rigid outline format in which you have to drag activities to change their grouping.

- Draw a relationship to any activity, whether or not it is visible; select a successor from a drop-down list.

- Establish group page breaks: when your activities are grouped into sets, you can start each group on a new page.

- Print all columns, or visible columns only (choose File, Page Setup).

- Context-sensitive help on demand, item-by-item (F1) or dialog-by-dialog (Help button).

Project Management Basics

In this chapter:

If you are new to formal project management techniques, or if you just want to review the concepts, read this section to understand project management and to identify the basic steps in project planning and controlling. This section provides an overview of building a schedule by creating activities necessary to achieve the project objective, adding project calendars, linking activities, and identifying and assigning the resources necessary to complete the project.

This section also provides an overview of refining the project schedule, including updating information data to show how the project is progressing, and calculating the effect of the schedule's current status on its outlook, including the completion date.

What is Project Management?

A project is a unique, one-time endeavor with a specific start and end, usually confined to a budget. Whether a project involves the creation of a new product, the relocation of a manufacturing facility, or the installation of a new computer system, successfully completed projects are the means by which a company builds its future. Projects "make things happen" for companies.

A project differs from ongoing work. Ongoing work focuses on repetitive activities—daily operations such as manufacturing, selling, distribution, or customer service—performed repeatedly, ideally with increasing productivity. A project is unusual. In many companies, a project is foreign to the daily routine. It may pull people away from their usual work, asking them to focus on achieving a deliverable result such as a new product design, a procedure for improving productivity, or a company-wide sales conference. Other enterprises are innately project-oriented—pharmaceutical research, aerospace, software development, construction, and most engineering disciplines, for example.

Project management helps you plan and control any kind of project by using a dynamic schedule—a schedule that provides a realistic model of a project's anticipated behavior, then changes to match the project's actual behavior. Because SureTrak uses your own project information to predict the effects of your decisions, you can be sure that each decision you make will move the project efficiently toward completion.

Project planning involves detailed consideration of all the activities needed to complete the project; realistic estimates of how long each activity will take; and relationships between activities. The relationships you establish between activities affect how the project proceeds, and how quickly it can be completed. Together, these elements of project management answer the questions, "What must be done?" and "When must it be done?"

Project planning also involves many other questions that you need to ask yourself, such as the following:

- What is the overall duration of this project?
- How much money will it cost to complete a project?
- How much equipment and materials are needed?
- How many people do we need at each stage of the project?
- How can we avoid scheduling conflicts?

- How will a delay affect labor requirements?

- Who needs to receive information about progress?

- What kinds of reports will I prepare?

The remainder of this chapter helps you understand the steps you should follow for planning and managing your own projects successfully.

Understanding the Process

SureTrak provides many tools that help you plan and control your project schedule. But where do you begin? What do you do first? As you become more familiar with project management and SureTrak, you will develop your own way of organizing projects and entering data.

The key elements that should guide your decisions in project management are planning, controlling, and managing.

Planning process Planning the project means thinking about and documenting what needs to be done—defining and coordinating specific activities and work tasks, establishing types of work and timeframes, assigning and allocating resources to activities, and developing an acceptable budget.

Controlling process Controlling the project means staying on course—tracking work progress and actual costs, comparing progress and costs to the baseline, devising workarounds, and recommending action.

Managing process Managing the project means communicating as accurately and timely as possible the schedule's progress—what has happened—and what may happen.

The flow chart on the next page shows the typical steps for creating a basic schedule. First, create a list of activities and tie them together using relationships. Calculate and review the schedule according to a timescale, assign the necessary resources required to complete the activity, then customize and print your presentation.

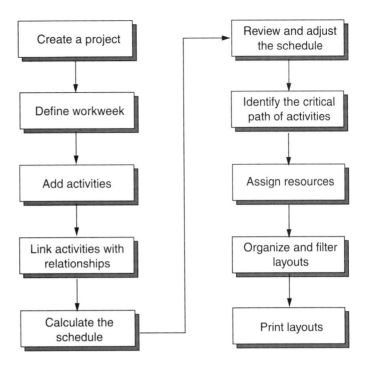

After you create a basic schedule, you may want to define and enhance dictionary data, such as activity coding, or refine the schedule by modifying calendar definitions.

The following topics provide more detail on each of these steps.

Building a Schedule

Begin building your schedule by creating a new project, adding activities, and defining relationships between them.

Defining the workweek Before you enter detailed project data, establish a general calendar for the project—a "global" calendar. The global calendar defines the project's holidays, typical workdays, and typical workhours. Then, create more specific calendars, called base calendars. Base calendars are copies of the global calendar which you modify to contain exceptions to, or differences from, the global calendar.

For more information about assigning calendars to activities, see the *Defining Project Calendars* chapter.

Use base calendars to schedule both activities and resources: work on some activities may occur during different hours and days than the rest of the project, and some resources, such as employees or difficult-to-operate equipment, may work different hours and days than the rest of the project. You can also specify calendars for project resources.

For information about activities, see the *Adding Activities* chapter.

Adding activities Once you create a project and its calendars, you're ready to divide the project into general kinds of work, and then into smaller pieces of work until you have pieces that are small enough to be discrete activities. You will know when you've arrived at the activity level, because an activity

- Comprises one kind of action,

- Has a predictable duration,

- Applies to one stage or portion of a project,

- Involves the same resources throughout,

- Is unlikely to be interrupted, and

- Is the responsibility of one person or entity.

Developing a network of activities You now understand the building blocks of your project—activities. Next, determine how activities logically connect to one another to build a schedule. Start by focusing on a specific activity: determine which other activity or activities control its start or finish.

For each activity, ask yourself what must be done before this activity can start, and what controls the start of this activity. Each answer—each activity that controls this activity—is a predecessor to it. An activity can have more than one predecessor—more than one activity that controls its start or finish.

For an easy-to-understand path through your project, avoid open-ended activities except for one at the beginning and one at the end of your project.

For more information about predecessors and successors, see the *Linking Activities with Relationships* chapter.

When considering how to link activities, focus on their sequence, not on their timing. At this point in the planning process, your purpose is to determine and model which activities control which other activities. Focus on logical relationships between activities (this-happens-before-that relationships). It is unnecessary to establish redundant relationships between activities, only those that involve direct control of one activity by another.

Avoid creating unnecessary open ends. An open end is an activity that has either no predecessors or no successors. The first activity or activities in your projects should be open ends—they should not have any predecessors. The last activity or activities should also be open-ended—they should not have any successors. All the activities between the first and last activities in a project should have predecessors and successors.

Identifying the critical path Once you establish links between activities, SureTrak calculates a schedule from the first activity to the last, and identifies the schedule's critical path—the sequence of activities that must be completed "on time" to ensure that the project finishes on time.

If you have several open-ended activities, SureTrak calculates the schedule on the premise that it has multiple stopping and starting points: the open ends. SureTrak regards each activity with no successor as the end of a miniproject within the project, and it has its own critical path through the project; a project with too many open ends has too many critical activities.

SureTrak uses the network of relationships you create between activities to calculate two sets of dates for each activity: early dates and late dates. First, it starts at each open-ended activity that has no predecessors, and calculates a forward pass, resulting in early start and early finish dates for each activity—the earliest dates an activity can possibly finish, based on its predecessors, its predecessors' predecessors, and so on.

Then, SureTrak calculates a backward pass. Starting at each open-ended activity that has no successors, which it considers the end of the project or an independent portion of the project, it calculates the late start and finish dates for each activity, based on when its successors must start, when its successors' successors must start, and so on.

SureTrak calculates the critical path based on activity durations and the relationships between activities. To shorten the critical path, you can adjust activity durations and relationships. Try some of these strategies to get your schedule back on track:

- Review duration estimates to identify the activities you can shorten.

- Add resources to critical activities so you can reduce their durations.

- Add more hours to each workday, or add more workdays to calendars. For example, make holidays or weekend days into workdays, or extend workday hours if you're managing a project in hours.

- Overlap activities by converting some critical finish to start relationships to start to start relationships. For example, if Documentation and Testing activities are linked finish to start, investigate whether testing can start some time (lag) after Documentation starts, rather than waiting for it to finish.

For more information about defining the critical path, see the *Creating and Fine-Tuning the Project Schedule* chapter.

- Divide long-duration activities into several shorter-duration activities so you can overlap them with start to start relationships.

Building a Schedule with SureTrak

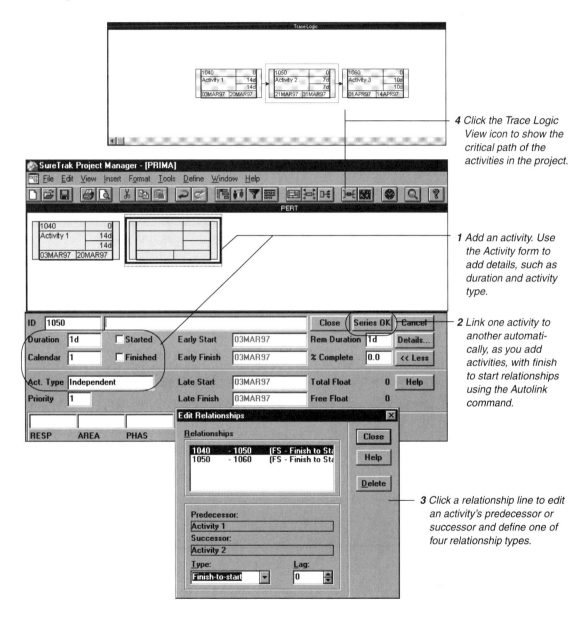

4 Click the Trace Logic View icon to show the critical path of the activities in the project.

1 Add an activity. Use the Activity form to add details, such as duration and activity type.

2 Link one activity to another automatically, as you add activities, with finish to start relationships using the Autolink command.

3 Click a relationship line to edit an activity's predecessor or successor and define one of four relationship types.

Adding Resources to the Schedule

Resources are what it takes to get the job done, such as labor, equipment, materials, or cash. You can use SureTrak to schedule a project without scheduling resources, and you may want to use it that way the first time. However, you'll eventually want to use SureTrak's powerful resource scheduling and management capabilities.

First, in the Resource Dictionary, define a list of resources needed to complete the project. To define a resource, specify a name, description, and unit of measure.

The unit of measure is the way you break down the resource when you assign it. The units for pipe might be LF for linear feet; units for labor resources might be HR for hour. If you want SureTrak to calculate costs for activities, assign these costs to resources as hourly values. For example, a salaried employee at $28,000 per year costs $13.46 per hour.

If a resource also generates revenue per hour, such as those for which you bill on a time-and-materials basis, enter an hourly revenue amount also. For example, you may pay a hydrological engineer $65 per hour, but you bill a client $100 for each hour of the hydrological engineer's time. Enter $65 as the cost, and $100 as the revenue, for this resource.

As part of the definition of a resource, indicate whether it is driving— whether it controls the duration of activities to which it is assigned, overriding any duration you may have specified for the activity. Think of a driving resource as an important or scarce resource whose work is preeminently important to the accomplishment of its activities. You can designate any resource as driving some activities and not driving others; this definition only establishes its default. For example, a manager might drive approval activities, but not documentation activities.

For more information about leveling, see the *Leveling Resources* chapter.

Indicate whether a resource should be leveled. Leveling resolves excess demands on resources by delaying lower-priority activities until the resources they require are available.

As you define a resource, assign a base calendar to it, then modify the resulting resource calendar to accommodate the resource's unique requirements. A resource calendar can be identical to the base calendar except for a worker's vacation or a machine's regular maintenance shutdown; or it can be quite different, with a longer or shorter workweek and different holidays.

For more information about assigning resources to activities, see the *Building a Resource Plan* chapter.

Set limits for any resources that are not unlimited—how much of this resource is available at any one time? The limits you provide enable SureTrak to graph resource overallocation on a Resource profile. If you level resources, SureTrak also uses these limits to adjust the schedule so that resource overallocation is reduced or eliminated.

Overallocating resources SureTrak schedules activities as though resources are unlimited: as though any number of people, any number of machines, any quantity of supplies is available when needed. If you want SureTrak to schedule activities based on limited resources, you can level resources; SureTrak identifies areas where resource demand exceeds resource supply, then delays lower-priority activities. The result is a leveled project, one that is achievable under current resource availability.

For more information about leveling a project, see the *Leveling Resources* chapter.

To level resources, you must establish the limit of each resource that has one. SureTrak levels only resources with limits. Establish limits when you define each finite resource; the Limits section enables you to define up to six different limits per resource, so you can model changing resource availability during the project. For example, four technicians may be available during the first month, five during the next 3 months, and only two for the last 3 weeks.

Adding and Assigning Resources

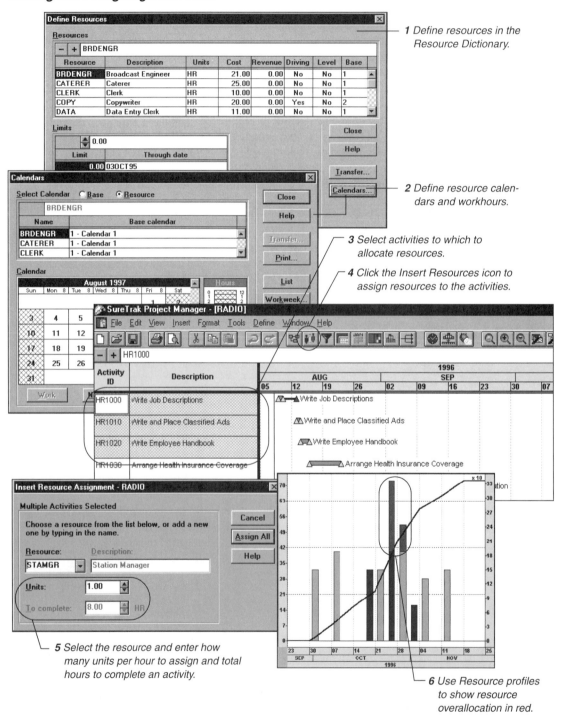

1 Define resources in the Resource Dictionary.

2 Define resource calendars and workhours.

3 Select activities to which to allocate resources.

4 Click the Insert Resources icon to assign resources to the activities.

5 Select the resource and enter how many units per hour to assign and total hours to complete an activity.

6 Use Resource profiles to show resource overallocation in red.

Organizing and Summarizing Your Project

SureTrak offers three tools to help you break down or group high-level work into smaller divisions, and eventually into activities: work breakdown structures (WBS), outlining, and activity codes. Although you can create complex projects without them, using one of these techniques may help you organize work more efficiently and thoroughly.

The primary difference between creating a WBS and outlining is that a WBS contains a dictionary; you define WBS codes that identify the levels, assign descriptions to identify the WBS codes on reports, and assign a specific WBS code to each activity. If you use an outline, SureTrak controls the outline numbering based on how you promote and demote activities within the outline; no descriptions are associated with an outline structure.

For more information on WBS codes, see the *Creating a Work Breakdown Structure* chapter.

Using a Work Breakdown Structure (WBS) A work breakdown structure is useful for complex projects, helping ensure that the resulting schedule accounts for every major component and detailed activity. High levels in the WBS organization summarize project information for management reports, while lower levels provide control of work performance.

For more information on outlining, see the *Adding Activities* chapter.

Using an outline Adding activities in outline form enables you to build your project's structure as you go, rather than defining a structure first. By specifying broad areas of the project and then narrowing down the work within each broad area, you will create a hierarchy of activities. Enter each level of the outline as if it were an activity. Then, indent levels that are subordinate to another level to create the outline. Continue this process as needed. The lowest levels consists of your project activities.

Using activity codes Another coding option, activity coding, is more commonly used to group activities, rather than divide them into smaller units of work. Activity codes are completely customizable; you decide how you want to group activities, then define those codes and assign them to groups of activities. Like WBS codes, you first define activity codes, then assign them to activities. After you assign these codes to groups of activities, you can categorize them in reports.

For more information on activity codes, see the *Creating Activity Codes* chapter.

SureTrak comes with three default activity codes: responsibility, phase, and area. When you assign codes to activities, you will be able to organize activities by responsibility, phase, and/or area—or by any other activity code you create that is appropriate for your company and project.

Organizing and Summarizing a Project

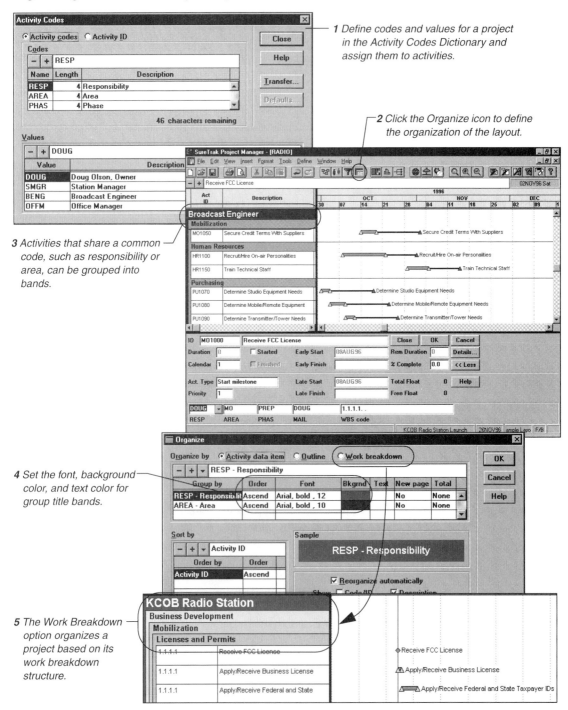

1 Define codes and values for a project in the Activity Codes Dictionary and assign them to activities.

2 Click the Organize icon to define the organization of the layout.

3 Activities that share a common code, such as responsibility or area, can be grouped into bands.

4 Set the font, background color, and text color for group title bands.

5 The Work Breakdown option organizes a project based on its work breakdown structure.

Updating to Show Progress

When enough progress has been made on a project that you suspect the original forecasts no longer accurately represent the project's outlook, it's time to update. Depending on the level of detail you are tracking, the update frequency can be daily, weekly, or monthly—or, for some short, highly intensive projects, even hourly.

Some companies use updating to keep historical records of each phase of a project, but most use it to look ahead. After you update a project to show when activities actually took place, SureTrak recalculates dates for each activity that is not complete. Some of those activities probably had predecessors among the activities that were updated, so they may be affected by any variation from the plan. Any activity that wasn't completed on its early dates may delay its successors, its successors' successors, and so on throughout the project.

You do not have to guess how these deviations and delays affect future activities. SureTrak calculates the results objectively: what's been accelerated, what's been delayed, and whether the project finish is affected. That's one of the most important benefits of precedence-based project scheduling.

You can follow either of two basic approaches to update a project: estimating progress for the entire project as though it is going as planned, and updating each activity individually to show how it meets or deviates from the plan. Many well-planned projects go mostly, but not entirely, according to plan, so you will probably use a combination of the two approaches: estimating progress for areas of the project that are approximately on schedule, and then updating each exception individually.

Both approaches to updating use the data date—the date through which your project is current. Before the project starts, the data date is the same as the start date, because the project is current as of its start. After the project starts, its data date changes every day; when you update the project to reflect the status of the real project, you decide the date to which you're updating it, and make that date the new data date.

Updating a project progressing according to plan If your project is going well, you can estimate progress for the entire project by clicking the Spotlight icon or by dragging the data date line. Then you can use the Update Progress dialog box to update as of the new data date. If only certain sections of it are on time, select those activities first and estimate progress only for them. You can also choose to estimate resource use as of the new data date; this information can be useful for later comparison to originally budgeted costs, especially if you separately update the resources that were used in greater or lesser quantities than expected.

Updating a project not progressing according to plan If your project is not going according to plan—many activities are occurring out of sequence or many activities are taking longer or shorter amounts of time than expected—you'll probably want to enter update information for each activity individually. When you update activities individually by using the Update Activity dialog box, you are concerned with these information items:

The actual start and finish dates may be earlier or later than originally planned.

- *Remaining Duration:* the amount of time in hours, days, weeks, or months an activity takes to complete.

- *Percent Complete:* the portion of the activity that is complete.

- *Actual Start Date:* the date the activity actually began.

- *Actual Finish Date:* the date the activity actually ended.

For more information on updating the project, see the *Updating Activities* and *Updating Resources and Costs* chapters.

You update all four of these items as of the data date. If you update on Tuesday morning, but you update the project as of Friday night, you'll want to record these items as of Friday night, even though some activities that were not complete as of Friday night are now complete. It's important for all activities in a project to be updated as of the same date—the new data date.

Updating a Schedule with SureTrak

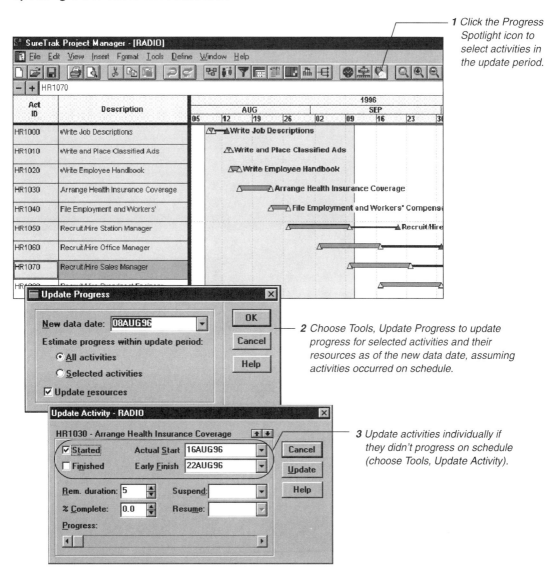

1 Click the Progress Spotlight icon to select activities in the update period.

2 Choose Tools, Update Progress to update progress for selected activities and their resources as of the new data date, assuming activities occurred on schedule.

3 Update activities individually if they didn't progress on schedule (choose Tools, Update Activity).

Developing Projects

In this part:

This part describes the steps involved with developing a new project. First, establish the project's objective, what it is you want to accomplish and the best way to achieve that goal. Then, define the activities needed to meet your goal and how long each activity will take; build relationships between them; establish project calendars and workperiods to reflect a typical workweek; and assign resources to activities. You will learn how to develop and present project data using both the Bar chart and PERT views.

After you establish the project, either as a standalone project or as part of a group, the next step is calculating a schedule, then adjusting and fine-tuning it by reviewing activity dates.

Creating SureTrak Projects

When you start SureTrak, you can create a new project or open an existing one. You can also open projects created using Microsoft Project and save them as SureTrak projects.

If you are working in a Concentric Project Management environment that includes using Primavera Project Planner (P3) in conjunction with SureTrak, SureTrak can open, save, back up, and restore projects in P3 format as well as projects in SureTrak format.

Adding a New Project

SureTrak enables you to add a new project in two ways. You can choose File, New and add your new project using the New Project dialog box. The New Project dialog box enables you to add a project for use in a project group or Concentric Project Management environment that includes P3. You can also create a new project using the Project KickStart Wizard when you first open SureTrak.

To create a new project using the Project KickStart Wizard
Click the Project KickStart Wizard icon in the welcome window when you first open SureTrak. Or, choose Tools, Wizards, Project KickStart Wizard to open the Wizard.

For detailed steps on using the Project KickStart Wizard, refer to the online help.

The Project KickStart Wizard guides you through eight steps that help you define the project phases, goals, tasks, anticipated obstacles, and people. It helps develop a clear overview of the project you want to create and the steps needed to complete it. With the Project KickStart Wizard, you can assign resources to activities and review the activity list in an outline format. After you have completed the eight steps to defining a project in the Project KickStart Wizard, you can open the project you created as a SureTrak file. Once in SureTrak, you can build on the project. For example, you can define relationships, and refine durations, calendars, and dictionaries.

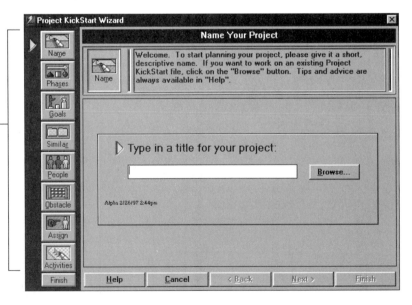

With the Project KickStart Wizard, you can easily define each aspect of your project.

To create a new project using the New Project dialog box
Choose File, New then type a unique project name in the Project Name
field. If you add a project that is a SureTrak type project, you can enter an
eight-character project name. If you add a project that is a Project Group
or Concentric (P3) type project, you can enter a four-character project
name only. Choose the type of project and specify a template. Identify
revisions to the project in the Number/Version field. Give the project a
specific title and identify the project's company or client. Click OK.

Specify the earliest date work can begin on the
project. If no date is specified, the start date
defaults to the computer's system date.

Enter a project finish date only if you
want to constrain the project end date.

Store the project anywhere
on your workstation or
network fileserver.

For more information about
SureTrak templates, see *Using*
Template Projects later in this
chapter.

Depending on the type of project
you create, specify whether you
want to measure activity durations
in days or hours.

For more information about
project groups, see the
Working with Project Groups
chapter.

Adding a project to a project group If the project you are adding is
part of a group, mark the Add This New Project To A Project Group
checkbox. Project group associates the project with an existing project
group. Project ID identifies the project with a two-character prefix that
precedes all Activity IDs for that project.

Choosing the project file type The Type field in the New Project
dialog box specifies whether the project will be a standalone project in
SureTrak, Project Groups, Concentric (P3), or in Finest Hour file format.

SureTrak displays the list of file types in the Open, Save As, Backup, Restore, and Project Check-in/ Check-out dialog boxes (access from the File and Tools, Project Utilities menus).

Choose SureTrak if the project is an independent project that is not part of a project group (also known as a standalone project). Choose Project Groups if the project is a collection of related or unrelated projects that share project data, such as Activity Code and Resource Dictionaries. Choose Concentric (P3) when you will exchange project data between SureTrak and P3. Choose Finest Hour when you will exchange project data with Finest Hour users.

For more information about the appearance of the project window, see the *Customizing the Bar Chart View* chapter.

When you create a new project, SureTrak opens a Bar chart view containing empty Activity columns on the left and an empty Bar chart on the right. When you add project Activity IDs and descriptions in the Activity columns, SureTrak creates the activity bars for the project.

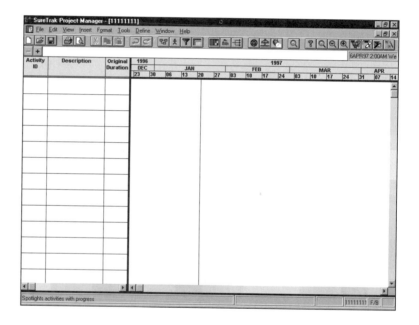

Setting Up Project Options

For more information about setting up default options for your project, see the *Customizing SureTrak's Default Options* chapter.

Before you add new projects or immediately after you create a new project, you may want to adjust some default options. You can customize how to display durations, a default activity type, rules for updating resources, how often to automatically save, along with many other options. Use the Options dialog box (choose Tools, Options) to set default options for your project.

Using Template Projects

If your projects involve work you've done in other projects, or if they share resources with other projects, you can use information from those projects. Any time you create a new project, you can use an existing project as the new project's template to reduce the time required to create a new project.

Select a template as a starting point for the new project.

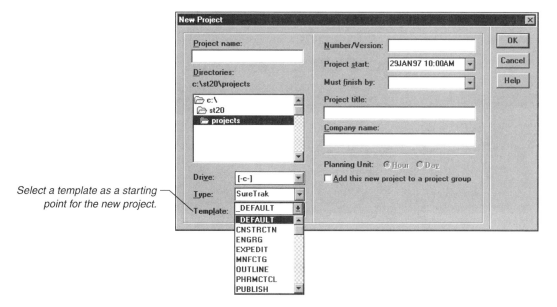

For more information about template projects, see *How to Create A Template Project* in SureTrak Help.

To open a template Choose File, New to display the New Project dialog box. Select a template from the Template drop-down list. SureTrak provides templates for various types of projects/industries that include a set of predefined activity codes. Use one of these templates, or use any existing SureTrak project as a template. Place the template's .DIR file, along with the files containing other information you want to include in the template, in the TEMPLATE directory under the SureTrak program directory.

Opening a Project

You can open any project originally created in SureTrak or in other applications. This enables easy communication between users of SureTrak and P3 and easy conversion of projects from other applications.

For more information about layouts, see the *Using SureTrak Layouts* chapter.

When you open an existing project, SureTrak loads the last layout you used with the project in the project window. The project window appears as it was formatted when you last saved the project. Layouts control the project window contents and the appearance of each item.

Select the project you want to open and click OK or double-click the project.

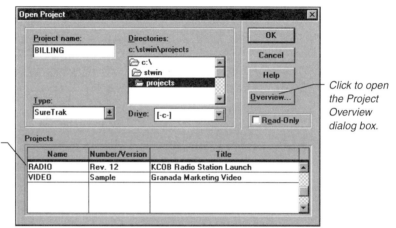

Click to open the Project Overview dialog box.

To open a project created in SureTrak or another application
Choose File, Open to display the Open Project dialog box. Select a project type from the Type drop-down list. Projects of the type you have selected appear in the Projects section. If necessary, change the drive and/or directory to locate the project.

Opening Concentric or Project Groups projects You can open a Project Groups project as a Concentric (P3) project and a Concentric (P3) project as a Project Groups project. When you do, SureTrak handles resource limits, target dates, and calendars differently for each type of project, as described in the following table.

Item	Project Groups	Concentric (P3)
Resource limits	Uses decimals.	Rounds values (integers).
Target dates	Uses standard SureTrak target dates.	Uses P3 target project dates; dates are not editable.
Calendars	Nonworkhours are customizable for each workday in the workweek.	Nonworkhours between workhours (such as lunch hours) are the same every day of the workweek.

For more information about layouts, see the *Using SureTrak Layouts* chapter.

To open several projects at one time You can open up to nine SureTrak projects at one time, depending on the size of the projects and the capacity of your computer. A project window contains each open project, identified by a title bar across the top of the window. The project you are working with is the active project, which SureTrak displays on top of any other open project windows. Use standard Windows operations to switch between projects or other applications.

Click the title bar of a cascaded project to make it the active project.

The project in front, RADIO, is the active project.

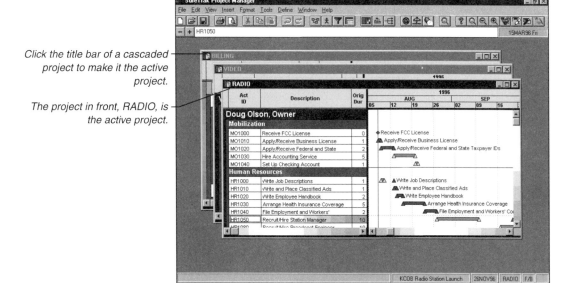

Accessing a Project used by Multiple Users

Several users can open the same project simultaneously. The first version is a Read Write version and all subsequently opened versions are Read Only; this means that more than one user can open a project, but only the first person to open it can save changes.

Similarly, one user can open the same project more than once, but can only make and save changes to the first version opened.

This feature is especially useful for "what-if" analysis on a project, because you can look at it with and without changes, or with different layouts, at the same time.

For example, to make changes to a project and compare the changed version to the project before those changes, open the project twice. SureTrak identifies the second version with a 2 in the title bar; make the changes to the first version, which has no number.

First version of RADIO opened.

Second version of RADIO opened.

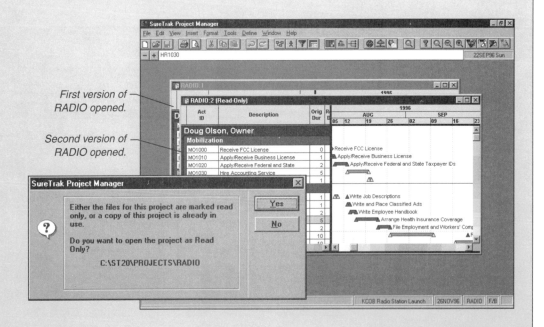

Previewing Project Overview Information

Without opening the project, you can review overall project information and specify information about the project as a whole. You can show this information in a page header or footer when you print project information.

Click to open the selected project.

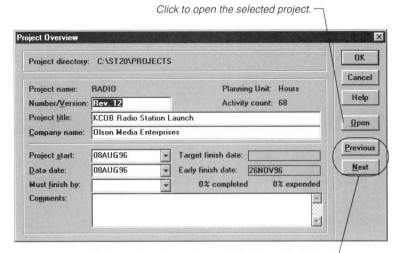

Click to review the previous or following project listed in the Projects section in the Open Project dialog box.

To display a project overview Choose File, Open and then click Overview. Select a project name from the Projects section, then click Overview. You can edit the project data date, start date, deadline, or version.

Much of this information is identical to that entered in the New Project dialog box when the project was created.

The Project Overview dialog box also provides information about the project's status, such as early finish date, target finish date, activity count, percent complete, and percent expended. These items are calculated by SureTrak and cannot be edited in this dialog box.

Saving a Project

 Since SureTrak is a memory-resident program, you need to save your changes to project data. You should also save your project to avoid losing data in the event of a hardware or power failure. Save a project to a new name if you want to perform "what-if" analysis on a copy of the project.

For more information about backing up projects, see Backing Up and Restoring a Project *later in this chapter.*

Saving the active project to the same file name Saving a project (choose File, Save) overwrites previous information, making old information irretrievable unless you make a backup copy before saving.

Saving a project to a new file name or type You can create a new project that is an exact copy of the active project as it exists at the moment by saving the active project with a new name. Choose File, Save As and enter the new filename for the copy in the Project Name field. Specify a file type in the Type field, then click OK.

If you select the P3 file type, SureTrak limits the project name to four characters.

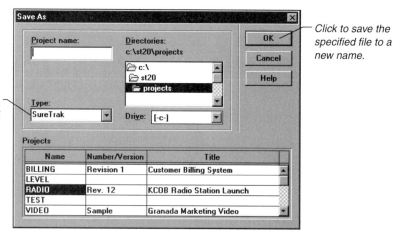

Click to save the specified file to a new name.

For details about automatically saving projects, see the Customizing SureTrak's Default Options *chapter.*

Saving all open projects When you configure SureTrak to save all open projects automatically (choose Tools, Options, then click the General tab), you needn't save your projects periodically. For example, you can specify that you want SureTrak to save your projects every 15 minutes; in the event of power failure, you won't lose more than 15 minutes of work.

Closing and Deleting a Project

To close a project, you can exit SureTrak, or you can close the active project and leave SureTrak open so that you can work on a different project. When a project finishes, you can delete it to free more space on your hard drive. If you create several "what-if" versions of your project, you can remove the projects you no longer need.

For more information about backing up projects, see *Backing Up and Restoring Projects* later in this chapter.

To close a project Choose File, Close to close a project without exiting SureTrak. Choose File, Exit to exit SureTrak. If you try to close or exit a project without saving, SureTrak prompts you to save the project. Saving a project overwrites previously saved information.

To delete a project You can delete projects from SureTrak, but, you must close an open project before you can delete it. Choose Tools, Project Utilities, Delete and select the project you want to delete.

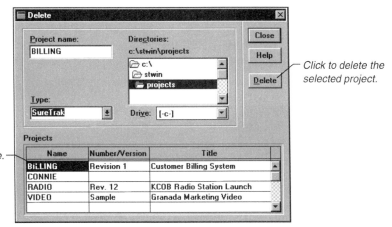

Select a project to delete.

Click to delete the selected project.

For more information about saving layouts, see the *Using SureTrak Layouts* chapter.

When you delete a project, SureTrak also deletes the project layout with the same name. To save the layout for use with other projects, use the Layouts dialog box (choose View, Layouts) to save the layout to a new name before deleting the project.

Backing Up and Restoring a Project

Although saving your project periodically provides a temporary backup, use a backup copy in the event of hardware failure or data loss caused by a power outage. You can also use backup copies of a project as records of project progress at specific times that can help you plan future projects.

SureTrak can create a backup copy of a project on any drive and directory on your computer or on a diskette. SureTrak can back up SureTrak, P3, and Finest Hour projects. Backup to diskette to send the project information to a client or to coworkers. You can also specify that you want SureTrak to save the project in a compressed format, which saves disk space and stores all project information in a single file with a .PRX extension.

If you back up the project in the compressed format, you must later use SureTrak to restore the project if you want to use the backup. If you back up the project in uncompressed format, the files are backed up individually and you can copy them with Windows Explorer, File Manager, or MS-DOS commands.

To make a backup copy of a project Choose Tools, Project Utilities, Backup, then select a project from the Projects section. Select a project type from the Type drop-down list. In the To field, select the drive and directory to which you want to copy the project. Click Backup.

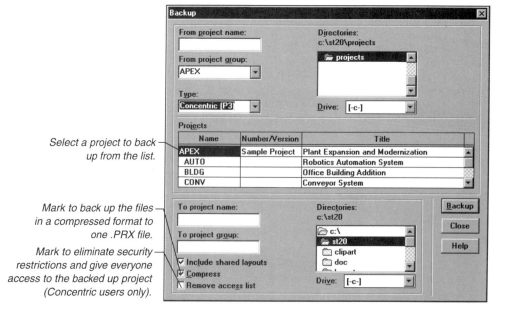

Select a project to back up from the list.

Mark to back up the files in a compressed format to one .PRX file.

Mark to eliminate security restrictions and give everyone access to the backed up project (Concentric users only).

For more information about backing up and restoring projects, see the *Working with Project Groups* chapter.

To restore a project from a backup Choose Tools, Project Utilities, Restore. Select the backed-up project name from the Projects section. Select a file type from the Type drop-down list. Specify the drive and directory where you want to restore the project. Click Restore. SureTrak restores the project with the project name it had when it was backed up.

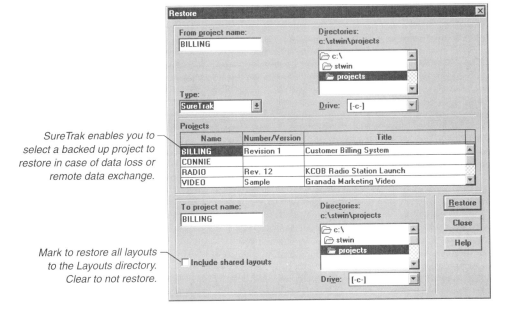

SureTrak enables you to select a backed up project to restore in case of data loss or remote data exchange.

Mark to restore all layouts to the Layouts directory. Clear to not restore.

Restoring member projects You must back up member projects using the Backup utility if you plan to move projects between offices or computers. SureTrak does not allow you to simply make a copy of the member project using Windows Explorer or File Manager. Backup enables you to extract the member project's activities, dictionaries, and calendars as a project that can be restored on another machine.

Adding Activities

With SureTrak, you can decide what activities are needed to accomplish your goal. An activity is one kind of action — such as design, build, or test — applied to one portion of a project.

You can easily add and modify activities and establish how long activities will take to complete. If some activities are repeated during the project, you can use copy and paste techniques to avoid re-entering them.

Read this chapter to learn how to enter activity information in the Bar chart and PERT views, and how to specify activity details for your project.

Assigning Activity IDs

Each Activity ID in a SureTrak project must be unique. Enter your own Activity IDs or use the IDs provided by SureTrak. You may want to structure these IDs to reflect cost codes, member projects, or similar activities. Activity IDs can consist of up to 10 alphanumeric characters.

To assign Activity IDs SureTrak automatically generates Activity IDs in increments of 10, starting with 1000 when you add a new activity. This increment enables you to add activities with IDs between those already entered, so you can preserve the correct sequence of Activity IDs when sorting them. For example, to add an activity between 1000 and 1010 when the activities are sorted by Activity ID, assign it an ID of 1001, 1002, or any other unused Activity ID between 1000 and 1010.

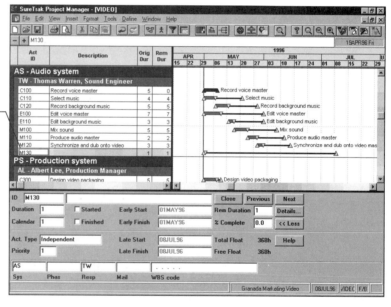

SureTrak adds new Activity IDs in increments of 10.

When SureTrak increments an ID by 10 to generate a new ID, it checks whether the new ID already exists in the schedule. If it exists, SureTrak moves in increments of 10 until it finds an unused ID. Deleting an activity or changing its ID frees that ID to be used by a new activity.

For more information on adjusting Activity IDs, see the *Customizing SureTrak's Default Options* chapter.

 If you want SureTrak to increment Activity IDs with a value other than 10, adjust the Increase Activity ID By field in the Options dialog box (choose Tools, Options, then click the General tab).

You can override the default starting ID to enter the Activity ID you want to start with. For example, if you enter AK2000, SureTrak increments subsequent Activity IDs as AK2010, AK2020, AK2030, and so on. If you then type over AK2030, replacing it with MP2000, SureTrak increments the next Activity ID as MP2010.

To change Activity IDs You can change an activity's ID by typing over the original ID in the Activity form. SureTrak automatically changes the ID everywhere it occurs in the project. For example, if the activity is assigned as a predecessor to another activity, SureTrak changes the ID in that activity's Predecessors detail form.

For more information about setting up intelligent IDs, see the *Creating Activity Codes* chapter.

Building intelligent Activity IDs You may want to build intelligence into Activity IDs by assigning letters or numbers that reflect cost codes, departments, member projects, or types of activities. Using Activity ID codes increases your ability to organize, select, and summarize activities.

The first two characters of a member project Activity ID identify the project group. The first character must be a letter; the second character can be either a letter or a number. You can use the remaining eight characters to create unique IDs for the member project.

Entering activity descriptions You can also identify an activity with a description of up to 48 characters. If you show the description in an Activity column, SureTrak wraps the displayed description if it doesn't fit on one line; widen the column or increase row height to show more of the description without scrolling.

Searching for Data Items

Use the Find dialog box as a quick filter to find Activity IDs, activity descriptions, activity codes, resource names and descriptions, log text fields, dates, and WBS codes in the Bar chart and PERT views, whether or not they are shown in the current layout. Find highlights any or all occurrences of the value you specify in the Value field; it selects the activity and highlights the column containing the value, if it is in the current view.

Choose Edit, Find, then specify a search on all data items or a specific data item in the Data Item field. Specify a value for the data item for which you are searching in the

Value field. Click Find Next to select the next item that meets the criteria you specified in the Data Item and Value fields. Click Find All to select all occurrences at once of the data item that you wish to find. SureTrak searches for data items beginning with the current activity and bases search order on the order of the items in the project window. If Find locates the value in an activity that is summarized, filtered, or hidden, SureTrak gives you the option to display the activity in the layout.

For more information about using filters, see the *Selecting Activities by Filter* chapter.

Search all data items or select a single data item from the drop-down list.

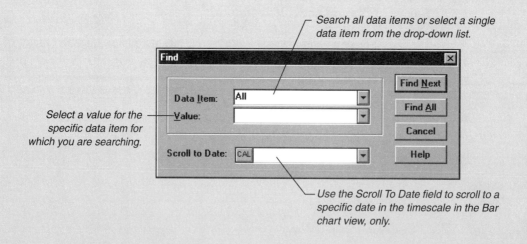

Select a value for the specific data item for which you are searching.

Use the Scroll To Date field to scroll to a specific date in the timescale in the Bar chart view, only.

Adding Activities in the Bar Chart View

The Bar chart view provides a spreadsheet-like method to add activities to the project. When you add activities in the Bar chart, specify only the data that appears in the Activity columns.

To add an activity in the Bar chart view

1 Choose Insert, Activity or click ⊞ in the edit bar to insert a new activity. SureTrak adds the new activity with a default duration of 1 day below the currently selected activity.

To delete an activity, choose Edit, Delete Activity or click ⊟ in the edit bar.

2 Enter an activity description and duration by clicking the appropriate cell in the Activity columns and typing the information in the edit bar.

3 Click ☑ in the edit bar to accept an entry in a cell or click ☒ to cancel. Use the left and right arrow keys to move to other cells.

SureTrak automatically assigns the Activity ID...

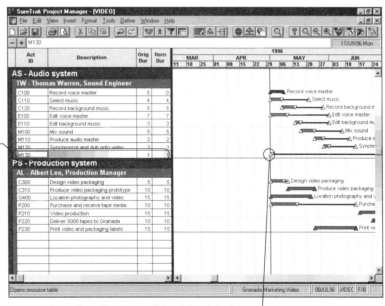

... and positions the new activity at the data date.

For more information about Activity IDs, see *Assigning Activity IDs* earlier in this chapter.

To add an activity using the Activity form You can enter and change information about an activity in the Activity form, located at the bottom of the project window. Use a full view of the Activity form to specify all activity information or a partial view to specify only the Activity ID, description, duration, calendar, early start, early finish, and percent complete.

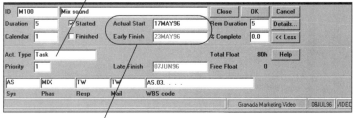

Click to specify information such as activity constraints, costs, dates, predecessors, and successors.

Click More to show more activity information, such as activity type, priority, float, and codes, in the Activity form.

Once you start an activity, the Late Start and Late Finish fields change to Actual Start and Actual Finish fields.

1 Choose View, Activity Form.

2 Choose Insert, Activity or click ⊞ to insert an activity row below the currently selected activity.

For more information about activity durations, see *Estimating Activity Durations* later in this chapter.

3 Enter information about the activity in the form. Accept the default Activity ID, enter a description, and estimate a duration in the Duration field.

4 Click OK when you have finished adding activity information.

To automatically link a series of activities in the Bar chart view Use the Autolink command to quickly add a chain of activities with finish to start relationships. If the activities you want to link already exist in the project, use the Link Activities command.

1 Choose Insert, Autolink then choose View, Activity Form to open an empty Activity form.

2 Click ⊞ in the edit bar to add an activity.

3 Enter activity description and duration for the first activity in the series; click the Series OK button.

Choose View, Relation-ships to display the relationship lines as they are being added.

SureTrak automatically adds the next Activity ID.

4 Add the other activities in the series, in the order in which they will occur, clicking the Series OK button after each activity. SureTrak links each activity to the one that was most recently added, with a finish to start relationship.

5 Choose Insert, Autolink to turn off Autolink.

For information about adding a series of activities in the PERT view, see the *Linking Activities with Relationships* chapter.

6 You can also add activities in a series without the Activity form open in the Bar chart view. Use the Activity columns to enter descriptions and modify durations.

Undoing Changes to an Activity

As you enter and edit activity information in the Bar chart or PERT view, you may want to undo a change you have made. Undoing a change restores the data to its previous value. Choose Edit, Undo to reverse the last change or set of changes you made to an activity.

Use the Redo command to reinstate the last change you made to an activity, reversing the previous Undo command. Choose Edit, Redo to reverse the reversal.

Adding Activities in the PERT View

Adding activities in the PERT view enables you to see the flow of logic as you build your project.

To add an activity in the PERT view Choose View, PERT. Double-click the area where you want to place the new activity. You can also choose Insert, Activity, or press the Insert key.

SureTrak adds the new activity and assigns an ID.

Use a full view of the Activity form to enter additional information for the newly added activity.

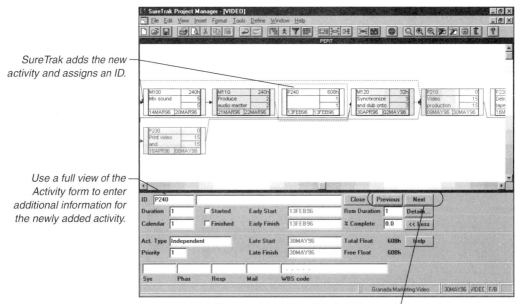

Once you add new activity information, Previous and Next change to OK and Cancel.

If you use the Insert Activity command, SureTrak places the new activity to the right of the selected activity. If you add an activity without an activity currently selected, SureTrak places the new activity in the position of the current focus, indicated by a dotted box.

If you add an activity without an activity currently selected, or if SureTrak is not set up to assign Activity IDs automatically, SureTrak places the cursor in the ID field in the Activity form for you to specify an Activity ID.

Estimating Activity Durations

Every activity has an original and a remaining duration. The original duration is the total time required to complete the activity. SureTrak automatically sets the remaining duration—the time left to accomplish the activity—equal to the original duration established when you add a new activity. When you update an activity, you can change the remaining duration, or have SureTrak recalculate it based on percent complete.

To enter durations in the Activity form Choose View, Activity Form. In the Duration field, enter an amount of time. Durations are expressed as hours, days, weeks, or a combination of all three.

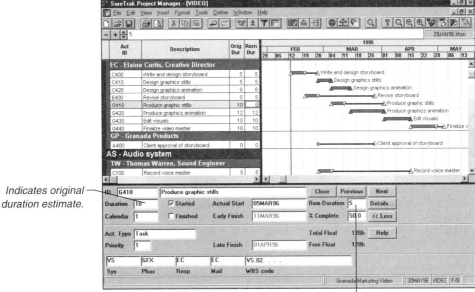

Indicates original duration estimate.

Indicates the duration left to complete.

For more information about calendars, see the *Defining Project Calendars* chapter.

Internally, SureTrak calculates all durations in hours; it keeps track of the number of hours represented by durations such as 2W3D. The number of hours available depends on the days in the workweek and the hours in the typical workday, which you set up on the global calendar. If the global calendar uses a 4-day workweek of 6-hour workdays, a week is 24 hours; the duration of 2W3D is 66 hours. If the global calendar uses a 6-day workweek of 10-hour workdays, a week is 60 hours; the duration of 2W3D is 150 hours.

To enter durations in the Activity columns Select the Original
Duration or Remaining Duration column. In the edit bar, enter a duration,
then press Enter.

To enter durations using the activity bar Point to the finish date of
an activity (the right end of the key bar) until the mouse pointer changes to
↤. Press the left mouse button and drag the end of the bar to the date you
want, then release the mouse button.

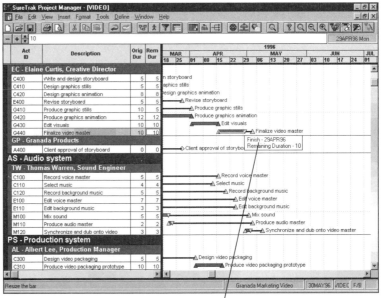

*When you drag the end of a bar, a date window —
shows the changing finish date and duration.*

The date window displays the revised duration and early finish date as you
stretch or shrink the bar. The early finish date and remaining duration for
the activity in the Activity columns also change when you finish dragging
the bar. You can drag the start of the activity bar in the same fashion.
Although it appears that you're changing the start date of the activity,
you're actually changing only the duration; when SureTrak calculates the
schedule, it recalculates the activity's start date.

 *If the activity has no progress (the percent complete is zero
and no actual resources or costs have been recorded), the
original duration also changes when you drag the start or
finish of a bar.*

Defining Activity Types

When you choose an activity type, you're specifying the method SureTrak uses to control duration (time consumption) and the calendar SureTrak uses to schedule it. Each of the seven types of activities models a different set of circumstances in a project.

If an activity requires time to complete (has a duration greater than zero) and is not merely a summary of other activities, it's one of three types: task, independent, or meeting. For any of these three activity types, you can specify a duration when you enter the activity or you can assign driving resources and let SureTrak calculate the activity's duration, based on how long its most important, or driving, resources must be assigned to it. (For the four other activity types, SureTrak always calculates the duration.)

If you're not tracking resources in a project, you can designate all activities with durations as task activities. Change the default activity type from independent to task in the Options dialog box (choose Tools, Options, then click the Project tab).

When choosing an activity type for an activity, consider the following:

- Should the activity's resources be scheduled according to the activity's base calendar? If so, it's a task activity.

- If resources should be scheduled by their own resource calendars, and the activity is scheduled according to when those resources can work on it, it's either a meeting or an independent activity.

- Finally, consider whether the resources must work simultaneously, as though they're in a meeting, or whether they can work separately—independently.

Choose View, Activity Form, then click More and select an activity type from the drop-down list.

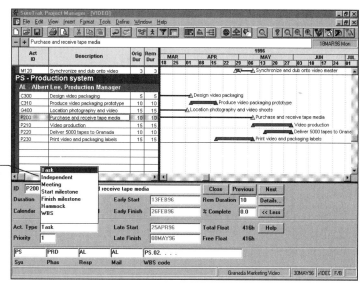

Creating task activities SureTrak always schedules task activities and their resources according to the activity's base calendar. A task activity starts according to network logic and finishes when its duration has elapsed. If you aren't assigning resources to the activity, are assigning only nondriving resources to the activity, or all resources are scheduled according to the activity's base calendar, then define an activity as a task.

When you change an activity type from Task to Independent, if none of the resources already assigned are driving, SureTrak makes all resources assigned to the activity driving.

Creating independent activities SureTrak schedules an independent activity according to predecessor logic and the times its driving resources are scheduled to work on it. Designate an activity as independent if resources can work independently of each other—according to their own resource calendars, and for their own durations, which you assign in the Resources detail form.

When driving resources are assigned to an independent activity, the time between the start of the first driving resource and the finish of the last driving resource determines the duration of the independent activity. Nondriving resources also work according to their own calendars, but they do not affect the activity's duration.

Creating meeting activities Meeting activities require that all resources work together simultaneously as a team to complete the work. They are useful for scheduling meetings and for any activities where resources cannot work independently.

SureTrak calculates the duration of a meeting activity with driving resources based on the driving resource with the longest duration. It uses a calendar that is a combination of the calendars for all driving resources. If no common time exists when all the driving resources can be scheduled to work on the activity, SureTrak uses the activity's base calendar and schedules all resources by that calendar, as though the activity were a task activity.

Creating start and finish milestones activity types Use milestones to indicate the beginning or end of a major event or phase, or any other important point in your project. Milestones have no original or remaining duration. When you add a zero-duration activity, SureTrak calculates a start and finish date for the activity. However, if you specify that the zero-duration activity is a start milestone (SM) or a finish milestone (FM), SureTrak shows only start dates or finish dates, respectively. Since a milestone represents only a point in time, it has no duration in the schedule. SureTrak always schedules a milestone according to its base calendar.

For more information about formatting milestones and the Bar chart, see the *Customizing the Bar Chart View* chapter.

Start and finish milestones appear on the Bar chart according to the milestone point styles, patterns, and colors specified in the Bar and Endpoint Options dialog box (choose Format, Bars, Options). If a milestone is critical, it is shown using the Critical Point style and color.

To create hammock activities Use hammocks to monitor the elapsed beginning-to-end duration of a group of activities. A hammock duration is the number of days between the beginning of the first activity and the end of the last one in the group—not the sum of the activities' durations. If many hammocked activities overlap, the hammock's duration will be smaller than the combined durations; if large gaps exist between the activities in the hammock, its duration may be longer.

A hammock activity differs from a WBS activity (described next) in that the activities in a hammock activity need not share any common coding element. The only shared characteristic of the activities in a hammock may be that you want to look at their collective elapsed time or check their collective start and finish dates.

A hammock activity should have one or more start to start predecessors (the first activities in the hammock group) and one or more finish to finish successors (the last activities in the hammock group). A hammock with no predecessors starts on the data date. A hammock with no successors ends on the project must-finish date, or on the calculated project finish date if no project must-finish date is defined.

1 Choose View, Activity Form to display the Activity form and select Hammock as the activity type for the activity.

2 Click Details to display activity detail, then choose Predecessors.

3 In the Predecessors detail form, specify start to start predecessors to be included in the hammock. The hammock begins at the earliest start date of the specified predecessors.

4 Choose Successors to open the Successors detail form and specify finish to finish successors to include in the hammock. The hammock ends on the latest early finish date of those successors. Its duration is its early finish minus its early start; its total float is its late finish minus its early finish.

To create WBS activities Like a hammock activity, the duration of a WBS activity extends from the start of the earliest activity in a group to the end of the latest one in the group. WBS codes control which activities are part of a WBS activity: SureTrak incorporates any activities that share a component of the WBS code into the WBS activity.

For more information about creating a WBS, see the *Creating a Work Breakdown Structure* chapter.

A WBS activity must have a WBS code to be meaningful. If it doesn't have a WBS code, or if no activities share an element of the WBS activity's WBS code, the WBS activity spans all activities from the data date to the finish date.

1 Choose View, Activity Form to open the Activity form and select WBS as the activity type for the activity.

2 In the WBS Code field in the Activity form, select the portion of the WBS code that you want to summarize. Select an upper-level code from the drop-down list.

3 Click OK.

Activity types and durations SureTrak calculates or records duration according to the type of activity. For some types of activities, you specify the duration; for others, SureTrak calculates it.

Activity Type	Description
Task, Independent, and Meeting activities	Enter the duration as the number of days, weeks, and/or hours required to accomplish the activity; or assign driving resources to determine duration.
Start Milestone (SM)	Leave duration as zero; occurs at start of day or hour and has no finish dates.
Finish Milestone (FM)	Leave duration as zero; occurs at end of day or hour and has no start dates.
Hammock	Leave duration as zero; SureTrak calculates duration from earliest predecessor to latest successor.
WBS	Leave duration as zero; SureTrak calculates duration from the earliest activity with a matching WBS code to the latest activity with a matching WBS code.

Assigning a Calendar to an Activity

Calendars determine the workdays and workhours on which an activity can be scheduled. You can define up to 31 of these calendars, called base calendars. By default, SureTrak uses Calendar 1 for activities, however, you can specify another calendar in the Activity form.

To select a base calendar Choose View, Activity Form.

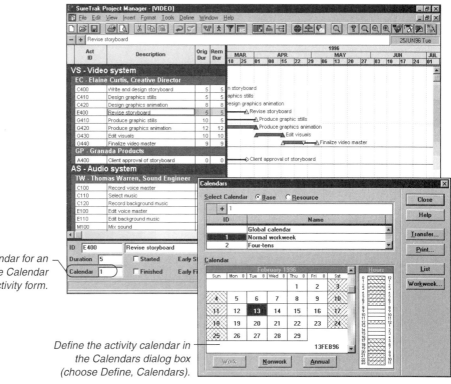

Specify a calendar for an activity in the Calendar field in the Activity form.

Define the activity calendar in the Calendars dialog box (choose Define, Calendars).

For more information about defining calendars, see the *Defining Project Calendars* chapter.

Using Scripts to Enter Activity Information

Scripts are programs that tell an application what to do. You can use them to automate tasks that you do repetitively or regularly. A script such as Global Change directly affects activities in SureTrak.

Global Change (GBLCHNG) performs one of four functions, either globally or based on a filter. It modifies durations or percent complete, deletes activities, modifies resource assignments, or modifies resource assignments and cost amounts.

To use a Basic script Choose Tools, Basic Scripts. Specify the script you want to use. Click Run.

If you use a specific script regularly, you can add it to the Tools menu and then click the Tools(#) button that corresponds to the script to launch it.

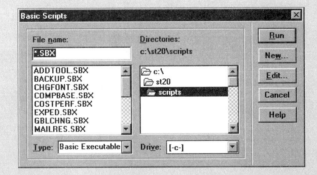

Deleting and Dissolving Activities

To remove an activity from a project, you can delete it or dissolve it. Deleting removes the activities and its relationships to other activities. Dissolving an activity joins the activity's predecessors and successors before the activity is removed, preserving schedule logic.

To delete activities When you delete an activity, SureTrak also deletes its relationships to other activities, both predecessor and successor. Check the activity's predecessor and successor activities to ensure that they remain correctly linked to other activities in the schedule before you delete the activity.

When you organize activities by resource, predecessor, or successor, the same activity may appear in several groups. For example, an activity to which three resources are assigned appears three times, once in each of the three resource bands, when the project window is organized by resource. When you try to delete the activity under these circumstances, SureTrak prompts you to specify whether to delete the activity itself or just the relationship or resource assignment.

1 Select an activity or activities in the Activity columns.

2 Choose Edit, Delete Activity.

3 Confirm that you want to delete the activity or activities.

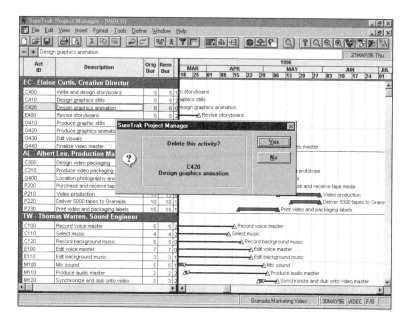

To dissolve activities Unlike deletion, dissolving activities maintains the project's logic by deleting an activity while joining its predecessor and successor activities with finish to start relationships. Dissolving several activities at once does not maintain all relationships that may have existed between the selected activities. Instead, SureTrak dissolves the first selected activity and connects its predecessors and successors; then it dissolves the next activity and connects its predecessors and successors. This process continues until all selected activities have been dissolved.

For information about dissolving activities in the PERT view, see the *Linking Activities with Relationships* chapter.

1 Select an activity in the Activity columns, or select multiple activities.

2 Choose Edit, Dissolve Activity.

3 Confirm that you want to dissolve the activity or activities.

Copying, Cutting, and Pasting Activities

Use SureTrak's copy and paste options to duplicate one or more activities. You can copy activities to save data-entry time, and you can cut or copy activities into a different application, edit them, and paste them back into your SureTrak project to update it. When you paste an activity, you must assign it a unique Activity ID. When you copy an activity, SureTrak copies any information on the Activity form as well as dates associated with the activity. You can also choose to copy relationship and/or resource and cost information.

Specify how you want SureTrak to handle duplicate Activity IDs.

Mark to have the copied activities inherit the codes, predecessor, and successor data of a particular group.

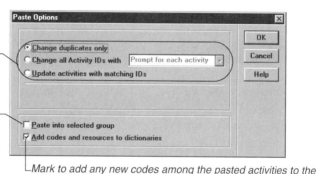

Mark to add any new codes among the pasted activities to the WBS, Activity Codes, and the Resource Dictionary.

 To copy and paste activities Select the activity or activities you want to copy and choose Edit, Copy Activity. Select the activity you want the copied activity to appear below and choose Edit, Paste Activity. If you are copying from and pasting to the same project, you will have to change the Activity IDs being pasted in the Paste Options dialog box. To copy and paste partial activity data, select the cell containing the data you want to copy. Choose Edit, Copy Cell. Select the cell or cells to which you want to copy this information. Choose Edit, Paste Cell.

 To cut and paste activities Select an activity or activities in the Activity columns and choose Edit, Cut Activity to remove the activity from the project window and copy it to the Clipboard. Select the activity that you want the copied activity to appear above and choose Edit, Paste Activity. You may have to specify how you want SureTrak to handle duplicate Activity IDs in the Paste Options dialog box.

If you add codes to the dictionaries when copying activities from one project to another, the best results occur if your dictionaries and codes are set up similarly. Set up each project's codes so that they appear in the same order, and so that the codes in each dictionary are the same length; otherwise, you may have to adjust the codes after you copy the activities.

Handling Duplicate Activity IDs When Copying Activities

When you paste copied activities, you must assign unique IDs to the copied activities. In the Paste Options dialog box, the Change Duplicates Only option enables you to copy activities as they exist. If a duplicate is encountered, SureTrak prompts you to specify a new ID for that activity. The Change All Activity IDs With Prompt For Each Activity option assigns a new ID to each activity. SureTrak displays each activity with an existing ID in a table, prompting you to enter a new ID for each one. The Change All Activity IDs with Prefix/Suffix option specifies a prefix and/ or suffix to add to the IDs.

The Change All Activity IDs with Auto-Increment option creates new IDs that are automatically incremented. Specify a start-at ID and indicate the amount by which SureTrak should increase each ID. For example, specify 100 as the start-at ID and 10 as the increment to obtain the new IDs 110, 120, 130, and so on.

The Change All Activity IDs with Arithmetic Add option increments IDs numerically, starting with a number you specify. For example, if you specify 10 as the increment for Activity IDs 100, 200, and 300, the new IDs will be 110, 210, and 310.

Choosing to add codes while pasting only adds codes; it does not paste dictionaries or descriptions. Pasting codes with activities works best when the dictionaries of the project from which you're pasting are in the same order as the dictionaries in the project to which you're pasting. You can set up the dictionaries in the project to which you are pasting so that they match before you paste activities. Then, when unfamiliar codes are pasted into the project, SureTrak will place them in the correct dictionary.

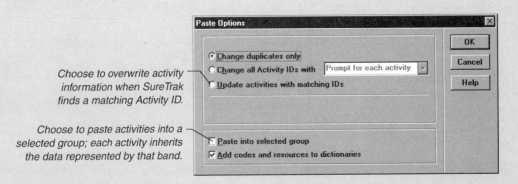

Choose to overwrite activity information when SureTrak finds a matching Activity ID.

Choose to paste activities into a selected group; each activity inherits the data represented by that band.

Moving Activities

You can use the mouse to drag an activity to another location in the same project. Relationships remain intact and SureTrak does not place the activity data on the Clipboard.

To move an activity in the Bar chart view First, organize the project (choose Format, Organize). Next, point to the left of the first column in the activity row. The mouse pointer changes to a ⊠. Drag the mouse up or down through the Activity columns until you reach the row where you want to move the activity, then release the mouse.

You can also use the keyboard to move activities in the PERT view. Select the activities you want to move, then choose Edit, Move Activity. Use the arrow keys to position the activities in the new location. Press Enter to place them.

To move an activity in the PERT view Drag the activity to the new location. If you move the activity to an occupied area, SureTrak moves conflicting activities to the right. You can also move several activities at once by selecting the activities you want to move then dragging them to the new location.

Moving activities between groups Moving activities between groups provides an easy way to modify activity data because SureTrak automatically reassigns the group values. You can move activities between groups based on activity codes, WBS codes, and calendar ID to modify these assignments.

Drag an activity between responsibility group bands, such as from Elaine Curtis to Albert Lee, to reassign responsibility code assignments.

Act ID	Description	Orig Dur	Rem Dur	FEB 05	12	19	26
EC - Elaine Curtis, Creative Director							
C400	Write and design storyboard	5	5				
C410	Design graphics stills	5	5				
E400	Revise storyboard	5	5				
G410	Produce graphic stills	10	5				
G420	Produce graphics animation	12	12				
G430	Edit visuals	10	10				
G440	Finalize video master	9	9				
AL - Albert Lee, Production Manager							
C300	Design video packaging	5	5				
C310	Produce video packaging prototype	10	10				
G400	Location photography and video	15	15				
P200	Purchase and receive tape media	10	10				
P210	Video production	15	15				
P220	Deliver 5000 tapes to Granada	10	10				

Using Log Text Data Items

Log Text data items are cells that contain your own free-form text notes about SureTrak activities. Use them to enter information that might not fit into any of SureTrak's defined data items for activities. For example, use Log Text cells to compare per-activity bid amounts from contractors, or to tag activities with special notes giving additional information, such as the telephone number for the contact person at the printing company handling your direct-mail advertising.

Ten logs are available; each can contain up to 48 characters per activity. SureTrak includes a layout for viewing logs called LOG, which has larger default row heights to display all information for each log in its own cell.

To display a log, choose Format, Columns and select the column data item you want to follow the Log Text. Select a Log Text item from the drop-down list. In the Column Title cell, label your Log Text columns to reflect the information you will enter. Click OK.

You can display, make an entry in, and edit logs in the Activity columns. You can also use logs as bar labels, filtering criteria, and for sorting. You can also display a noneditable Log Record column, which combines all 10 logs in one column. Display a Log Record in the same manner you display a Log Text field.

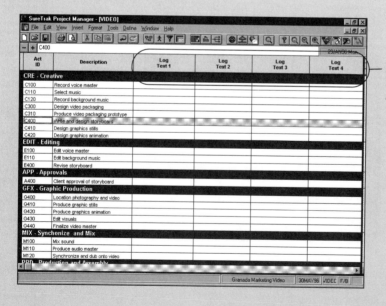

Enter any type of information in the Log Text cells in the Activity columns.

Using an Outline to Build a Project

Add activities in outline form to build structure into your project as you go. By specifying broad areas of the project and then narrowing down the work in each area, you can create activities of greater detail at each step. When you create an outline of activities, you create a hierarchy of topics and activities. You can use up to 10 levels in an outline hierarchy, although you will most likely use only four or five levels.

You enter each level of the outline as if it were an activity. Then, when you indent an activity ("demote" the activity in the hierarchy), SureTrak changes the activity above it to a topic activity. You can add activity information such as duration and activity type only to activities at the lowest level. Topic activities at higher levels of the outline accumulate, or summarize, the durations of their associated activities.

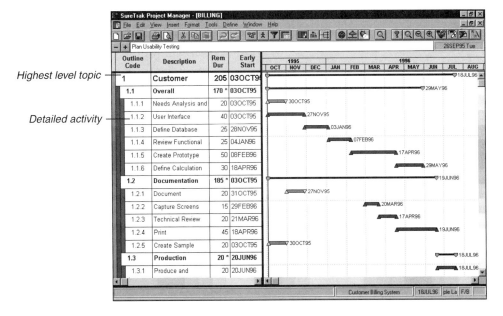

Highest level topic

Detailed activity

For detailed steps about how to outline a project, see the *Organizing and Summarizing Activities* chapter.

Adding activities as an outline Before outlining activities, set up the Organize dialog box for outlining. As you outline a project, SureTrak automatically assigns an outline code.

Choose Outline to display the project in outline mode.

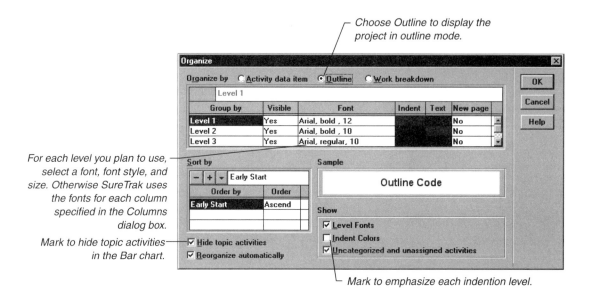

For each level you plan to use, select a font, font style, and size. Otherwise SureTrak uses the fonts for each column specified in the Columns dialog box.

Mark to hide topic activities in the Bar chart.

Mark to emphasize each indention level.

Add the outline code as a column in the Activity columns by choosing Format, Columns.

Creating relationships in an outline As you indent and outdent activities in an outline, you are establishing logic in a project as well as a hierarchy of activities. You should be aware of several considerations as you outline a project.

You can create links between topics at the same level in the hierarchy. For example, if you have a project with Design, Build, and Test as level-1 topics, you can enter relationships among the three topics. When you create a link between topics, you create relationships between all the activities in the predecessor topic and all the activities in the successor topic. In this example, Build has no predecessor specified; however, since its topic, Build, has Design as a predecessor, Build is also scheduled as if a direct relationship existed between Build and Design.

For more information about linking activities and specifying relationships, see the *Linking Activities with Relationships* chapter.

The following rules also apply when creating relationships in an outline:

■ You can create relationships between any activities that aren't topics, whether they are subordinate to the same topic or different topics.

■ You cannot create relationships between a topic and any of its subordinates.

■ Topics can only have finish to start relationships. The finish of a topic is always determined by the durations of its subordinate topics and activities.

■ You can constrain only the start of topics.

For more information about dragging activities, see the *Customizing the Bar Chart View* chapter.

Renumbering an outline You can use dragging techniques to help organize your outline. Turn off automatic reorganizing by clearing the Reorganize Automatically checkbox in the Organize dialog box, then drag activities so they appear in the order you want. Use the Renumber Outline icon to renumber the outline codes in sequence. SureTrak compensates for nonexistent levels by outdenting activities so that no outline levels are missing.

Organizing outlines in project groups You can set up SureTrak to organize the project group by the member project activity prefixes, then by the outline numbers. This keeps each member project's activities together. Choose Tools, Options and click the Project tab.

Mark to organize outline codes by project.

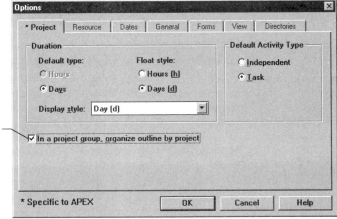

Creating Projects Using Fragnets

Fragnets—fragments of networks—simplify building a project. A fragnet is a set of activities that you copy from a project, save, and apply elsewhere in the same project or to another project. When you work in an environment where projects are similar, you can save time by using fragnets instead of completely recreating the activities they contain each time.

When you view a fragnet in the Clipboard Viewer, the format will be jumbled. When you paste it in a SureTrak project, however, it will retain the original format.

Using fragnets is more powerful than conventional copy-and-paste techniques because you can copy, store, and retrieve as many fragnets as you need, whenever you need them. When you use copy-and-paste techniques, you can store only one set of activities. The next time you copy or cut an activity, the new data irretrievably overwrites any existing data in the Clipboard. Fragnets enable you to copy and store information without being limited to the temporary contents of the Clipboard. SureTrak copies most activity data, including Activity IDs, durations, relationships, resources, and costs, with the fragnet.

To store a fragnet

1 Select the activities you want to store as a fragnet.

2 Choose Edit, Copy Activity to copy the activities to the Clipboard.

3 Open the Clipboard.

Your copied activities and their relationship and resource information appear in the Clipboard Viewer.

4 Choose File, Save As to open the Save As dialog box for the Clipboard Viewer. In the File Name field, type a name for the fragment, followed by the .CLP extension. In the Directories and Drives field, specify the location where you want the fragnet stored.

5 Click OK, then choose File, Exit.

To retrieve a fragnet

1 In the project window, select the activity you want the fragnet to appear below.

2 Open the Clipboard.

3 Choose File, Open to display the Open dialog box for the Clipboard Viewer and select the fragnet (.CLP file) from the drive and directory in which you stored it.

4 Click OK to open the fragnet file in the Clipboard.

If other information already appears in the Clipboard, Windows asks whether to overwrite it with the .CLP file (the fragnet) you have chosen. Click Yes to overwrite any existing data in the Clipboard, or click Cancel. You can then save any existing data in the Clipboard as a .CLP file to be retrieved later.

5 Choose File, Exit.

6 Return to the SureTrak project window.

7 Choose Edit, Paste Activity to insert the fragnet in the project window.

Switching Between the Bar Chart and PERT Views

Switching to the Bar chart view
When you add activities in the PERT view and then switch to the Bar chart view, SureTrak places the new activities at the bottom of the Activity columns. If an activity other than a new activity is currently selected, SureTrak reorganizes the Bar chart view and positions new activities in the appropriate rows, based on the current sort and group criteria in the bars Organize dialog box.

Switching to the PERT view When
you add activities in the Bar chart view, then switch to the PERT view, SureTrak rearranges all activities in the PERT view and places the new activities based on their relationships. SureTrak positions activities without relationships at the bottom of the network. If activities are organized into groups in the PERT view, SureTrak places the new activities in the appropriate group.

If you do not want SureTrak to rearrange all activities when moving to the PERT view, you can have SureTrak place only the new activities, or ask how to rearrange activities.

Choose Format, Organize to set the arrangement options for the PERT view.

In the Activity Placement and Spacing section in the Organize dialog box, choose Ask How To Reorganize to have SureTrak ask you to choose a method for arranging activities when moving to the PERT view.

Choose Reorganize Unplaced Activities to have SureTrak position only new activities. Choose Best Fit to have SureTrak place new activities to the right (or in the first empty spot) of the right-most predecessor. If a new activity has no predecessor, SureTrak places it to the left of the leftmost predecessor. Choose Bottom to have SureTrak place new activities at the bottom of the network.

Switching views after changing activities If you change activities in one view, and then switch views, the changed activities may no longer belong in their original position. For example, suppose activities in the Bar chart view are grouped by department. While working in the PERT view, you change the department code values for several activities, then switch to the Bar chart. Choose Format, Reorganize Now to place the changed activities in the appropriate rows.

Linking Activities with Relationships

By identifying relationships between activities and linking them, you create a network that represents the sequence in which activities perform. SureTrak bases the project schedule on these activity relationships.

SureTrak provides several methods for defining relationships: visualize and define logic in a nontimescaled PERT view, link activities directly on bars in a Bar chart view, name predecessors and successors in detail forms, or use the Autolink command.

Understanding Relationship Types

An activity can have predecessors—activities that occur before it, and it can have successors—activities that occur after it. The set of sequences of activities connected by relationships is called the "network," and it determines when SureTrak schedules each activity in the project. SureTrak also uses the network of predecessor/successor relationships among activities to calculate the project's critical path—the sequence of related activities that determines the earliest possible completion date for the project.

In SureTrak, each predecessor or successor is related to other activities in one of four ways: finish to start, finish to finish, start to start, or start to finish, as described and illustrated below.

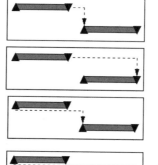

Finish to start (FS). The successor activity can begin only when the predecessor activity finishes. This is SureTrak's default relationship type.

Finish to finish (FF). The finish of the successor activity depends on the finish of the predecessor activity.

Start to start (SS). The start of the successor activity depends on the start of the predecessor activity.

Start to finish (SF). The successor activity cannot finish until the current activity starts.

Creating Relationships Using the PERT View

You can define relationships in the PERT view by dragging the mouse between any two activities that you want to connect.

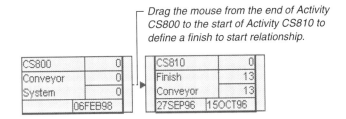

Drag the mouse from the end of Activity CS800 to the start of Activity CS810 to define a finish to start relationship.

To create relationships in PERT Point to the left or right of the predecessor activity. When the mouse changes to a ↘⋹, drag the mouse to the left or right of the successor activity. Click to select a successor activity; SureTrak lists the activities included in the current view.

You can also drag the mouse to the edge of the window to scroll to the successor activity.

If the successor activity is not displayed onscreen, drag the mouse to an unoccupied area of the view. When you release the mouse, SureTrak displays a dialog box where you specify the successor activity and type of relationship.

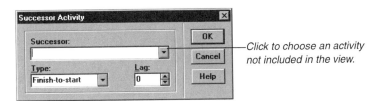

Click to choose an activity not included in the view.

To automatically link a series of activities in the PERT view

Use the Autolink command to quickly add a chain of activities with finish to start relationships.

1 Choose Insert, Autolink.

2 Double-click a blank space in the project window to add the first activity. SureTrak displays the Activity form.

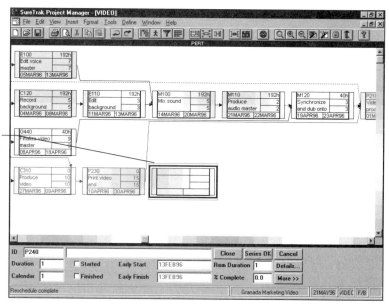

When you add a series of activities in PERT, SureTrak automatically links each activity with a finish to start relationship.

3 Enter an activity description and duration for the first activity in the series.

4 Click Series OK.

5 Add the other activities in the series, in the order in which they will occur; click Series OK after each activity. SureTrak links each activity to the one that was most recently added with a finish to start relationship.

6 Choose Insert, Autolink to turn off Autolink.

Creating Relationships Using the Bar Chart View

After you add activities, you can define relationships between them in the Bar chart by dragging the mouse between any two activities you want to connect.

To identify the key bar, check the setting by choosing Format, Bars.

To create relationships in the Bar chart Choose View, Relationships. Point to the start or finish of the predecessor activity bar. When the mouse pointer changes to ↘⋲, press and hold the mouse button. Click the end of the bar or endpoint designated as the key bar; no other bar will change the mouse pointer to the relationship shape. Drag the mouse to the start or finish of the successor activity bar.

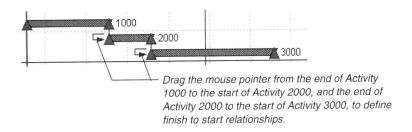

Drag the mouse pointer from the end of Activity 1000 to the start of Activity 2000, and the end of Activity 2000 to the start of Activity 3000, to define finish to start relationships.

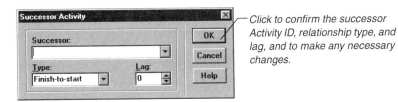

Click to confirm the successor Activity ID, relationship type, and lag, and to make any necessary changes.

You do not need to display relationship lines in the project window to create relationships between activities.

To create a relationship to an activity not visible on the Bar chart You can link an activity to a successor even if the successor activity doesn't currently appear on the Bar chart. Click the predecessor and drag the pointer to any empty space on the Bar chart, then release the mouse button. SureTrak opens the Successor Activity dialog box with a suggested successor for the activity. Click the drop-down arrow to replace it with a different successor, and specify the relationship type and lag time.

Defining Lag Time Between Activities

When a successor's start or finish doesn't coincide exactly with its predecessor's start or finish, you can specify a lag time for the relationship in days, weeks, hours, or a combination of duration units. Lag time can be positive or negative; use abbreviations for durations. For example, if Activity 2000 can begin 2 days after Activity 1900 finishes, the relationship between 1900 (the predecessor) and 2000 (the successor) is finish to start with a lag time of 2D.

SureTrak displays lag according to the project's duration style (w, d, h) you select in the Options dialog box (choose Tools, Options, then click the Project tab).

You can create relationships with negative lag. If the dependent activity occurs before the activity on which it depends, the dependent activity is considered a successor activity with negative lag. For example, if successor Activity 3000 should start 2 days before its predecessor, Activity 2900, starts, the relationship is start to start with a negative lag time of 2D.

SureTrak interprets lag times according to the predecessor activity's base calendar. Consider two activities that have a start to start relationship with a 2 day lag. If the predecessor activity uses a 7-day workweek and finishes on a Friday, SureTrak schedules the 2 days of lag time on Saturday and Sunday (workdays for the predecessor), even if those days are nonworkdays for the successor; the successor activity is then scheduled to start on Monday.

Automatically Linking a Series of Activities

The Link Activities command in the Bar chart and PERT views enables you to select several activities and assign finish to start relationships to them all at once, so that they form a sequence, or series. The activities are linked in the same sequence as they appear in the Activity columns or are linked from left to right and top to bottom in PERT. For example, if you select three consecutive activities, A, B, and C, SureTrak links A as a predecessor to B, and B as a predecessor to C. However, if you select only two activities, SureTrak designates the second one (the activity with the selection box around one of the cells) as the successor.

The Unlink Activities command enables you to select a series of activities and remove all relationships among the selected activities.

For example, if you select activities A, B, and C, SureTrak unlinks any relationships that A has with B or C, any that B has with A or C, and any that C has with A or B. Relationships to activities that were not selected remain intact.

To unlink a series of activities in the Bar chart or PERT, select a series of activities then choose Edit, Unlink Activities. To remove all relationships between all activities in the project, choose Edit, Select All, then choose Edit, Unlink Activities. If you have not added the activities you want to link into a series with finish to start relationships, use the Autolink command in the Bar chart or PERT view to add the activities.

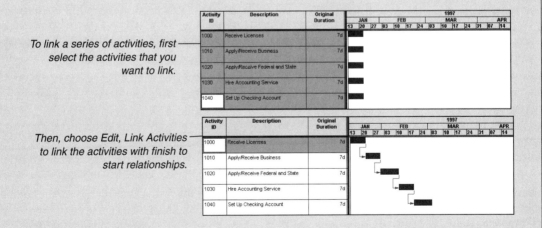

To link a series of activities, first select the activities that you want to link.

Then, choose Edit, Link Activities to link the activities with finish to start relationships.

Creating Relationships Using the Predecessors and Successors Forms

 The Predecessors and Successors forms show the relationships for the activity currently selected in the Activity columns or in PERT. SureTrak identifies the activity by its ID and description located on the top line of the form.

Use the Predecessors and Successors forms to assign multiple predecessors or successors to an activity without using the mouse. These forms make it easy to review all activity relationships simultaneously, and to quickly change the relationship type or lag.

 To assign relationships using Predecessors or Successors forms In the Activity columns or in PERT, select the activity to which you are assigning a predecessor or successor. Choose View, Activity Detail, then Predecessors or Successors to display the Predecessors or Successors detail forms. Right-click in the Predecessor or Successor column and select a predecessor or successor from the drop-down list.

In the Type column, select a relationship type from the drop-down list.

Click to see the successors or predecessors for the previously selected activity.

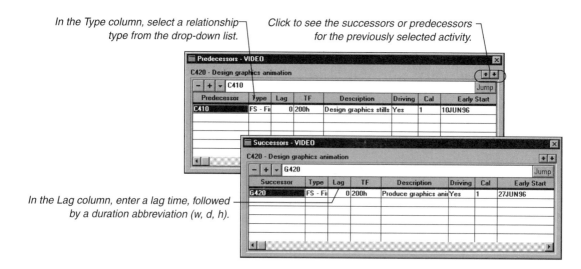

In the Lag column, enter a lag time, followed by a duration abbreviation (w, d, h).

To jump back to an activity in the Activity form, click Previous or Next.

Click Jump to jump to the predecessor or successor activity in the edit bar. When you jump to an activity, SureTrak highlights the activity from which you jumped. Use ▲ ▼ to return to the previously highlighted activity.

Scroll to see other columns, such as early or late dates, percent complete, remaining duration, and float, in the Predecessors or Successors form. When you scroll, the first three columns always remain in view so you can refer to the Activity ID, type, and lag as you review additional data columns.

Tracing Logic

You can step your way through a sequence of linked activities forward or backward through the schedule, moving from an activity to its predecessor, to that activity's predecessor, or from an activity to its successor, to that activity's successor. You can choose any successor or predecessor for each step and you can trace as much or as little of the path as you want. SureTrak selects each activity traced so that you can keep track of the activities on the path you trace.

Tracing logic is useful when you are trying to determine why a particular activity has negative float. You can also open the Constraints detail form to display each activity's constraints simultaneously.

To zoom the Trace Logic view without affecting the PERT view, click in the Trace Logic view, then choose View, Zoom.

To trace logic in the PERT view Select the activity from which you want to begin tracing logic, then choose View, Trace Logic. SureTrak displays the Trace Logic view below the PERT view. If the Activity form is displayed, SureTrak places the Trace Logic view above the form.

SureTrak displays the selected activity in the PERT view and its immediate predecessor and successor in the Trace Logic view.

To move through the chain of activities, click a predecessor or successor of the selected activity or use the arrow keys. SureTrak moves along the driving relationship path.

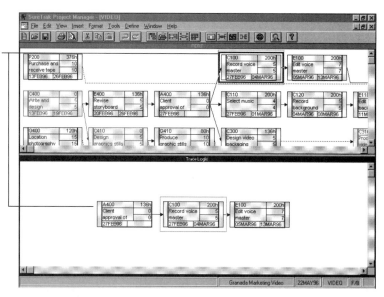

Drag the horizontal split bar up or down to resize the Trace Logic view. To close the Trace Logic view, right-click in an empty area in the Trace Logic view, then choose Hide Trace Logic, or choose View, Trace Logic again.

Changing the Trace Logic view to a movable window You can change the Trace Logic view to a window that can be placed anywhere in the project window. Right-click in the Trace Logic view, then choose Undock Trace Logic. To change the Trace Logic view window back to a full view, right-click in the Trace Logic window and choose Dock, Trace Logic.

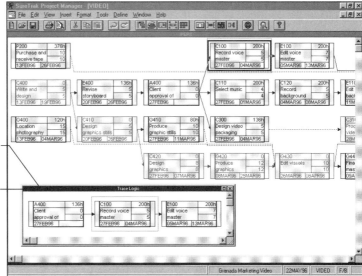

Resize the Trace Logic window and place it anywhere onscreen.

Double-click the Trace Logic band to toggle between a docked and floating window.

Setting Trace Logic options You can control the number of predecessors and successors SureTrak displays in the Trace Logic view by choosing Format, Trace Logic Options.

You can choose to show only activities with driving relationships if you want to focus on the critical paths in your project. SureTrak does not show activities that have nondriving relationships to and from the selected activity.

Modify the amount of detail SureTrak shows by increasing or decreasing the level of predecessors and successors.

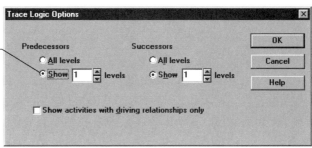

To trace logic using the Predecessors and Successors forms
Open the Predecessors or Successors forms. In the Activity columns or in PERT, select the activity from which you want to begin tracing schedule logic. Press the Ctrl key while double-clicking a predecessor or successor in the detail form. SureTrak selects this activity, highlights it in the columns, and displays its predecessors or successors in the window. Press Ctrl and double-click another predecessor or successor to move to that activity.

Click Jump to quickly jump to the predecessor or successor activity in the edit bar.

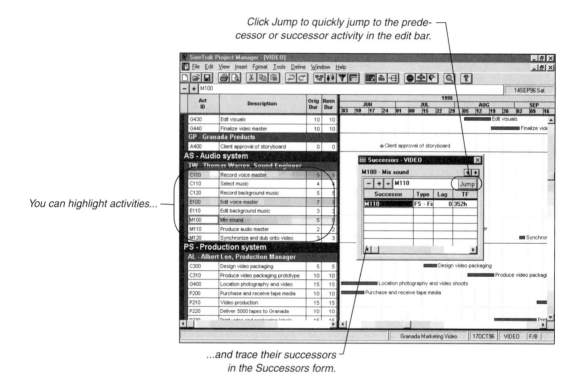

You can highlight activities...

...and trace their successors in the Successors form.

Editing and Deleting Relationships

As you add activities and make adjustments to your project, you may need to modify or delete relationships between activities. You can make these changes to relationships in a variety of ways.

 When you review, change, or delete activity relationships, be sure to display all relationships by choosing View, Relationships.

To edit a relationship on the Bar chart or PERT Point to a relationship line. When the mouse pointer changes to ⚲ in the Bar chart or ↖ in PERT, click the mouse button to display the Edit Relationships dialog box.

Select the relationship you want to edit.

Change the relationship to one of four types.

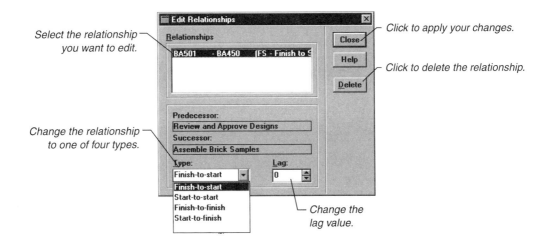

Click to apply your changes.

Click to delete the relationship.

Change the lag value.

 When you delete a relationship from the Edit Relationships dialog box or the Predecessors and Successors forms, SureTrak displays a confirmation box. You delete only the relationship, not the activities.

Dissolving Activities to Preserve Logic

Dissolving differs from deleting in that it deletes the activity and then links the deleted activity's predecessors to each of its successors with a finish to start relationship. For example, activity A is the predecessor to B, and B is the predecessor to C. If you dissolve activity B, SureTrak links its predecessor, A, to its successor, C. If B had two successors, A becomes the predecessor of both of them.

To dissolve activities Select one or several activities in the Activity columns or in PERT and choose Edit, Dissolve Activity. SureTrak deletes the first activity or activities, linking its predecessors to its successors. If more activities were selected, SureTrak then deletes the second selected activity, linking its predecessors and successors, and so on.

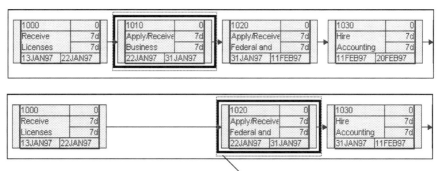

When you choose to dissolve an activity in PERT, SureTrak automatically links the predecessor to the successor.

Displaying Critical and Driving Relationships

An activity can have multiple predecessor relationships. SureTrak identifies the predecessor(s) that control, or drive, the early start and finish dates for the activity. The link between this predecessor and the activity it controls is called the driving relationship; if two or more predecessors share this control, they are both driving. Any relationships from predecessors to successors that do not control the early dates for the successor activity are nondriving relationships.

A driving relationship between two critical activities—activities which, if delayed, delay a deadline or the entire project—is considered a critical relationship. SureTrak identifies driving relationships and critical relationships when it calculates the schedule, based on the information you enter for each activity and relationship.

For more information about formatting relationship lines, see the *Customizing the PERT View* chapter.

To display driving and nondriving relationships in PERT
Choose View, PERT and then choose Format, Relationship Lines. Specify whether SureTrak displays driving and nondriving relationships in the Display section. You can also specify a line style and color for the driving and nondriving relationship lines.

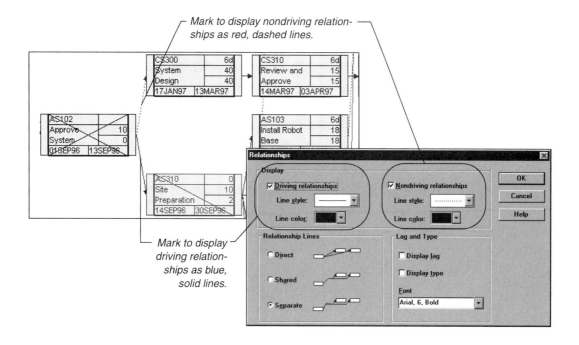

If the project contains driving relationships that are critical, SureTrak displays the color for the relationship lines as critical. Choose Format, Activity Box Ends and Colors to define the relationship line color for critical activities.

For information about formatting relationship lines, see the *Customizing the Bar Chart View* chapter.

To display driving, and nondriving relationships in the Bar chart In the Bar chart view, choose Format, Relationship Lines. You can control how SureTrak displays the relationship line types and colors. For driving and nondriving relationships, set the Visible cell to Yes to display relationship lines. If you set the Visible cell for critical relationships to No, SureTrak still displays the relationship line if it is a driving relationship; the relationship line appears in the color and line style you choose for driving relationships.

Choose Draft quality to have lines appear onscreen faster but some vertical and horizontal segments overlap. Choose Presentation quality to have SureTrak draw each relationship line individually; lines overlap only if they originate from the same predecessor.

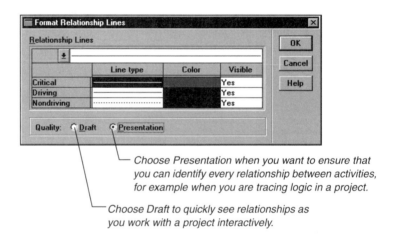

Choose Presentation when you want to ensure that you can identify every relationship between activities, for example when you are tracing logic in a project.

Choose Draft to quickly see relationships as you work with a project interactively.

Displaying a Timescaled Logic Diagram

A timescaled logic diagram shows the relationships among activities and the flow of work through a project. Once you enter activities with durations and relationships, and SureTrak has calculated the schedule, you can see a timescaled logic diagram in the Bar chart view by displaying relationships and then summarizing the activities into bands that show individual activities.

For more information about summarizing activities, see the *Organizing and Summarizing Activities* chapter.

SureTrak includes several reports based on timescaled logic diagrams, named SUM5 through SUM9. Each one is organized and summarized by a different activity code; one is summarized for the entire project, in case you're not using the Area, Phase, or Responsibility codes. To apply any of these reports, choose Reports, Define, select any TSL (timescaled logic) report ID SUM5 through SUM9, and click Apply.

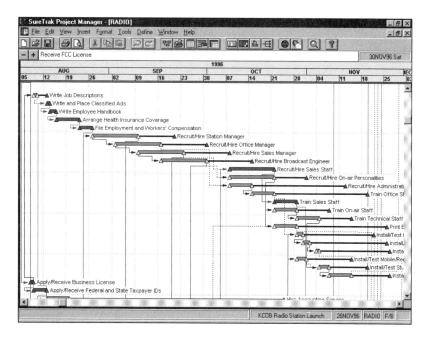

For more information about timescaled logic reports, see the *Creating SureTrak Reports* chapter.

To create a timescaled logic diagram

1 Choose View, Bar Chart, then choose View, Relationships to show relationships in the Bar chart.

2 Choose Format, Organize to organize your activities by any activity data item.

3 Choose Format, Summarization, Summarize All.

4 In the Summarize To field, click the drop-down arrow and select the level below Project Name—the highest level you can summarize to without summarizing the entire project—then click OK.

5 Choose Format, Summarization, Format Summary Bars. Choose the Show Individual Bars and Arrange Bars to Avoid Text Clipping options. Click OK.

6 In the Activity columns, drag the row height pointer of the summa-rized band down to increase the amount of space for the bars on the Bar chart. Reposition activity bars within the vertical space of the summarized band. Position the mouse pointer over a bar until it changes to ⵑ. Then click and drag the bar up or down within the band.

7 To show only the timescaled logic diagram, drag the vertical split bar to the left until the columns are hidden.

To control the location of the bar labels, choose Format, Bars, select a bar in the Graphic Element section, and specify the location of its label(s) in the Label Text section. The Top, Bottom, Rightmost, and Leftmost choices look better than Right or Left in a timescaled logic diagram.

Defining Project Calendars

You can set up multiple calendars in SureTrak that designate different periods as workdays and workhours, and assign the calendars to activities or to resources.

Read this chapter to learn how to use global, base, and resource calendars, and how to transfer calendars from SureTrak, P3, Finest Hour, and other projects.

Defining the Global Calendar

SureTrak supports three kinds of calendars: global, base, and resource. The global calendar is the basis for all other calendars. In effect, it is a "behind-the-scenes" calendar that controls the default workdays, holidays, and worktimes of all new calendars. The global calendar is never assigned to activities; it serves only to establish defaults for all new calendars.

The global calendar affects all new calendars. Set up the global calendar to reflect the typical workweek and workhours for your project, as well as holidays and other nonworktimes.

The default global calendar contains a 5-day, 8-hour workday from 8:00 a.m. to 12:00 noon and from 1:00 p.m. to 5:00 p.m. The default global calendar also contains three annual holidays: New Year's Day (January 1), U.S. Independence Day (July 4), and Christmas (December 25), plus three U.S. holidays that occur on different dates each year (Memorial Day, Labor Day, and Thanksgiving).

When you create a project, SureTrak creates three calendars with default settings: global, Normal Workweek, and a round-the-clock calendar. Before creating more calendars and assigning calendars to activities, customize the global calendar to meet your project needs.

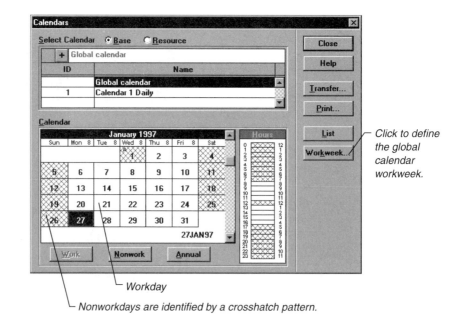

Click to define the global calendar workweek.

Workday

Nonworkdays are identified by a crosshatch pattern.

You can also double-click an hour to switch it from work to nonwork or from nonwork to work.

To define the global calendar workweek Choose Define, Calendars. Choose Base and select the Global Calendar. Click Workweek. Specify the days to include in the global workweek and the hours of work then click OK. The workhours you designate apply to all selected days.

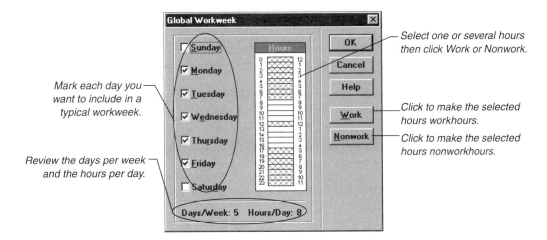

Mark each day you want to include in a typical workweek.

Review the days per week and the hours per day.

Select one or several hours then click Work or Nonwork.

Click to make the selected hours workhours.

Click to make the selected hours nonworkhours.

For more information on defining exceptions, see *Specifying Holidays, Vacations, and Exceptions on Calendars* later in this chapter.

After you define the global calendar workweek, define exceptions to that workweek, such as holidays, either on the monthly calendar display or on a list of exceptions.

Printing Calendars

You can print one month or a span of months from any calendar by choosing Define, Calendars and selecting the calendar you want to print. Click Print in the Calendars dialog box, then specify the dates to include in the From and To fields. If you leave the From field blank, SureTrak prints the calendar from the project start date. If you leave the To field blank, SureTrak prints the calendar through the end of the project. Choose Print To File to send the output to a file for printing later, either from the current computer or from another one.

Defining Base Calendars

All projects have a global calendar and a default base calendar (Normal Workweek). You can create up to 31 base calendars for a project.

SureTrak assigns the default Normal Workweek calendar to all activities except those for which you choose a different base calendar.

Base calendars are altered versions of the global calendar that reflect work schedules for various activities. For example, work may occur on some activities 24 hours a day. However, most of the company's employees work Monday through Friday, from 8:00 a.m. to 5:00 p.m, so define the global calendar to reflect these hours.

A base calendar is identical to the global calendar until you change the new base calendar's workweek and workdays, creating exceptions to the inherited holidays and other nonworktimes for the new base calendar.

Any standard workweek changes you make to the global calendar do not affect existing base calendars; changes only establish defaults for future calendars. However, any specific workday and nonworkday exceptions you change on the global calendar will be made to all existing base and resource calendars.

To define a base workweek Choose Define, Calendars. Choose Base. Add a new calendar using the following steps. SureTrak assigns the base calendar a numerical ID; you can edit it, assigning any one character letter or number that you want.

1 Choose Base.

2 Click to add a new calendar.

3 Type a name for the new calendar. Then click ☑ to save it.

4 Click to define the workweek for the calendar.

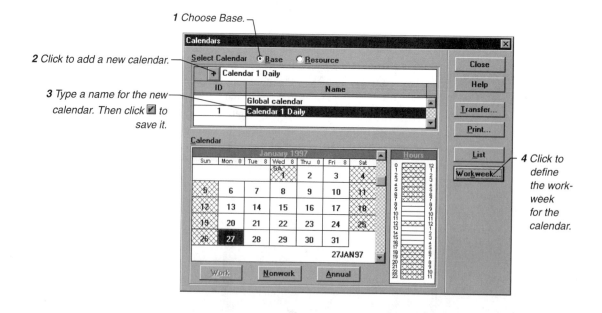

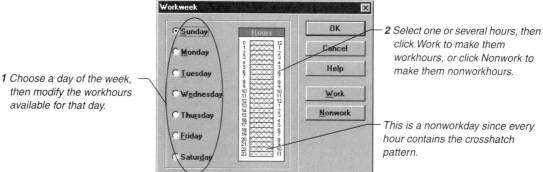

1 Choose a day of the week, then modify the workhours available for that day.

2 Select one or several hours, then click Work to make them workhours, or click Nonwork to make them nonworkhours.

This is a nonworkday since every hour contains the crosshatch pattern.

You can also double-click an hour to switch it from work to nonwork or from nonwork to work.

After you define the base calendar workweek, you can define any exceptions to that workweek, such as holidays. You can also define exceptions to the exceptions inherited from the global calendar, such as a global holiday that you change to worktime on this base calendar.

Editing Calendars

You can edit workweeks and exceptions for the global, base, and resource calendars at any time. Select the calendar you want to edit and change it. When you change a calendar, SureTrak displays the following message.

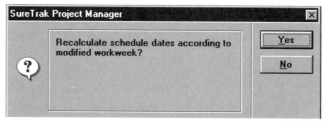

For more information about defining exceptions, see *Specifying Holidays, Vacations, and Exceptions on Calendars* later in this chapter.

To recalculate activity durations based on the new workweek, click Yes. To recalculate activity dates based on the new workweek, click No. For example, assume that you change a base calendar from a 5-day to a 6-day workweek; an activity 10 days long is 2 weeks according to the existing base calendar. Do you want SureTrak to recalculate its duration (so that it is now 12 days, but still 2 weeks long) or change its finish date to show that it will finish earlier because of the longer workweek?

Defining Resource Calendars

Each resource can have a unique calendar, enabling you to accommodate different work schedules for individual people, pieces of equipment, and materials. A resource calendar is a copy of a base calendar that you modify to meet a resource's special schedule. SureTrak creates a new resource calendar each time you define a resource; until you customize it for the resource, it is an exact copy of the base calendar you select for it.

The resource calendar inherits the worktimes and holidays from the base calendar. You can specify a new workweek or use the base calendar's workweek. You can then modify the base calendar's worktimes and holidays to fit the unique worktimes of the resource. For example, to meet a deadline, some resources may work on a day that is normally a nonworkday. For example, the Testing department may work Saturdays—normally a nonworkday—for the last month of a project. In this case, associate the resource with a base calendar, then add the Saturdays that the department will work as exceptions to that base calendar.

You can also choose Define, Calendars, then choose Resource to display a list of resources and the associated base calendars.

To define a resource workweek Choose Define, Resources, then click Calendars; SureTrak lists all resource calendars. In the Select Calendar section, select the resource whose calendar you want to define.

If you have not associated a resource with a base calendar, SureTrak automatically associates the resource with calendar 1, the Normal Workweek calendar.

Choose Resource, and define a base calendar that corresponds to each resource.

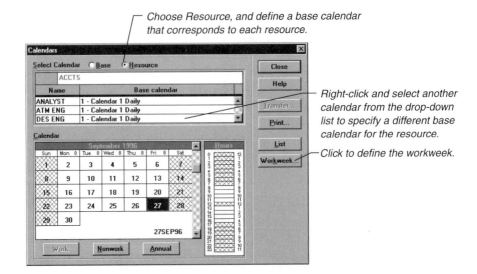

Right-click and select another calendar from the drop-down list to specify a different base calendar for the resource.

Click to define the workweek.

In the Calendars dialog box, click Workweek. By default, the resource calendars use its base calendar's workweek. To modify the workweek, clear the Use Base Workweek checkbox. Select the workhours or nonworkhours for this resource, then click Work or Nonwork to make them workhours or nonworkhours, respectively. Click OK.

Double-click an hour to switch it from work to nonwork or from nonwork to work.

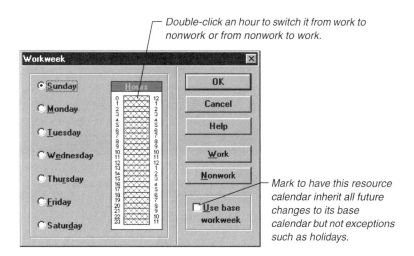

Mark to have this resource calendar inherit all future changes to its base calendar but not exceptions such as holidays.

For more information about resources and resource calendars, see the *Building a Resource Plan* chapter.

After you define the resource calendar's workweek, you can define any exceptions to that workweek, such as vacations or machine downtime. You can also define exceptions for this resource to the exceptions inherited from the base calendar, such as weekend days that this particular resource will work.

Specifying Holidays, Vacations, and Exceptions on Calendars

After you define the workweek for the global, base, or resource calendar, you can define exceptions, such as holidays, vacations, or machine downtime. Define exceptions on the monthly calendar, or display them in a list. First, define holidays for the global calendar that will apply to all base calendars, then define those for each base calendar.

In the base calendar, you can also define exceptions to the exceptions inherited from the global calendar, such as a global holiday that you change to worktime on this base calendar—meaning that work on activities assigned to this base calendar can occur on this day. In the resource calendar, you can also define exceptions for this resource to the exceptions inherited from the base calendar, such as weekend days that this particular resource will work.

To define exceptions to the calendar using the monthly calendar display Choose Define, Calendars. Select the global calendar or a base calendar, then click Calendar to display the monthly calendar. Specify the exceptions. Click Close when you finish.

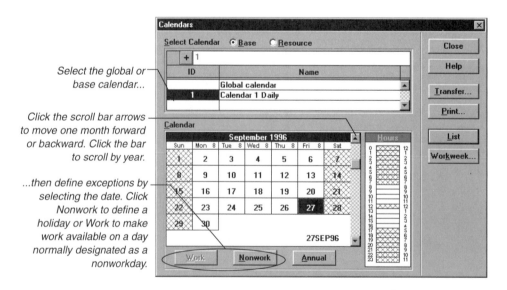

Select the global or base calendar...

Click the scroll bar arrows to move one month forward or backward. Click the bar to scroll by year.

...then define exceptions by selecting the date. Click Nonwork to define a holiday or Work to make work available on a day normally designated as a nonworkday.

If the exception is a workday, a number showing the scheduled hours for that day appears in the upper right corner of the date field in the calendar. You can change these hours in the Hours table. Double-click an hour to change its status.

If the exception occurs every year on exactly the same date, click Annual. The letter A in the upper left corner of the calendar date field identifies annual exceptions. For example, New Year's Day always occurs on January 1, so it is an annual holiday.

To define exceptions to the calendar using the list calendar
Choose Define, Calendars. Select a calendar, then click List. Add or change exceptions as needed. To designate an annual exception, use the monthly calendar display to select the date, then click Annual. Press Enter to save each exception defined.

Click and select a date from the pop-up calendar to add workday and nonworkday exceptions to the selected calendar.

Right-click and select Yes or No from the drop-down list to change the workday setting for an exception.

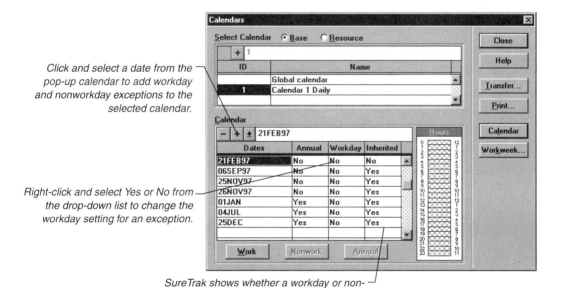

SureTrak shows whether a workday or non-workday is inherited from the global calendar.

 Holidays that occur on a different date each year, such as Labor Day, are not considered annual holidays. Enter these kinds of holidays on the global calendar for each year the project spans.

To change workhours for an exception Select the exception on the list calendar and double-click each hour you want to be a workhour in the Hours section; or select several hours and click Work or Nonwork.

Deleting Calendars

SureTrak projects always have a global calendar and calendar 1, the Normal Workweek calendar. You cannot delete the global calendar or calendar 1, but you can edit them so that the global calendar describes the workweek, workhours, and exceptions for your project team; and the Normal Workweek calendar describes the workweek, workhours, and exceptions common to most activities.

You can delete any other base calendars that you no longer need. When you delete a base calendar, SureTrak associates any activities and resources that were associated with the deleted calendar with calendar 1.

To delete a base calendar Choose Define, Calendars and select a base calendar. Click ⊟.

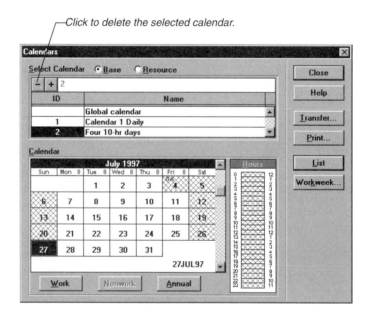

Click to delete the selected calendar.

You cannot delete a resource calendar from the Select Calendar section; SureTrak deletes it when you delete the resource. You can, however, change the base calendar a resource is associated with, which changes the workweek and exceptions the resource calendar inherits.

Transferring Calendars from Other Projects

Separate projects may use identical calendars. For example, perhaps all projects in a certain company work the same days and have the same nonworkdays. You can transfer global and base calendars, including holidays and other nonworkperiods, from any SureTrak project to the current project, rather than define them for each project. You can also transfer calendars from projects created by P3 and Finest Hour.

SureTrak maintains calendar assignments in the current project by calendar number, so that an activity assigned to base calendar 3 of the old calendars is now assigned to base calendar 3 of the newly transferred calendars.

To transfer calendars from SureTrak, P3, and other projects
Choose Define, Calendars, then click Transfer. Enter your specifications. Click OK to confirm that you want to transfer the calendars.

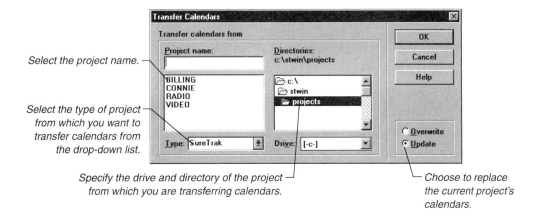

Select the project name.

Select the type of project from which you want to transfer calendars from the drop-down list.

Specify the drive and directory of the project from which you are transferring calendars.

Choose to replace the current project's calendars.

Overwriting project calendars when transferring If you choose the Overwrite option, SureTrak deletes all the current project's calendars.

SureTrak transfers resource calendars only when you transfer the resources themselves.

Updating project calendars when transferring If you choose the Update option, SureTrak copies calendars from the other project over calendars with matching numbers in the current project, replacing them; adds calendars whose numbers don't exist in the current project; and ignores calendars whose numbers exist in the current project but not in the project you are transferring from.

For more information about transferring resources, see the *Building a Resource Plan* chapter.

For example, assume that the current project contains calendars numbered 1, 2, and 3, and the other project contains calendar numbers 1, 2, and 5. If you choose Overwrite, the current project contains calendars 1, 2, and 5 from the other project. If you choose Update, the current project contains its own calendar 3, which was not updated, plus calendars 1, 2, and 5 from the other project. SureTrak updated Calendars 1 and 2 with calendars 1 and 2 from the other project, and added calendar 5.

Building a Resource Plan

In addition to having a network of activities required to complete a project, successful project management requires that you carefully plan and control resources—people, equipment, and materials—and budgets throughout the project. Using resources enables you to track your project's costs and revenue.

Begin by building a dictionary of resources necessary to complete the project; for each resource, set an availability limit, limit prices, and a calendar to define its standard worktime. Then, allocate resources to the activities that require them. You can assign more than one resource to each activity.

Creating a Resource List

Anything required to accomplish an activity can be considered a resource—labor, materials, equipment, or money. SureTrak enables you to define the resources required to accomplish the activities in your project.

You can identify a pool of resources for your project by entering a resource name, description, and unit of measure for each resource. If you want SureTrak to calculate costs and revenue for the project, you can also define a unit cost and a revenue unit value.

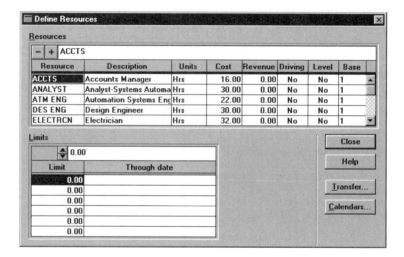

To add a resource to the project

1 Choose Define, Resources.

2 Click ⊞ in the Resources section to add a resource to the list.

3 In the Resource cell, enter a resource name of up to eight characters. In the Description cell, enter a full title for the resource.

4 In the Units cell, enter the unit of measurement, using up to four letters.

   For example, the units for pipe may be LF, for linear feet, or the units for labor resources may be HR, for hour.

5 In the Cost cell, enter the amount the resource costs per hour.

   For example, PVC pipe at $0.10 per linear foot can be installed at a rate of 350 feet per hour for an hourly cost of $35. A salaried employee at $28,000 per year costs $13.46 per hour.

6 In the Revenue cell, enter the amount of money each unit of the resource earns per hour, if anything.

Typical examples of revenue-earning resources are those for which you bill on the basis of time and materials or those for which you charge lump sums.

For more information about driving resources, see *Defining Driving Resources* later in this chapter.

7 In the Driving cell, enter Yes if the amount of the resource assigned to an activity determines the duration of that activity, overriding any duration you may have specified for the activity.

Enter No if you do not want the resource to drive the duration of activities to which it is assigned.

8 In the Level cell, enter Yes if you want SureTrak to level this resource.

Enter No if SureTrak should ignore this resource when leveling. Leveling resolves excess demands on resources by delaying lower-priority activities until the resources they require are available.

9 Right-click in the Base cell to select a base calendar to use as the basis for creating a work calendar for the resource.

10 Click OK.

To delete a resource from the project If you define a resource and later decide that it is no longer needed, you can delete it. In the Define Resources dialog box, select the resource in the Resources section, then click . SureTrak deletes the resource from the list and from all activities it is assigned to.

After you incorporate resources into your project plan, you can show resource requirements and overallocations. For more information, see the Analyzing Resource Use with Profiles and Tables *chapter. To have SureTrak resolve excess resource demands by leveling resources, see the* Leveling Resources *chapter.*

Setting Resource Availability Limits

SureTrak uses the limits you establish for resources and the dates through which the limits are in effect to determine the amount of a resource that is available at any time. Although entering limits for project resources is not mandatory, you must specify resource limits if you want to show resource limits in the Resource profile or Resource table or if you plan to level resources.

For more information about the Resource profile or the Resource table, see the *Analyzing Resource Use with Profiles and Tables* chapter.

To define resource limits Choose Define, Resources. Select a resource and specify an hourly limit in the Limits section, then press Enter. For example, establish a limit of two sound engineers per hour. Right-click in the Through Date cell and select a closing date for this limit from the pop-up calendar. If the limit is valid through the end of the project, leave the Through Date cell blank. Specify another limit and Through Date for this resource or select another resource. Save your changes by clicking Close.

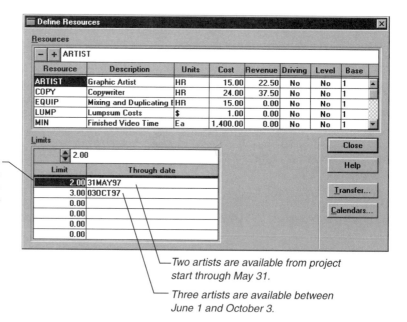

For each resource, you can define up to six timeperiods with different limits and a date through which that limit applies.

Two artists are available from project start through May 31.

Three artists are available between June 1 and October 3.

When specifying limits and through dates, remember these effects. To indicate that:

■ The resource is readily available in unlimited amounts through the end of the project, enter a limit of zero *without* a through date.

■ None of the resource is available through a given date, enter a limit of zero *with* a through date.

■ The number of resources is available each hour through the end of the project, enter a limit of any number other than zero without a through date.

Defining a Resource's Work Schedule

Each resource can have its own unique calendar, so you can accommodate different work schedules for individual people, equipment, and materials. A resource calendar is simply a copy of any base calendar that you can modify to meet a resource's special schedule.

To meet a deadline, some resources may have to work on a day that is normally a nonworkday. For example, the Testing department may work Saturdays—normally a nonworkday—for the last month of a project. In this case, associate the resource with a base calendar, then add the Saturdays as exceptions to that base calendar.

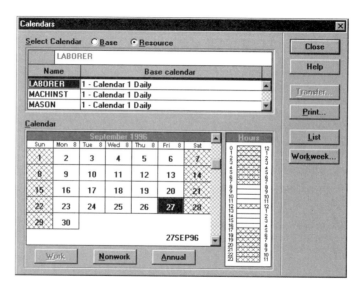

For detailed information about resource calendars, see the *Defining Project Calendars* chapter.

To define a resource calendar Choose Define, Resources, then click Calendars. Choose the Resource option and select the Base Calendar from which you will start to define this resource's calendar. Customize the calendar to show the resource's workweek, workhours, and exceptions.

Transferring Resources from Other Projects

Separate projects can use identical resources. Instead of entering identical or near-identical resources twice, transfer these resources between the projects.

When you transfer resources, SureTrak also transfers their resource calendars. You also can transfer the base calendars associated with each resource calendar. If the calendar on which any transferred resource is based does not already exist in the current project, based on calendar number, and you choose not to transfer base calendars, the resource calendar uses calendar 1 from the current project.

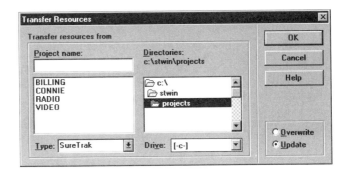

To transfer resources from another project

1 Choose Define, Resources, then click Transfer.

2 Right-click in the Type field and select a project type from the drop-down list.

3 Specify the drive and directory of the project from which you want to transfer resources.

4 Select the name of the project from which you want to transfer resources.

 If the project you are looking for is not listed, make sure the drive and directory are correct and that you have specified the correct type of project in the Type field.

5 Choose Overwrite or Update.

Choosing Overwrite deletes all existing resources in the current project and adds all the resources from the other project. SureTrak does not remove current resource assignments for activities.

Choosing Update adds and replaces resources based on resource ID: if the other project has some resources not defined in the current project, transferring adds them; if the other project has some resources with matching IDs, transferring replaces their current information with information from the other project; if the current project has some resources that the other project does not have, they are unaffected by an Update transfer.

6 Click OK. When prompted, confirm your decisions to transfer resources and the associated base calendars.

Defining Driving Resources

The duration of an activity sometimes depends on the amount of a specific resource assigned to it. Generally, the more labor resources assigned, the less time it takes to complete the activity. If you reduce resources, the activity takes longer to complete. Resources that control an activity's duration in this way are called driving resources.

When you reduce the units per hour of a driving resource, SureTrak recalculates the resource's duration accordingly, increasing it; when you increase the quantity of a driving resource, SureTrak calculates a correspondingly shorter duration. The driving resource with the longest duration controls the activity's duration.

Choose Define, Resources and enter Yes in the Driving cell to make a resource drive the duration of activities to which the person is assigned.

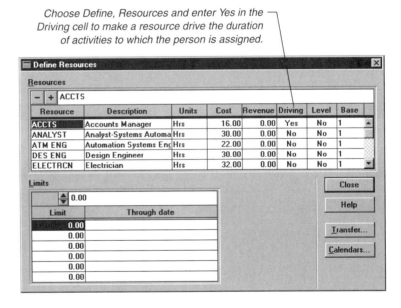

Driving resources determine the method SureTrak uses to perform several calculations. Driving resources assigned to a task, independent, or meeting activity determine the activity's duration. If you enter a total at completion amount for a driving resource assignment, SureTrak calculates resource duration; if you enter a total at completion amount for a nondriving resource assignment, SureTrak calculates the number of units required per hour. Calendars of driving resources combine to determine the time SureTrak schedules a meeting activity.

To automatically designate a resource as driving You can have SureTrak automatically set a resource to driving when resources are created. Choose Tools, Options, then click the Resource tab. Mark the Make Resources Driving By Default checkbox. If you mark this checkbox in the Options dialog box, SureTrak sets the Driving column in the Define Resources dialog box for the resource to Yes.

You can assign several driving resources to the same activity. The following table describes how SureTrak calculates activity durations from driving resources for the three main activity types.

Activity Type	Duration
Task with driving resource	Equal to duration of the driving resource with longest resource duration, plus its resource lag
Independent with driving resource	From the earliest early start of a driving resource through latest early finish of a driving resource
Meeting with driving resource	Equal to duration of the driving resource with longest resource duration, plus its resource lag

When you change an activity type from Task to Independent, SureTrak makes all resources assigned to the activity driving resources, if none of the resources already assigned are driving.

The activity type determines whether SureTrak assigns resources to activities according to their own calendars or according to the activity's base calendar, as described in the following table.

Activity Type	Base Calendar
Task	Activity's base calendar for all resources, both driving and nondriving
Independent	Individual resource calendars; both driving and nondriving resources use their own calendars
Meeting	A conglomerate calendar of common worktime among driving resources; both driving and nondriving resources use this conglomerate calendar

Editing Remaining Duration of Activities with Driving Resources

You can change the remaining durations of activities that have driving resources the same ways you edit activities with nondriving resources: on the Bar chart, by dragging the end of the activity bar to the new finish date; in the Update dialog box; in Activity columns; or in the Activity form.

SureTrak changes the activity's duration to the amount you specify and proportionately changes the amounts of driving resources—which control the activity's duration. It recalculates either the Units Per Hour or the total Quantity At Completion, depending on the project option selected in the Options dialog box (choose Tools, Options, and click the Resource tab).

For details about Autocost rules and their impacts on resources, see the *Updating Resources and Costs* chapter.

If you mark the Freeze Resource Units Per Hour checkbox, the resource Units Per Hour remain unchanged; SureTrak increases or decreases the total Quantity To Complete proportionately as the resource duration increases or decreases. If you clear the Freeze Resource Units Per Hour checkbox, the total Quantity To Complete remains the same; SureTrak increases the Units Per Hour as the duration decreases or decreases the Units Per Hour as the duration increases.

How Do Resources Affect Activities with Fixed Durations?

Independent, meeting, and task activities have specific durations. You specify their duration by entering a specific duration for the activity itself, and assigning only nondriving resources to it, which defer to the activity's duration; or by assigning one or more driving resources to the activity, and letting SureTrak calculate the activity's duration as equal to the longest duration of any assigned driving resource.

If you assign only nondriving resources to a task activity, SureTrak uses the duration you specified for the activity; it schedules the activity according to its base calendar.

If you assign only nondriving resources to an independent activity, SureTrak uses the duration you specified for the activity; it schedules each resource separately, or independently. Individual resources' durations are made equal to the activity's duration, but since each resource is scheduled by its own resource calendar, it may or may not coincide with the scheduling of the activity itself.

If you assign only nondriving resources to a meeting activity, SureTrak uses the duration you specified for the activity; it schedules all resources together, so that they all start and finish at the same time the activity starts and finishes.

If the duration of an activity depends on how much time a specific resource can devote to it per day, assign those resources as driving resources. SureTrak calculates the activity duration equal to the longest duration of the driving resources assigned to it. When you assign a driving resource to a task activity, SureTrak calculates the activity's duration according to the amount of time the longest driving resource will work on it; it schedules the activity during worktime defined on the base calendar you assign to the activity, forcing the resource to work by the activity's calendar, not its own.

When you assign a driving resource to an independent activity, SureTrak calculates when each driving resource will work on the activity, based on its own calendar. Then SureTrak checks the start and finish dates of each driving resource for this activity, and calculates the activity's duration from the start date of the first resource to the finish date of the last resource.

When you assign a driving resource to a meeting activity, SureTrak calculates the duration of each driving resource's work on the activity, then calculates the duration of the activity and all nondriving resources as being equal to the longest duration of those driving resources. It schedules the activity during nonworktime in a calendar it derives by calculating worktime common to all of the driving resources' calendars.

Assigning Resources to Activities

All projects require resources—people, equipment, materials, or money—to accomplish the work. After you define the resources a project requires, use the Insert Resource Assignment dialog box or the Resource column to quickly assign them to activities.

When you assign a resource to an activity, you are describing how much of that resource is required to accomplish that activity. An activity can require several resources and the same resource can be assigned to several activities. After you've assigned a resource to an activity, use the Resources detail form to review resource data for each activity. Resources can be allocated so they drive the activity duration (driving), or they can be spread across a specified activity duration (nondriving).

 To assign a resource using the Insert Resource Assignment dialog box

1 Select the activity to which you want to assign resources.

2 Choose Insert, Resource Assignment.

You can assign the same resource to multiple activities by first selecting the appropriate activities.

Insert Resource Assignment - RADIO	
PU1000 - Determine Facility Needs	Cancel
Choose a resource from the list below, or add a new one by typing in the name.	Assign
Resource: Description:	Help
BRDENGR Broadcast Engineer	
Units: 1.00	
To complete: 16.00 HR	

3 Select a resource from the drop-down list. SureTrak provides the description for the resource that you entered in the Resource Dictionary. Or, type a new resource name and description, which is automatically added to the Resource Dictionary.

For more information about driving resources, see Defining Driving Resources *earlier in this chapter.*

4 Enter the quantity of resource assigned to the activity, that is, the number of resources required per hour for work on the activity. If the resource is driving, also enter the total required to complete the assignment, that is, the number of hours required to complete the entire task. SureTrak calculates the duration of the activity automatically.

For example, if you have one designer to allocate to a Design New Feature activity, which requires 80 hours of work, enter 1.00 in the Units field and enter 80.00 in the To Complete field. SureTrak will calculate the activity duration as 10 days, assuming an eight-hour workday.

5 Click Assign to allocate the specified resource to the designated activity. Or, click Assign All when allocating a resource to more than one activity at the same time (multiple activities are selected).

6 Select another activity and continue to assign resources, or click Close to close the Insert Resource Assignment dialog box.

 Use the Insert Resource Assignment dialog box to make initial assignments only. If you need to revise an assignment, use the Resources detail form.

To allocate a nondriving resource, specify either the quantity of resource (units), or the total estimated effort (to complete). When you change one value, SureTrak automatically calculates the other for you, based on the default duration and the activity duration.

For details about organizing the project, see the *Organizing and Summarizing Activities* chapter.

To assign a resource in the Activity columns You can also assign or edit resources directly in the Activity columns. First, set up the Activity columns to be organized by resource and include a column for the resource name. Click the resource cell for the activity to which you want to assign a resource, then type the resource name in the edit bar. Press Enter or click ☑ to confirm or ☒ to cancel.

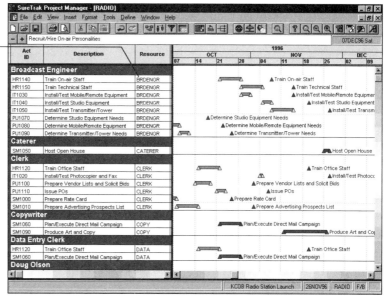

When typing the resource name in the Resource column, just type the first one or two characters. SureTrak "types ahead" for you to make entering data easier.

To assign or change a resource using the Resources detail form Use the Resource detail form to review or modify all the data about an activity's resources.

1 Select the activity to which you want to assign resources.

2 Choose View, Activity Detail, Resources.

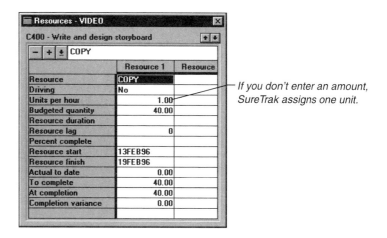

If you don't enter an amount, SureTrak assigns one unit.

3 Click ⊞ in the Resources detail form to add resource assignments. Click ⬇ to select a resource from the list. SureTrak automatically calculates default values for the remaining cells.

4 In the Driving cell, enter Yes if the resource drives the activity's duration.

A driving resource indicates that the resource drives the duration of the activity to which it is assigned.

5 In the Units per Hour cell, enter the amount of the resource that is required per hour for the activity.

If you know the total amount of the resource required for the entire activity, enter that amount in the At Completion cell.

6 If the resource is nondriving, SureTrak calculates the information for the Budgeted Quantity cell. If the resource is driving, SureTrak calculates the remaining duration of the activity.

Budgeted quantity is the total quantity of resource budgeted to the activity and is calculated as Quantity Assigned x Resource Duration.

7 For nondriving resources only, enter a resource duration in the Resource Duration cell if the resource's duration is different from the activity's duration.

When a resource is assigned to an activity, some cells for that resource may be blank, including, Actual to Date, To Complete, and Percent Complete. Fill in these cells when you update project progress.

8 For nondriving resources only, in the Resource Lag cell enter the amount of time after the activity starts that the resource should start.

For example, a resource will not start work on an activity until 3 days of its work are complete.

9 Click ▲ or ▼ to move to the next activity or to the next selected activity.

10 Click OK.

SureTrak always calculates resource start and finish dates based on either the activity's duration or the resource's assigned duration and lag time. Nondriving resources assigned to task and meeting activities have resource start and finish dates identical to the activity start and finish dates, unless you enter a specific resource duration and/or lag. Nondriving resources assigned to independent activities work according to their own scheduled days and hours. SureTrak calculates the duration of the activity from the date the first resource starts to the date the last resource finishes.

Assigning resources by moving activities You can also assign resources to an activity by moving activities to different bands when the project is organized by resources. If you drag an activity having no resource assignment from the uncategorized band to a group banded by resource, the moved activity inherits the resource with a Units per Hour equal to 1.

For more information about dragging activities, see the *Organizing and Summarizing Activities* chapter.

You can add more specific resource assignment information in the Resources detail form. Several layouts supplied with SureTrak have resource bands: RES1, RES2, RES3, and RES4.

Assigning a Resource Multiple Times

You can assign the same resource to an activity more than once. The data item called Resource Designator/Cost Account differentiates between resource assignments when a resource is assigned to a specific activity more than once. For example, define Boxes as a resource, then assign Boxes to one activity several times with a different cost each time to represent the costs of different-sized boxes.

You can display the resource designator as a noneditable column in the Activity columns by adding it in the Columns dialog box (choose Format, Columns); SureTrak displays values for this column when you group activities by resource. An activity in a P3 project that has only a cost account with no resources assigned will be assigned a "resource" named COSTACCT in SureTrak; this resource is a placeholder for the cost account information from P3.

Assigning Costs and Revenue

You can work with resources that have no monetary values. If you are interested only in resource scheduling and availability, define them with no associated costs or revenue. Alternatively, you can define resources as cost- and/or revenue-bearing, and let SureTrak calculate the cost and/or revenue for each assignment of each resource to an activity. You can also define lump sum resources and assign these specific quantities of money to activities.

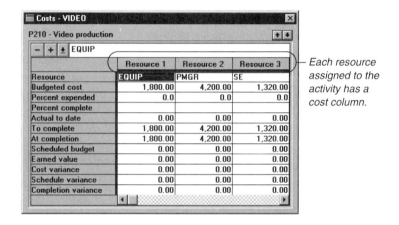

Each resource assigned to the activity has a cost column.

To assign costs to a resource Choose Define, Resources. Enter the amount each unit of resource will cost in the Cost column. After you define costs for resources, SureTrak calculates the values and displays the information in the Costs detail form. Choose View, Activity Detail, Costs to display the Costs detail form.

You can enter an activity's budgeted cost for a resource directly or have SureTrak calculate it for each resource assignment based on the resource's unit cost (defined in the Resources dialog box) and the resource's units per hour (assigned in the Resources detail form).

Add lump sum costs in the Costs detail form even if no hourly resource quantities are generating the costs.

To assign lump sum costs to a resource If you know the exact amount a resource assignment will cost or the exact amount it will earn, you can enter these amounts directly as lump sums, rather than by defining the resources as having associated hourly costs and revenues. For example, perhaps your company has agreed to install its product at a customer site for a specific fee. It doesn't matter how long the installation takes or how many people are required; you have agreed to a specific revenue amount for this activity.

1 Select the activity to which you want to add a lump sum cost.

2 Choose View, Activity Detail, Costs.

3 Select a blank Resource cell and type a name for the lump sum, such as MISC for Miscellaneous Costs.

4 Type the lump sum amount in the At Completion cell.

5 If a portion of the lump sum has been spent as of the data date, enter the percent spent in the Percent Complete cell or enter the actual amount in the Actual to Date cell.

SureTrak calculates the other cost cells for the lump sum, but does not recalculate cost percent complete.

6 Click ▲ or ▼ to move to the next activity, or click ✖ to close the form.

To add a lump sum revenue to an activity

1 Select the activity to which you want to add a lump sum revenue.

2 Choose View, Activity Detail, Revenue.

3 Select a blank Resource cell and type a name for the revenue, such as GRANT or LUMP.

Add lump sum revenue in the Revenue detail form even if no hourly resource quantities are generating the revenue.

4 Type the lump sum amount in the Revenue At Completion cell.

5 If a portion of the lump sum has been accrued as of the data date, enter the percent accrued in the Percent Complete cell or enter the actual amount in the Revenue to Date cell.

SureTrak calculates the other cost cells for the lump sum.

6 Click ▲ or ▼ to move to the next activity, or click ✖ to close the form.

For information about updating lump sum costs and revenue, see the *Updating Resources and Costs* chapter.

 Resource, cost, and revenue amounts can be shown without a decimal or with two decimal places. You may want to suppress the decimal places for projects that involve large amounts (choose Tools, Options, then click the Resource tab).

Creating and Fine-Tuning the Project Schedule

A project's schedule is its logic network: the order activities occur. SureTrak uses the Critical Path Method (CPM) to create a schedule. You can control whether SureTrak schedules a project automatically whenever you enter or update activity information, or only when you initiate it; how SureTrak handles out-of-sequence activities; and the amount of float that defines the criticality of activities.

Because network logic alone cannot reflect all project conditions, you may sometimes need to impose constraints on specific dates.

This chapter discusses calculating and fine-tuning a schedule.

Building a Schedule

 You create a schedule by adding activities to your project, then establishing relationships between those activities. SureTrak schedules your projects either automatically or on demand when you press F9, assigning early and late dates and tracing a path through the activities from the beginning of the project to the end. You can constrain certain activities, which affects the way SureTrak schedules them—sometimes pushing back the project's finish date, sometimes creating negative float or out-of-sequence activities.

A project schedule is dynamic; when you make changes to the project, SureTrak recalculates the schedule incorporating these changes.

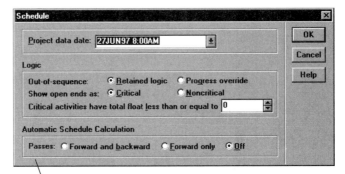

Choose Tools, Schedule to display the Schedule dialog box, where you can control certain aspects of the way SureTrak schedules your project.

For information about adding activities to a project, see the *Adding Activities* chapter.

To learn how to assign relationships to activities, see the *Linking Activities with Relationships* chapter.

Setting Schedule Calculation Options

Set scheduling options for the project in the Schedule dialog box. You decide how to handle out-of-sequence progress, and whether or not you want SureTrak to schedule automatically. You can also specify a data date that is different from the date on which you enter the information. Choose Tools, Schedule to display the Schedule dialog box.

Click and select a new data date from the pop-up calendar or type a date.

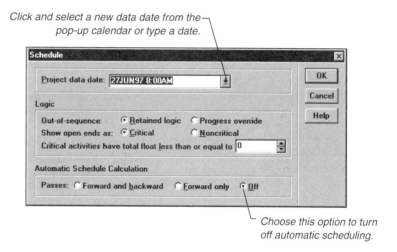

Choose this option to turn off automatic scheduling.

For more information on the data date and updating, see the *Updating Activities* chapter.

Specifying the project data date The project data date, which is the date SureTrak uses as the starting point for its current schedule calculations, appears in the Schedule dialog box. SureTrak uses the project start date as a data date until you specify a new data date. If you change the data date in the Schedule dialog box, SureTrak reschedules the project as of the new data date but does not update progress on the project; activities are rescheduled after the data date, as though delayed until then.

Specifying out-of-sequence logic By default, SureTrak uses retained logic to schedule an activity that occurs out of its logical sequence—before its predecessors. It schedules the remaining duration of the out-of-sequence activity according to network logic; any remaining duration of an activity that started out of sequence is scheduled after its predecessors finish. If you specify Retained Logic, SureTrak starts the activity out of sequence, but does not permit its remaining duration to start until its controlling predecessor completes.

If you specify Progress Override, SureTrak schedules the out-of-sequence activity as though it has no predecessors; its remaining duration is scheduled at the data date, so that it proceeds without delay. The out-of-sequence activity's successors will also occur earlier in the schedule, unless they are prevented by other predecessors.

Setting automatic scheduling preferences In the Schedule dialog box, you can specify which schedule calculations SureTrak automatically performs after each modification to an activity or relationship. The forward pass calculates activity early start and finish dates; the backward pass calculates late start and finish dates. By default, SureTrak calculates both the forward and backward passes.

By default, SureTrak recalculates the schedule after each change to a relationship or activity duration. Before you enter update information, choose Off in the Automatic Schedule Calculation section of the Schedule dialog box (choose Tools, Schedule).

When you change the data date by dragging the data-date line or by using the Progress Spotlight feature, SureTrak turns off automatic scheduling, then turns it on again when you finish estimating progress with the Update Progress Now icon or the Update Progress dialog box.

Defining the Critical Path

SureTrak offers two choices for identifying critical activities: one for open-ended activity paths and one defining criticality. Typically, a project has one open-ended activity (with no predecessors) at the beginning of the project and one open-ended activity (with no successors) at the end of the project.

By default, an activity without a successor (one with an open end) is shown as noncritical, with float to the project's must-finish deadline date if one exists, or to its calculated finish date if no deadline was established. If you prefer, you can show these open-ended activity paths as critical, creating more than one critical path. SureTrak determines the critical path by comparing early and late dates. The critical path is the longest path of activities in the project—the path that determines the project's finish date. This path of activities is also the path with the least amount of float, usually zero or negative.

If you make open ends noncritical, SureTrak sets the late finish dates for open-ended activities to the project's early finish date. If the project's must-finish date is earlier than its calculated early finish date, SureTrak uses the must-finish date instead.

Choose this option to display open-ended activities as critical.

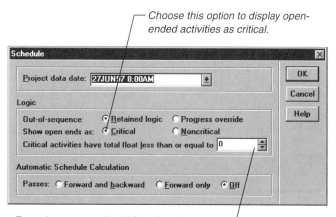

Enter the amount of total float that determines the criticality of an activity and indicate if you're measuring float in hours (h) or days (d).

To define the amount of float that makes an activity critical

You can show activities with some float as critical to emphasize the importance of on-time completion. Or, if a project is significantly behind schedule, set a higher threshold for criticality, showing as critical only those activities that have less than a specified quantity of negative float—those that are the most behind schedule, or most critical.

These activities are critical even though they have positive float.

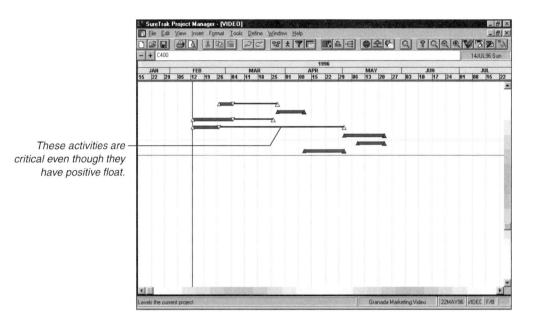

For more information on tracing the critical path in the PERT view, see the *Customizing the PERT View* chapter.

Reviewing Activity Dates

Depending on the type of date, you can review activity dates in the Activity columns, Dates detail form, Update Activity dialog box, bars and labels on the Bar chart, or in the Activity form, and in PERT.

For information about entering actual start and finish dates, see the *Updating Activities* chapter.

When scheduling, SureTrak calculates early and late dates for each activity, based on the relationships you create between activities. You can attach certain activities to specific dates, overriding these calculated dates. The following table describes activity dates used in SureTrak. SureTrak calculates some dates, while you can enter others.

Activity Date	Description
Early start	Earliest date activity can begin; calculated by SureTrak.
Early finish	Earliest date activity can finish; calculated by SureTrak.
Late start	Latest date activity can start without delaying project's finish or an established deadline; calculated by SureTrak.
Late finish	Latest date activity can finish without delaying project's finish or an established deadline; calculated by SureTrak.
Target start	Target date activity should start; entered by user.
Target finish	Target date activity should finish; entered by user.
Start constraint	Restriction placed on activity's start date that specifies when it can or must start; entered by user.
Finish constraint	Restriction placed on activity's finish date that specifies when it can or must finish; entered by user.
Actual start	Date activity actually started; entered by user, or calculated by SureTrak if estimating progress.
Actual finish	Date activity actually finished; entered by user, or calculated by SureTrak if estimating progress.
Unleveled start	Date activity was scheduled to start before user leveled resources; calculated by SureTrak.
Unleveled finish	Date activity was scheduled to finish before user leveled resources; calculated by SureTrak.
Suspend date	Date work on activity is suspended; requires an actual start date; entered by user.
Resume date	Date work on activity will or did resume; requires a suspend date; entered by user.

For information about adding activity date columns to the project, see the *Customizing the Bar Chart View* chapter.

To review dates in the Activity columns You can display any activity dates in the Activity columns pane of the Bar chart view. For example, list the early start and finish dates to show when activities are currently scheduled to occur. This display is particularly useful if your timescale uses a broad increment, such as months, which does not show exact dates on the Bar chart.

To review dates in the Dates detail form Choose View, Activity, Detail, Dates to display the Dates detail form. The Dates form lists all dates associated with an activity. Use it to assign target or actual dates, and to compare them to the calculated early, late, and unleveled dates.

When you open the Dates form, SureTrak shows dates for the activity selected in the Activity columns. Use the ▲ ▼ buttons to move to the next or previous activity in the Activity columns (or the previous or next selected activity, if several activities are selected) and display its dates.

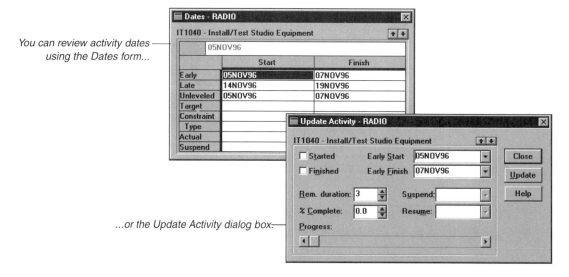

You can review activity dates using the Dates form...

...or the Update Activity dialog box.

To review dates in the Update Activity dialog box Choose Tools, Update Activity to display the Update Activity dialog box. The Update Activity dialog box shows an activity's early dates. When an activity has started or finished, SureTrak replaces these dates with actual start and/or finish dates. The Update Activity dialog box also displays suspend and resume dates if you've recorded an interruption, in addition to the activity's remaining duration and percent complete.

For more information about updating activities, see the *Updating Activities* chapter.

When you open the Update Activity dialog box, SureTrak shows dates for the activity selected. Use the arrow buttons to move to the previous or next activity (or the previous or next selected activity, if several activities are selected) and display its dates.

To review dates on the Bar chart You can customize the Bar chart to show bars and endpoints for dates you want to review or compare. Use the timescale and the Bar chart legend to interpret early dates, late dates, target dates, unleveled dates, free float, or total float.

You may need to click the More button in the Activity form to display late dates, if they are not displayed.

To review dates in the Activity form Open the Activity form (choose View, Activity Form) to view the date fields that show an activity's early and late start and finish dates. Once you indicate that an activity has started, the actual start date replaces the early start date; no late start date exists. When you indicate that an activity has finished, the actual finish date replaces the early finish date; no late finish date exists.

SureTrak calculates the early and late dates for the activity. You can edit them in the Activity form, if permitted in the Forms tab of the Options dialog box (choose Tools, Options). However, SureTrak recalculates these dates each time it schedules, overwriting your edits.

To edit activity dates To change any date in a detail form, Activity form, or in the Activity columns, move the insertion point to the date field. Type the new date over the existing date, using the date format you specified in the Options dialog box in the Dates tab.

If the date appears dimmed in the edit bar, it cannot be edited.

Using Constraints on Activity Dates

Network logic alone cannot reflect all project situations. For example, perhaps an activity is delayed due to a deferral in funding, or a manufacturer notifies you that a piece of equipment will be delivered earlier than scheduled. Or perhaps certain outside activities must be completed before the start of winter. These activities depend on dates, rather than other activities—or in addition to their dependence on other activities.

To model dependence on specific dates, assign constraints to activities. SureTrak uses the constrained dates instead of calculated dates when determining the project schedule.

SureTrak implements 10 types of constraints. The following constraints constrain an activity to a particular date. The expected finish, as late as possible, and zero total float constraints constrain duration or determine whether the activity is scheduled as early as possible, or as late as possible without delaying its successors.

Early start constraint Use this constraint for a potential delay. It pushes early start forward (later) to a specified date and prevents the activity from starting too early. It affects the schedule only if the specified constraint date is later than the calculated early start date.

Late start constraint Use this constraint to meet a deadline. An activity must start by a specified date. It pulls the late start back (earlier) if the calculated late start is later than the specified constraint date.

Early finish constraint Use this constraint for a potential delay. It pushes early finish forward (later) to a specified date and prevents an activity from finishing too early. It affects the schedule only if the specified constraint date is later than the early finish date.

Late finish constraint Use this constraint for a deadline. An activity must finish by a specified date. It pulls late finish back (earlier) if the calculated late finish is later than the specified constraint date.

Start on constraint Use this constraint for a specific start date. It forces early and late start dates to a specified date. (It works the same as applying both start no earlier than and start no later than constraints.) Unlike the mandatory constraints, it does not violate network logic; activities will not be scheduled ahead of their predecessors.

Mandatory start constraint Use as a specific start date. It forces early and late start dates equal to a specified date and ensures leveling does not delay the activity. This constraint can violate network logic; a successor with a mandatory start constraint might be scheduled before its predecessors.

Mandatory finish constraint Use as a specific finish date. It forces early and late finish dates equal to a specified date and ensures leveling does not delay activity. It can violate network logic; a successor with a mandatory finish constraint might be scheduled before its predecessors.

 Use caution when you apply mandatory start and finish dates. SureTrak uses these dates whether or not they are consistent with network logic. If the mandatory dates you assign are earlier than the early dates calculated by SureTrak, an activity may be scheduled earlier than its predecessors.

A constraint assigned to one activity may affect other activities: if an activity must or definitely will occur before or after a specific date, that restriction could affect the dates of other activities. If a date constraint has been assigned, SureTrak uses that date for calculations, regardless of any other dates.

For example, if an activity is scheduled to start January 15 and has a start no earlier than constraint of January 20, SureTrak schedules it to start on January 20, and delays its successors accordingly. If an activity is scheduled to finish June 19, but has a finish no later than constraint of June 3, SureTrak schedules it to finish June 3, and schedules its predecessors in time for it to finish on that date.

Using the expected finish constraint to calculate duration
When you assign an expected finish constraint to an activity, SureTrak calculates the remaining duration as the difference between the activity's early start date and the expected finish date. If the activity is underway, the remaining duration is the difference between the data date and the expected finish date. If the expected finish date is earlier than the scheduled early start, SureTrak sets the remaining duration to zero.

Use the expected finish constraint to revise remaining durations for long-duration activities that overlap many update periods, so you don't have to continually update with new remaining durations. You can also use it to estimate an activity's initial duration by entering an actual start and expected finish. Then, when the duration has been calculated, delete the actual start date, so that the activity is not shown as underway.

Using the zero total float constraint to make an activity critical To make an activity critical, use the zero total float constraint. When you apply the zero total float constraint to an activity with positive float, SureTrak sets the activity's late dates equal to its early dates. The activity may be delayed or scheduled earlier, as its predecessors are rescheduled, but it will always have zero or negative float.

When you assign a zero total float constraint to an activity, it affects that activity's predecessors as well; it may reduce or even eliminate any positive total float they have. This constraint does not affect activities that already have zero or negative float.

Using a constraint to delay an activity as much as possible
To force an activity to occur as late as possible, use the as late as possible constraint. When you apply the as late as possible constraint to an activity, SureTrak sets the early dates as late as possible without affecting successor activities, eliminating the activity's free float. You may want to use this constraint on activities involving payments you must make, or deliveries that should arrive just in time.

Assigning Constraints to Activities

You can assign constraints directly on the Bar chart or in the Constraints detail form. If a date in an Activity column is associated with a constraint, SureTrak displays an asterisk (*) next to the date in the Activity column.

To assign constraints on the Bar chart

1 Scroll around the Bar chart until you can see the activity you want to constrain.

2 Press the Ctrl key until the mouse pointer changes to ⌐. Position the mouse pointer over either end of the activity bar until the ·ェ· pointer appears.

3 Press and hold the left mouse button as you drag the pointer across the Bar chart to the date that you want to force the activity to. Release the mouse button to display the Constraints detail form.

4 In the Constraints detail form, verify or change the constraint type and date.

5 Click ⊠ to close the Constraints form.

SureTrak applies the constraint to the activity and, if automatic scheduling is turned on, SureTrak recalculates the schedule.

 You cannot assign constraints to activities by dragging the activity bar if your project is organized by resources.

 ### To assign constraints using the Constraints form

1 Select one or more activities in the Activity columns.

2 Choose View, Activity Detail, Constraints to display the Constraints detail form.

3 Select the type of constraint you want to impose on the activity.

4 If you're assigning one of the eight types of date constraints, click ▣ in the associated date box and select the date you want the activity constrained to from the pop-up calendar.

5 Click ⊠ to close the Constraints form or use the ▲ ▼ buttons to move to another activity.

Enter constraint information in the Constraints form.

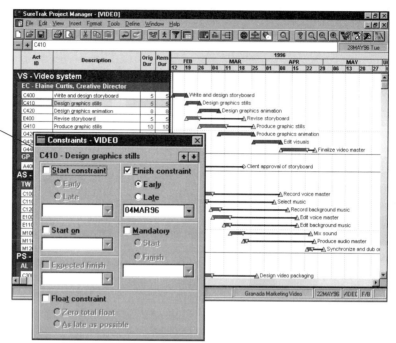

Changing the Duration and Dates of Activity Bars

SureTrak enables you to adjust the schedule by dragging the duration of some activities in the Bar chart view. Changing the duration or dates of one activity can affect the schedule dates for preceding or succeeding activities. It is helpful to show relationship lines in the Bar chart view so you can easily identify any related activities that your changes may affect (choose View, Relationships).

1 To change the duration of an activity, position the mouse pointer at the end of the activity bar until the mouse pointer changes.

Act ID	Description	Orig Dur	Rem Dur	FEB			MAR			1997
				24	03	10	17	24	31	07
1080	Install computer system	20d	20d							
1090	Test computer system	13d	13d							
1100	Install photocopier	14d	14d					Finish - 21MAR97 Remaining Duration - 15d		

2 Drag the end of the bar until you reach the duration you want. The Datometer displays the finish date and duration as you move the endpoint.

To view the constraint placed on the activity, select the activity and choose View, Activity Detail, Constraints. To view the actual dates assigned, select the activity and choose View, Activity Detail, Dates.

You can also move an entire bar to an earlier or later timeframe. When you change the dates of an activity, and then you calculate the schedule, SureTrak returns the activity to its logically scheduled timeframe. To anchor an activity to a specific timeframe, you can apply a constraint when you change the start and finish dates.

To change the start and finish dates for an activity

1 Position the mouse pointer in the center of the activity bar whose dates you want to change. The pointer changes to +.

2 Drag the bar to the right or left until you reach the date you want and release the mouse button.

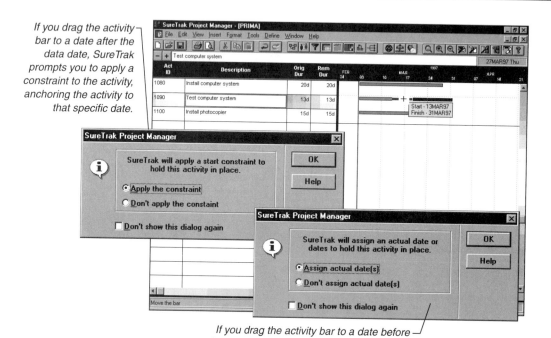

If you drag the activity bar to a date after the data date, SureTrak prompts you to apply a constraint to the activity, anchoring the activity to that specific date.

If you drag the activity bar to a date before the project data date, SureTrak prompts you to set actual dates for the activity.

3 Choose whether to assign constraints or actual dates for the activity. Assigning constraints or actual dates anchors the activity to that timeframe. If you do not assign constraints or actual dates, SureTrak returns the activity to its previous date.

4 Click OK.

When you calculate the schedule, SureTrak uses the constraint to anchor the activity to the specific timeframe.

 To display the constraint and actual dates message boxes each time you drag the bar or to turn off having SureTrak automatically assign constraints/actual dates in the Bar chart, set the options in the Options dialog box (choose Tools, Options, and click the General tab).

Working with Project Groups

In most companies, projects affect, and are affected by, other projects. They may share resources, one project's activities may depend on completion of another project's activities, and upper management may want consolidated reports that show the status of all projects together.

With SureTrak's Project Groups feature, you can schedule, update, and manage interrelated projects separately and together.

Why Use Project Groups?

Using SureTrak, you can plan, schedule, and control multiple projects independently. You can also combine them as necessary for overall corporate reporting and planning, and for company-wide decision making at higher levels of management.

Project groups are especially useful in organizations where several projects are underway simultaneously. These projects may be related: they may compete for the same resources, or certain activities in one project may have to be finished or underway before activities in another project can begin. By including these related projects in a project group, you can globally resolve potential resource conflicts and see the interrelationships between activities in the projects.

An organization may also have projects that are too large to manage as single projects. For example, a complex project may consist of several phases, and each phase may have subphases. Using project groups, you can divide the complex project into several phases, making each phase more manageable for individual project managers, department heads, or team leaders.

Project Group Terminology

Project Group: a collection of related or unrelated projects. Select Project Groups from the drop-down list in the Type field in the New, Open, Save As, Backup, Restore, and Transfer dialog boxes.

Member Project: a project that is a part of a project group. A member project is also known simply as a project.

Standalone Project: a project that is not a member of a project group.

Source Project: a project that is added to or removed from a project group.

Destination Group: a project group into which a project is being added.

Project ID: a two-character code comprising the first two characters of the Activity ID, used to differentiate member projects within a project group.

Concentric (P3) file type: a file in Primavera Project Planner format; also known as the P3 file type.

Project Group Scenarios

As your organization's project controls coordinator, use this section to familiarize yourself with some ways you can use project groups. Each example uses SureTrak's grouping features in a different way.

Project group with interrelated projects Assume that you are the project manager for a cable television company expanding its coverage area into two new states. In the project group, you define activity codes for Responsibility, Site, Legal, Hookup, and Step. You add to these codes values that pertain to activities in both projects. Later in the planning process, the member project managers can add more values that pertain to their projects' unique activities.

You also define resources that will be used in both projects, such as purchasing, satellite installation, and real estate resources. Each member project manager also can add local resources, such as excavation, testing, and marketing.

After you define the project group's Activity Codes and Resource Dictionaries, create a member project for each of the two states into which the company is expanding.

For more information on checking a project out of a project group, see *Keeping Track of Projects within a Project Group* later in this chapter.

Because the member project managers in charge of the service expansion will travel from your main headquarters to the two expansion states, they check out their member projects from the project group using Check-in/Check-out. Both managers start with empty projects you created, which contain copies of the Activity Code and Resource Dictionaries to use when they add activities. The project managers create their schedules, then back up the member projects and return them to you. When you receive the member projects, you check them back into the project group so you can see them together.

After the member project managers schedule their projects and return or save them, you create relationships between the member projects, and between the member projects and the project group, where necessary. Then send the member projects back to the project managers; each schedule now reflects the interrelationships between activities in the member projects.

The member project managers change the schedule and update progress as necessary. Project managers not at headquarters back up their updated projects and send them to you via electronic mail (E-mail) so you can merge them into the project group. If project managers work locally, they update their projects directly. These regular updates help you keep the status of each project current, as well as the overall status of the expansion.

Complex project Your company is preparing to manufacture and market a new line of cellular telephones. As the product manager preparing to plan the project, you realize that it is quite complex. In addition to the several stages and corresponding substages, the production and assembly portions of the project have been outsourced to two third-party manufacturers.

You start by creating a project group, and defining the basic WBS coding structure, which includes the first three levels of the structure, for the project group.

You also define activity codes for Responsibility, Stage, Area, and Mail, and add general values for these codes, including E-mail addresses for the Mail code. You also define resources for the stages of the project for which your company will be directly responsible.

After defining the project group, create member projects for the planning and design, plant retooling, assembly, production, and product delivery stages. Then, define default activity code values and a default WBS code in the project group.

Since you have outsourced the cellular telephone production and assembly to two different companies that use SureTrak, you can back up the contract manufacturers' projects and send them via diskettes; they can add their activities, lower-level WBS codes, specific activity code values, and resources, and then create their own schedules. They schedule their respective projects and return them. You then restore the projects to the project group for overall scheduling.

This process is beneficial from a management standpoint because project managers can control their parts of the project, while you as the product manager can report overall progress and forecast the date the cellular telephones will be ready to sell. You also can customize reports for upper management by summarizing activities of the member projects to show progress for each major stage, instead of the progress for each activity.

Many distinct projects in the same organization Assume that you are the corporate project manager for a documentation company, and have developed processes that you follow to complete each project; in general, all projects share the same resources—your employees.

As the corporate project manager, create a project group and define all the resources used for documentation projects. Also, define a standardized set of activity and WBS codes. One important benefit of this approach is that member project managers can quickly create their projects without defining resources, activity codes, or WBS codes, since all documentation projects use resources from the same resource pool.

Another benefit is that you can use the project group to determine whether you have enough resources to complete all concurrent projects. If resources are insufficient, you can develop "what-if" scenarios by leveling the resources. Leveling eliminates resource overallocations across all projects, and you can see the impact on each project's finish dates using the new resource allocations. You can then determine whether you can complete the projects by the required dates, or whether you need to add temporary resources to remain on schedule.

In addition, since a project group shares its database with the member projects, you can easily track cash flow for all projects to make sure the projects are collectively progressing on time and within budget.

Access Rights to a Project Group

If you are working in a project group or in a member project, you have exclusive modification rights to the project group data. If someone else attempts to open the project group or one of its member projects, SureTrak displays a message indicating that the project group is either Read Only or in use. Another user can open the project group or the member project in Read Only mode, but cannot save it with the same name.

You can also choose to open a project in Read Only mode even if the project is not in use by another user. Mark the Read Only checkbox. You cannot save any changes you make to the project, but you can make temporary changes to perform "what-if" schedule analyses. Choose File, Save As and assign the project a new name to save the changes.

Creating a Project Group

The first step to setting up a project group is to create the project group—the project that will serve as a "container" for all the member projects you're tracking together. The second step is to add member projects to the project group.

 The Project Groups and Concentric (P3) project types are equivalent.

To create a project group Choose File, New.

Type a four-character project name.

Specify the drive and directory where SureTrak will store the project group files.

Specify Project Groups as the project type.

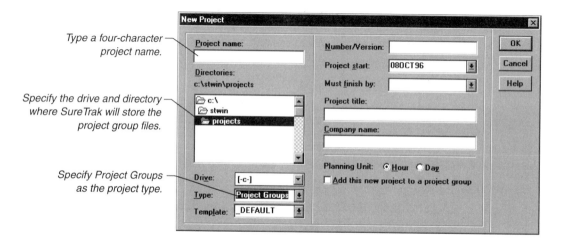

Identify any revisions to the project group in the Number/Version field. Assign the project group a title. Identify the project group's company or client. Specify the project group planning unit (hours or days) for activity durations. Click OK.

You can also use the Project Groups Wizard to create project groups.

SureTrak creates the project group and opens the Bar chart view. You can now define the project group's common project items.

For more information about project group items, see *Planning Your Own Project Groups* later in this chapter.

 Project groups must be saved in the Project Groups format. To use an existing project in SureTrak format as a project group, first save it in the Project Groups format.

Project IDs

When you add a member project to a project group you assign it a unique, two-character project ID. SureTrak automatically inserts this project ID as the first two characters of each Activity ID in the member project. The project ID distinguishes activities in the member project from other activities in the project group.

Adding a Project to a Project Group

SureTrak's Project Group Wizard helps you collect standalone projects into a project group. It also helps you remove a project from a project group, converting the member project into a standalone project.

For information on creating a project group, see *Creating a Project Group* earlier in this chapter.

The Project Group Wizard requires that the project group must already exist and must be the Project Groups or Concentric (P3) type.

To add an existing project to a project group using the Project Group Wizard Close all open projects. Choose Tools, Wizards, Project Group Wizard.

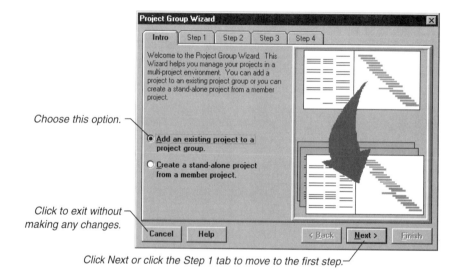

Choose this option.

Click to exit without making any changes.

Click Next or click the Step 1 tab to move to the first step.

To create a project group with member projects manually, see *Manually Grouping Projects* later in this chapter.

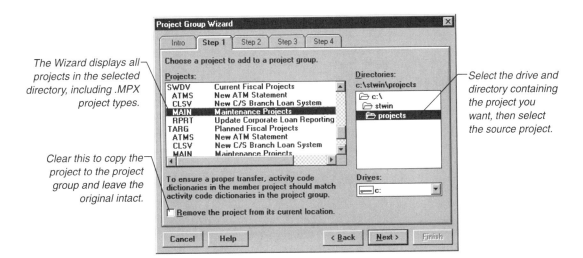

The Wizard displays all projects in the selected directory, including .MPX project types.

Clear this to copy the project to the project group and leave the original intact.

Select the drive and directory containing the project you want, then select the source project.

After selecting the project to insert into a project group, click Next or the tab for Step 2 and select the project group that will receive the new member project.

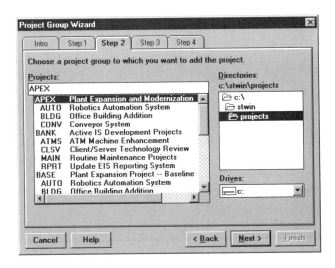

In step 3, SureTrak verifies that there are no conflicts between the name or project ID of the new member project and the project group. If SureTrak detects a duplicate project name or project ID, it suggests a replacement name and/or replacement project ID for the project you are adding. Even if no duplicates are detected, you can change the project name and/or project ID. If you change the project name or ID so it matches another project in the group or directory, SureTrak displays a message box asking whether to overwrite the existing project with the current project. Click Yes if the project is a more current version of the same project; otherwise, click No and change the project name and ID.

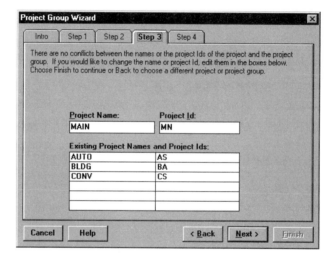

Continue to step 4, where SureTrak reviews your specifications and advises you that the new member project will use the project group's dictionaries. Resources and code values in the new member project that do not already appear in the project group's dictionaries will be added to the group dictionaries. After confirming that the operation is correct, click Finish.

 After you click Finish, you cannot return to previous steps or undo the operation. You can, however, remove the project from the project group. Choose the Create A Standalone Project From A Member Project option in the Project Group Wizard to perform this action.

Creating a Standalone Project from a Member Project

If you add a standalone project to a project group, SureTrak automatically adds the standalone project's resources and activity codes to the group. All member projects have access to the added project items.

You may want to convert a member project to a standalone project if it is best handled as a distinct project with no interrelationships or shared resources, or if its calendars and codes should be different from those of the project group.

1 Choose Tools, Wizards, Project Group Wizard.

2 Choose the Create A Standalone Project From A Member Project option.

3 Select the drive and directory containing the project you want to use, then select the source project—the one you want to convert to a standalone project.

4 To remove the project from the group, mark the Remove The Project From Its Current Location checkbox.

If this checkbox is unmarked, SureTrak copies the project as a standalone project, but leaves the original project intact.

5 Proceed through the rest of the Wizard.

Removing/Deleting a Project from a Project Group

You can remove a member project from a project group without deleting it or you can delete the entire project.

To remove a member project from a project group Convert the member project into a standalone project using the Project Groups Wizard. Choose Tools, Wizards, Project Group Wizard.

Choose to remove a member project from a project group. Then click Next.

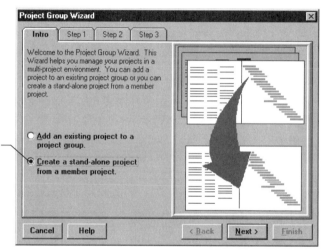

If you do not mark this checkbox, two copies of the project result. One is a member of the project group; the other is a standalone project.

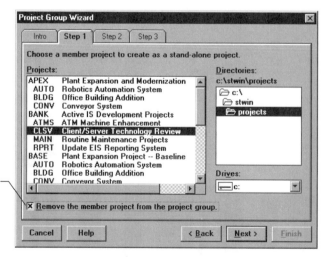

To delete a project that is a member of a project group Choose
Tools, Project Utilities, Delete.

Right-click and select
Project Groups, then right-
click in the Project Group
field and select a group.

Select the member project
you want to delete.

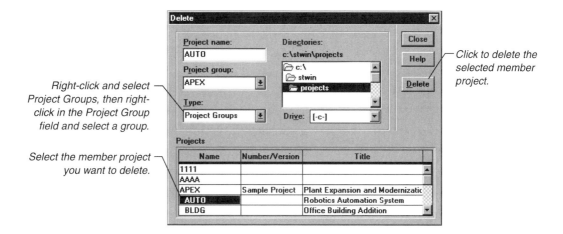

Click to delete the
selected member
project.

 If you delete a project group, SureTrak also deletes the
member projects in that group.

Manually Grouping Projects

In SureTrak, you can manually group projects if you are creating a new project group and creating new projects to add to the new group. If you are collecting existing projects into a group, rather than creating a new project group, use the Project Group Wizard.

To add new member projects to a project group

1 Choose File, New.

2 Assign the project a four-character name in the Project Name field.

3 Right-click in the Type field and select Project Groups from the drop-down list.

4 Mark the Add This New Project To A Project Group checkbox.

5 Right-click in the Project Group field, then select the project group to which you want to add the new project.

6 Type a two-character code in the Project ID field to identify the member project.

   The Project ID becomes the first two Activity ID characters for each activity in the project. For example, if you add activity 100 to the C1 project, the new Activity ID is C1100. The first character of the Project ID must be a letter.

7 Click OK.

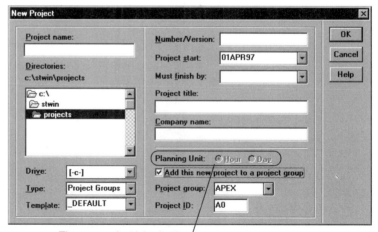

The new project inherits the planning unit of its project group.

Planning Your Own Project Groups

Before creating or modifying project groups, consider how you will use data structures common to all projects, such as activity codes and work breakdown structure (WBS) codes; how you will use calendars; and whether to place activities in the project group or in a member project. This section discusses some important decisions you should consider when planning and implementing project groups in your organization.

Identifying common project group items After you create a project group, define project items that are common to the project group and the member projects. The following project items are shared among projects in a project group: the Resource Dictionary, base calendar, resource calendars, activity codes and values, Activity IDs, and WBS codes.

Setting up the project group coding structure Create at least one coding structure that will be used in the project group. If you use a WBS, set up the structure for the entire WBS, but define the top two or three levels of the WBS in the project group. Managers of member projects can add the lower levels. Be sure to agree on a structure beforehand, since member project managers will not be able to change it.

Also, set up standard activity codes and add them to all member projects. You may want to reserve some activity codes for the member project managers. For example, define generic codes (Code 1, Code 2) that each member project manager can use in a different way, as appropriate for his or her project. Alternatively, define activity codes unique to each member project, and each member project manager need only work with the codes relevant to his or her project.

Default activity and WBS codes After you create a project group and add projects to it, you can define default activity codes and values and WBS codes for its member projects, so that each activity added to a member project contains a default set of activity code values specific to that member project.

 You can define default codes only for Project Groups or Concentric (P3) projects.

For example, define a default department code value in the project group for each member project, so a new activity in any member project inherits the value representing the department responsible for that member project.

For more information about activity codes, see the *Creating Activity Codes* chapter.

You can define default values for some or all the activity codes for each member project. You can also define a default WBS code for each member project.

For more information about project group outlines, see the *Adding Activities* chapter.

Project group outlines If you build projects using outlines, SureTrak can separate project group outline numbers from member project outline numbers. You can outline all project group activities together, as well as separately within each member project.

Adding an activity to the project group Some activities may belong to the project group as a whole, instead of pertaining only to a member project. You can add those activities in the project group. Follow these general guidelines when determining whether activities belong in the project group:

■   Include an activity in a *project group* if it has no clear departmental responsibility; if it incurs costs across departments; if it is a key milestone for several member projects; or if it will be linked to activities in several member projects.

■   Include an activity in a *member project* if one department is responsible for it; if it will be updated by the manager of a member project; or if its budget is from a single department.

Defining relationships between member projects After you create the project group and add member projects to it, you can create relationships between the member projects to show their interrelationships. Create these relationships when the start or finish of an activity in one member project controls an activity in another member project or in the project group.

For more information about relationships, see the *Linking Activities with Relationships* chapter.

To create relationships between member projects, open the project group so you can access all member projects, and then create the necessary relationships.

When calculating a schedule, SureTrak treats a relationship between a project group activity and a member project activity, or between activities in different member projects, as internal early start and late finish constraints in the member project. However, it does not actually assign a constraint; the Constraints detail form shows no constraint for the activities.

SureTrak uses the early start constraint during the forward scheduling pass and the late finish constraint during the backward pass to maintain the interrelationship between the project group and the member project. To change the way SureTrak schedules activities that depend on these constraint dates, open the project group and change the relationship type or lag.

Workgroup considerations Depending on how your company is set up, you can use any of several methods to share and exchange project information. Project participants may be located within an area accessible by the same computer network, or they may be located at remote sites that require that the member project managers travel.

For more information about E-mail, see the *Updating Project Data Remotely* chapter.

If member project managers and team members are accessible via a local area or wide area network, you can use E-mail to request and collect project information.

If a member project manager must travel to a project location, use the Check-in/Check-out feature so other network users know that this project is unavailable, and to ensure that project data modifications are not lost.

Modifying the Project Group

You can make changes to a project group and apply those changes to all member projects. In a project group, you can modify the global or base calendar, add new activity codes, change default activity code values, and change existing resource names and their cost and revenue values.

To make changes to the project group Choose File, Open. SureTrak lists project groups with member projects indented under each project group. Select the project group that you want to change. Click OK.

In a member project, you can add activity code values to activity codes, define new WBS codes using the existing structure, add new resource definitions, change resource assignments, and modify resource calendars. SureTrak reflects all additions and changes throughout the project group, because the dictionaries are shared. While in a member project you cannot modify relationships to activities in other member projects, but you can add, delete, or change relationships in the member project.

To update a project group Each member project can have its own data date. However, for overall reporting and consistency, Primavera suggests that you establish the same time each week, month, or other interval for each member project manager to update his or her project.

For more information on summarizing, see the *Organizing and Summarizing Activities* chapter.

When each member project has been updated, the project group manager can open the project group and summarize all the member projects for a "big picture" view of the project group's progress. If one member project seems behind schedule, the project group manager can unsummarize that project to look more closely at how the work is being accomplished.

Keeping Track of Projects within a Project Group

SureTrak's Project Check-in/Check-out feature enables you to keep track of member projects that are used outside the project group. This feature is useful when a member project manager travels to a project site and updates or modifies the member project while at that site, or when member project managers work on projects at home.

SureTrak notes when a member project manager checks-out a project from a project group. When anyone tries to open that member project or the project group, SureTrak informs the user that the project is checked-out. Users can make changes and save the project, but SureTrak overwrites those changes when the checked-out project is checked back into the project group.

When you check-out a project to diskette(s), SureTrak creates a compressed backup that spans all necessary diskettes.

 Before you can check the project back into the project group, you must restore it to a temporary directory on your hard drive (choose Tools, Project Utilities, Restore).

For more information on backing up projects, see *Backing Up and Restoring a Project Group* later in this chapter.

If you don't need to inform other users that the project is checked-out, and you want to store the project on diskettes, consider using the Backup feature rather than project check-out.

If you check-out a project to a directory on a hard drive, SureTrak does not compress the project. To use the project, open it using SureTrak.

To check-out a project from a project group Choose Tools, Project Utilities, Check-in/Check-out, then click the Check Out tab.

1 Select the project group drive and directory.

2 Select the project you want to check-out.

3 Select the drive and directory where you want to store the checked-out project.

4 Click to check-out the selected project and copy it to the location you specified.

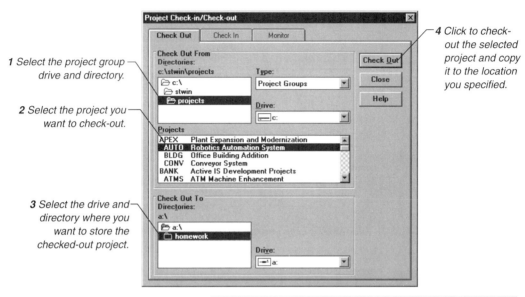

When you check-out to a diskette, SureTrak displays this reminder.

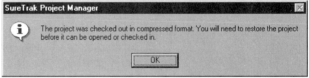

To check a project back into a project group When the member project manager finishes with a project, check the project back into the project group. SureTrak overwrites any changes that may have been made locally to the member project while it was checked-out.

 If the project was checked-out to a diskette, you must restore it to a temporary directory before running project check-in.

Choose Tools, Project Utilities, Check-in/Check-out, then click the Check In tab.

1 Specify the drive and directory where the project was being worked on while checked-out.

2 Select the project to check-in.

3 Specify the final path and directory to which the project is being checked-in.

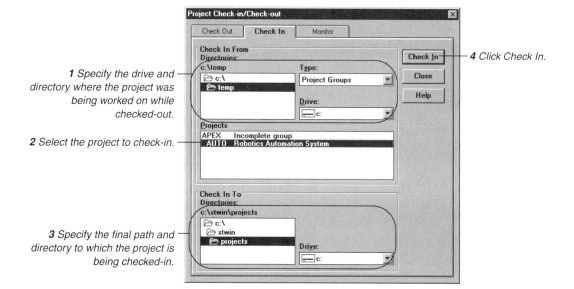

4 Click Check In.

To determine whether a project is currently checked-out

Choose Tools, Project Utilities, Check-in/Check-out, then click the Monitor tab.

Specify the drive and directory where the project of interest is located.

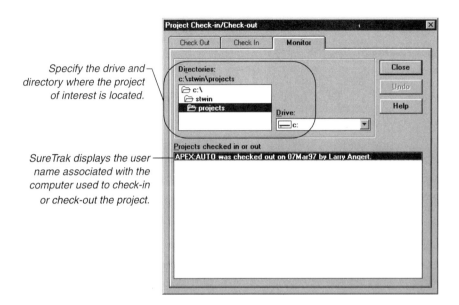

SureTrak displays the user name associated with the computer used to check-in or check-out the project.

To reverse the check-out status of a project   When a project has been checked-out for an extended period, you may want to disable the warning message that displays each time you open the project. Choose Tools, Project Utilities, Check-in/Check-out then click the Monitor tab. Select the project and then click Undo.

Backing Up and Restoring a Project Group

Use Backup and Restore to copy project groups to diskettes or from drive to drive, as well as to preserve copies of your project data. Use Backup and Restore to copy an entire project group or an individual member project that you can restore, along with its dictionaries and external relationships, into a project group.

 When you back up both SureTrak and P3 projects to diskettes—especially when those projects share a common project name—be sure to back them up to different diskettes or to different directories on a diskette.

Backing up project groups When you back up a project group, SureTrak automatically backs up its layouts, reports and graphic specifications, as well as all other activity information, such as project dictionaries and filter specifications. Back up a project group using the Back Up command (choose Tools, Project Utilities, Backup).

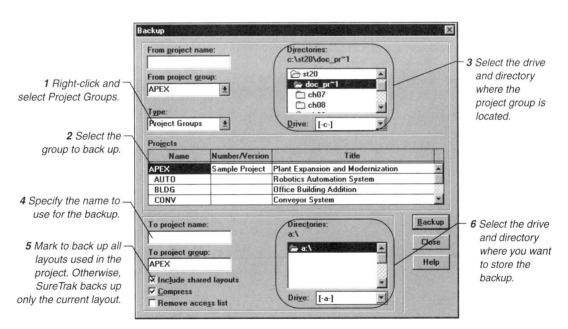

1 Right-click and select Project Groups.

2 Select the group to back up.

3 Select the drive and directory where the project group is located.

4 Specify the name to use for the backup.

5 Mark to back up all layouts used in the project. Otherwise, SureTrak backs up only the current layout.

6 Select the drive and directory where you want to store the backup.

Removing the access list Mark the Remove Access List checkbox if the backup will be restored to a single-user system.

Backup log Along with the backup files, SureTrak creates a file called PBACKUP.LOG that contains the project group name, the backup date, and an indication of whether the backup was compressed.

Restoring project groups Choose Tools, Project Utilities, Restore to restore a project from the backup diskettes or directory to the selected directory.

Identify the source drive and directory, and the name of the project group to restore.

Select the drive and directory where you want to restore the backup files.

Mark to restore all layouts referenced in the backed up project group's reports.

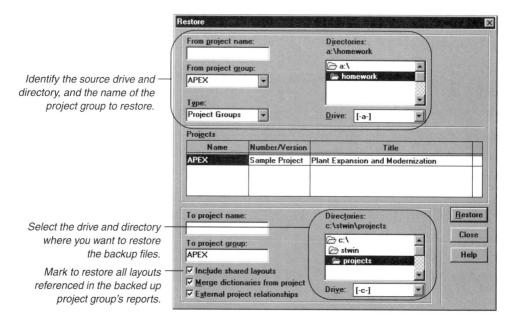

Include shared layouts A project group you restore may contain layouts with the same names as existing project group layouts, although the layouts themselves may differ. Mark the Include Shared Layouts checkbox and SureTrak prompts you before it replaces the current layout with the one being restored.

Merge dictionaries from project The Merge Dictionaries From Project checkbox is not relevant when restoring project groups because the restored dictionaries always overwrite the current dictionaries.

External project relationships The External Project Relationships checkbox is not relevant when restoring project groups because all relationships are always restored.

Overwriting an existing project group If a project group using the same name (for example, an older version of the backed-up project group) already exists in the directory you select, confirm that you want to replace it with the restored project group.

Organizing Project Information

This part discusses how to structure project data so you can organize and present it in a variety of ways. Use activity codes to categorize work into groups, such as phase and responsibility. Create a work breakdown structure (WBS) to organize data into a hierarchy of work to be accomplished. Use outlining to break down a project into large work segments and then into smaller work segments. Filters can make analysis easier by enabling you to display only the activities that match the criteria you specify.

This part also discusses ways to summarize activity data.

Creating Activity Codes

Use activity codes to categorize the activities in your project however you want—any way that will clarify the "what kind, who, where, why" of those activities. Activity codes help present the information you need in your SureTrak reports and graphics to manage your project effectively.

Use activity codes to filter out a set of activities for reviewing or updating, to organize activities for analysis and presentation, and to calculate subtotals for numeric fields.

Creating an Activity Code Dictionary

Activity coding consists of defining codes, or categories; creating a list of values for each code; and assigning the values to activities. In SureTrak, you can define up to 20 activity codes.

The default activity codes are Responsibility, Area, Phase, and Mail. You can add codes or replace these with others that are more relevant to your projects.

You can use activity codes to organize, summarize, sort, and filter activities in a project. For example, perhaps all 200 activities in a project belong to a certain department; Department is the name of the code, and it can have the values Engineering, Operations, or Marketing. A department code is assigned to each activity. Assume that 20 activities have Marketing as their department; you can then organize, filter, or summarize information for these activities separately from the information for activities of the other departments.

If you define several codes, you can organize, filter, sort, or summarize by any combination. For example, if you define Responsibility, Site, and Business Unit codes, you can organize by Business Unit and Responsibility, by Site and Business Unit, by Site and Responsibility, or by any other combination of those codes. You can also combine actions; for example, you can organize by one code and sort within that group by another code.

To define activity codes Choose Define, Activity Codes. Specify each code's name, length, and description. Click Close. Code names can be one to four characters long. The maximum code value length is 10 characters.

Click and type an activity code name, then click ☑.

Specify the maximum length for values of this code then click ☑. The default length is four characters.

Enter a description using up to 48 characters, then click ☑.

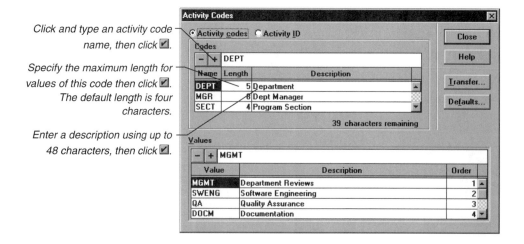

You can define up to 20 activity codes with a combined length of 64 characters. Divide the available 64 characters among the activity codes any way you want. For example, you can have eight 8-character codes, one 8-character and fourteen 4-character codes, or any other combination of codes up to 64 characters. As you specify activity code lengths, a reminder in the Codes section of the dialog box shows you the number of unused characters.

Defining Code Values

The activity code length is the maximum number of characters you can use for any value of a particular activity code—not the maximum number of characters in the code's name. As you add activity code values, SureTrak sorts them alphanumerically. However, you can control the order of the values, both in this listing and in the project window, by assigning each value a number from 1 to 999 in the Order column. SureTrak uses this order when you organize or sort activities by activity code. For example, in a Department code with ENGRG and R&D code values, use Order 1 for the R&D code and 2 for ENGRG to place R&D activities before ENGRG activities.

To add code values Choose Define, Activity Codes.

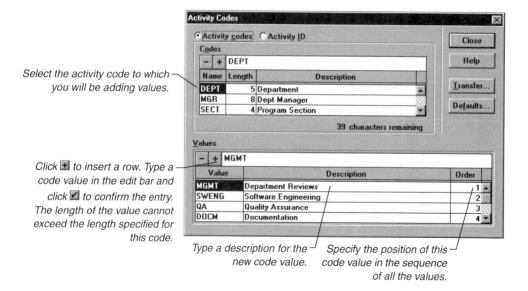

Select the activity code to which you will be adding values.

Click ⊞ to insert a row. Type a code value in the edit bar and click ☑ to confirm the entry. The length of the value cannot exceed the length specified for this code.

Type a description for the new code value.

Specify the position of this code value in the sequence of all the values.

Changing activity code lengths You may need to change the length of a code after it has been established. For example, suppose you originally specified four characters as the code length for the System code, and you now want to decrease that length to two characters. When you decrease the code length, SureTrak truncates all values for that code and asks you to confirm each of the revised values. Each truncated value must be unique.

To print activity codes You can print activity codes or a list of
Activity ID codes using the PRNCODES Basic script provided with
SureTrak. This script enables you to keep printed copies of the contents of
the Activity Code Dictionary. Choose Tools, Basic Scripts. Select the
PRNCODES script so that PRNCODES.SBX appears in the File Name
field. Click Run to open the Print Dictionary dialog box.

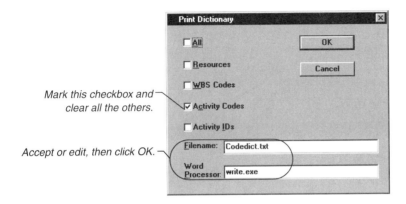

*Mark this checkbox and
clear all the others.*

Accept or edit, then click OK.

 *By default, SureTrak creates the output file using Microsoft
Write. You can specify any other word processor; SureTrak
uses it by default the next time you print dictionaries.*

To transfer activity codes If you use the same codes in several
projects, transfer the Activity Code Dictionary from one project to
another. Transferring another project's Activity Code Dictionary to a
project overwrites the existing activity codes and values in the current
project. Choose Define, Activity Codes and click Transfer to open the
Transfer Activity Codes dialog box.

*If the project you want does
not appear in the list, make
sure the drive and directory
are correct and that you
have specified the correct
type of project in the Type
field.*

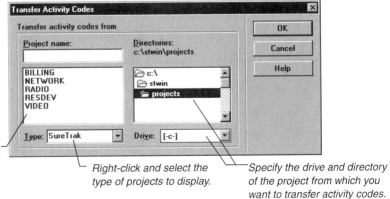

*Select the name of the
project from which you want
to transfer activity codes.*

*Right-click and select the
type of projects to display.*

*Specify the drive and directory
of the project from which you
want to transfer activity codes.*

Creating Activity Code Templates

If you work with essentially the same activity codes in each project, establish your own set of template codes so that you do not have to redefine or transfer them each time you create a new project. When you create your own code template, existing projects are not affected.

To create an activity code template

1 Choose File, New and enter a name for the new project.

2 Choose Define, Activity Codes. Define the activity codes you want to use in the template and close the dialog box.

3 Choose File, Save to save the project using the SureTrak format; then exit SureTrak.

4 Use Windows File Manager or Explorer to locate the file with the extension .TTL for the newly created project. For example, if you named the new project DICTIONARIES, look for the file named DICTIO-NARIES.TTL among your SureTrak project files. SureTrak stores activity codes in this file.

5 Using File Manager or Explorer, copy this file to TEMPLATE.TTL, and store it in the STWIN directory or move it to the same directory as STW.EXE.

6 If an existing project already contains the activity codes you want to use as defaults, copy the .TTL file for that project to the SureTrak program directory, then rename the copy TEMPLATE.TTL.

 If you create a project named TEMPLATE, place it in a directory other than the one that contains SureTrak. If you create a project called TEMPLATE in the SureTrak directory (usually the STWIN directory), you may overwrite all the existing SureTrak template files.

Assigning Activity Codes Using the Activity Form

You can assign up to 20 activity codes to each activity. Your coding system will be most useful if you assign a value for every code you use to each activity.

You can assign activity codes to activities using the code fields in the Activity form. The Activity form displays a field for each activity code you create. Use this method to assign activity codes at the same time you add or modify an activity.

To assign activity codes using the Activity form Choose View, Activity Form to open the Activity form for the currently selected activity. Click More if codes are not displayed. Assign the codes you want and click OK.

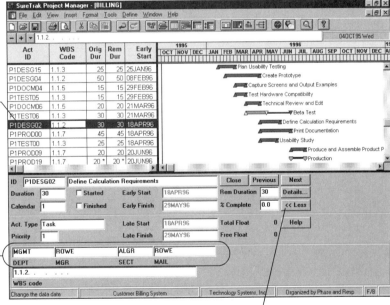

Select an activity and choose View, Activity Form to show the activity in the Activity Form.

Right-click in any activity code field to display a drop-down list; select the value you want to assign to the current activity for each code.

Click to hide some of the Activity form. The button changes to More; click it to expand the Activity form.

Assigning Activity Codes Using Activity Columns

You can also assign activity codes using the Activity columns. Use this method to quickly assign or change codes for activities shown in the Activity columns.

For details about adding Activity columns to a layout, see the *Customizing the Bar Chart View* chapter.

To assign activity codes using the Activity columns Add columns to the layout for the activity codes you want to work with. Select the activity code cell in the row for the activity whose code value you want to assign or modify. Click ⬇ in the edit bar to select the value from the drop-down list. Click ☑ to confirm your choice.

Newly assigned activity code.

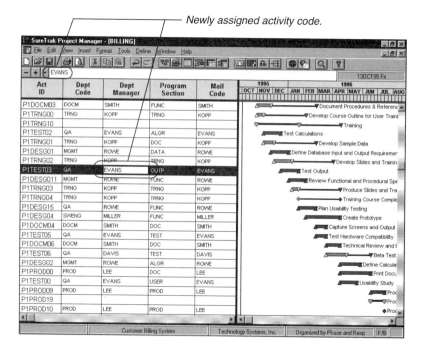

To assign an activity code value to several selected activities
Click the cell you want to copy and choose Edit, Copy Cell. Select the activities to which you want to assign the code value. Be sure the cell in focus is the column you want to copy to, then choose Edit, Paste Cell.

*Right-click an activity on
the Activity columns, Bar
chart, or PERT view and
choose Activity Detail,
Codes to open the form.*

To assign activity codes using the Codes form Use the Codes
form to assign or review all the values associated with an activity. Choose
View, Activity Detail, Codes. Assign a value for the code, click the up and
down arrows to move to another activity; or close the form.

*Right-click and select a value
for the code from the
drop-down list.*

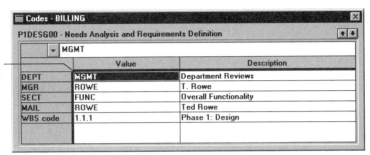

Coding Activity IDs

You can divide the characters of an Activity ID into parts, giving each part special meaning. By building "intelligence" into Activity IDs, you can increase your ability to organize, select, and summarize activities. For example, if a project involves producing several products, each of which requires similar development phases, code Activity IDs so that each activity is easily identified by product and phase.

You can set up the Activity ID codes the same way you set up other activity code fields. An Activity ID can contain up to 10 characters, which you can divide into a maximum of four parts, and define the length of each part. For example, the first two characters identify the department, the next four characters store cost coding information, and the last four characters remain uncoded.

To define Activity ID codes and values Choose Define, Activity Codes.

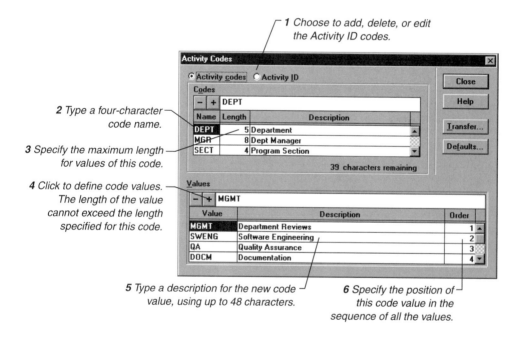

1 Choose to add, delete, or edit the Activity ID codes.

2 Type a four-character code name.

3 Specify the maximum length for values of this code.

4 Click to define code values. The length of the value cannot exceed the length specified for this code.

5 Type a description for the new code value, using up to 48 characters.

6 Specify the position of this code value in the sequence of all the values.

SureTrak sorts values alphanumerically as you add them. However, you can control the order of the values by assigning each value a number from 1 to 999 in the Order column. SureTrak uses this order when you organize or sort activities by Activity ID code.

Changing an Activity and Its Codes

When you add an activity or drag an activity to an activity code-banded group, the added or dragged activity inherits the activity codes of that group. To change them, overwrite these inherited codes in the Activity form, Codes form, or the Activity columns.

To add an activity with inherited codes Organize your project into bands whose codes you want to assign to new activities. Select an activity row under the band or bands that represent the codes you want to assign to the new activity. Add an activity. Complete the Activity form, keeping or changing any inherited codes. Click OK to save the new activity and any changes made on the Activity form.

Dragging activity codes To change activity codes by dragging activities, organize your project into bands whose codes you want to assign to moved activities. Select the activity or activities you want to move. Point to the left edge of the activity you want to move. The mouse pointer changes to ⊕, indicating the "Drag-and-drop" feature is active.

Drag the selected activities to the appropriate band. SureTrak places the activities below the activity row or band, and sorts them according to current sorting specifications.

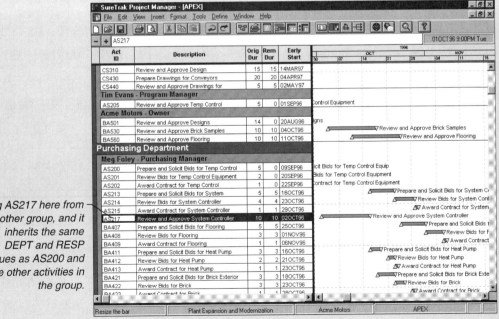

Drag AS217 here from another group, and it inherits the same DEPT and RESP values as AS200 and the other activities in the group.

Defining Default Activity Codes

You can define default activity code values for activities in member projects that are part of Project Groups or Concentric (P3) projects. Define default values for some or all of the activity codes for each member project. SureTrak automatically assigns the values you specified when you add activities to a member project. For example, define a default Department value for each member project of a project group, so that new activities in member projects automatically inherit the department value you specify.

You can change the values assigned to any activity in any project.

To define default member project codes Choose File, Open, then open the Project Group you want. Choose Define, Activity Codes and click Defaults. SureTrak automatically chooses the Activity ID option, selects the SUBP code field, and opens the Default Codes dialog box.

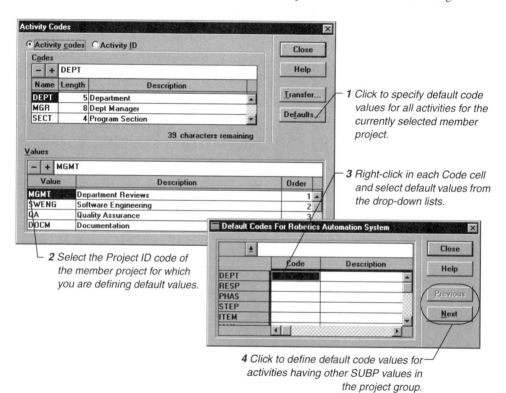

1 Click to specify default code values for all activities for the currently selected member project.

3 Right-click in each Code cell and select default values from the drop-down lists.

2 Select the Project ID code of the member project for which you are defining default values.

4 Click to define default code values for activities having other SUBP values in the project group.

Creating a Work Breakdown Structure

Like activity codes, work breakdown structure (WBS) codes enable you to categorize the activities in your project. You design a work breakdown structure in levels of detail that help you "break down" the work of a new project.

Summarize activities with similar WBS codes and prepare high-level, overview reports that generalize project information for management.

Defining WBS Codes

A WBS organizes a project so you can report and summarize project data at different levels of detail. Graphically portrayed as an inverted tree, create a WBS by establishing a hierarchy of work to be accomplished, beginning with the final project objective or work product at the top, and subdividing to individual activities at the bottom.

When you start planning a project, use WBS codes to divide the project into major components and their subcomponents. Break down the subcomponents until you have defined discrete activities that can be assigned a duration (the amount of time required for completion). This may require one or more levels of subcomponents.

Each company can tailor a WBS to its own approach to managing projects. A WBS can also vary from project to project.

First develop a hierarchical coding system that corresponds to each level and component. Then assign WBS codes to activities so you can easily track each component.

Use WBS codes to filter out a set of activities for reviewing or updating on a report, to organize activities for analysis and presentation, or to calculate subtotals for numeric fields.

The figure on the next page shows a partial WBS for the sample project APEX. In this project, three major components must be completed to achieve the goal of an expanded and modernized automobile production plant: an automated system, a new conveyor system, and an office building addition. Each major component is separated into smaller components.

The highest level represents the project itself; it is assigned a unique primary character code—AM. At the next level, AM.01, AM.02, and AM.03 represent the three highest-level divisions of the WBS. The WBS codes at subordinate levels incorporate the higher-level WBS codes and represent general tasks to be performed.

All levels of the structure are assigned codes. Longer WBS codes represent lower levels—more detailed descriptions of work. The lowest level of the structure consists of the most specific activities required to complete the project; these are the activities you'll add to your SureTrak project.

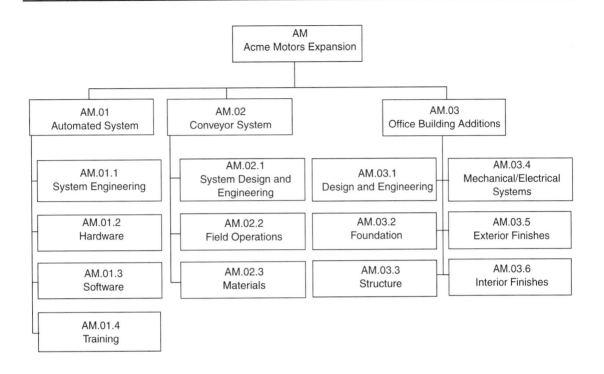

This diagram is for illustration only and cannot be reproduced in SureTrak.

Setting Up WBS Levels

If you develop a similar project later, you can transfer, or copy, the WBS to the new one.

When you begin a new project, first define a structure for the WBS codes. You will generally set up the WBS code structure once per project, although you can change it later if necessary.

When you set up the structure of WBS codes, define the number of sections in the WBS code, the acceptable number of characters for each section, and the character used to separate the sections. Consider ways to build intelligence into the project codes such as having the first letters of the WBS indicate the overall project or client.

You can create a WBS containing up to 20 levels with a maximum of 48 total characters, excluding separator characters such as dashes. If your WBS has only a few levels, the levels can contain more characters. The WBS structure of the APEX sample project uses four levels and a total of six characters.

To define WBS codes Choose Define, WBS Codes. Click Structure. Specify character widths and separators. Do not specify a separator for the last level you define. Click OK.

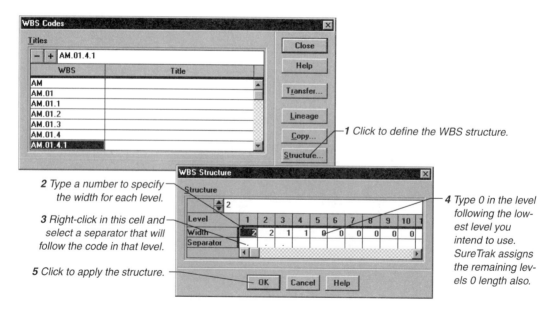

1 Click to define the WBS structure.

2 Type a number to specify the width for each level.

3 Right-click in this cell and select a separator that will follow the code in that level.

4 Type 0 in the level following the lowest level you intend to use. SureTrak assigns the remaining levels 0 length also.

5 Click to apply the structure.

For more information about outlining, see the *Adding Activities* chapter.

If your WBS codes consist of one number at each level of the structure, and if you don't need descriptions of the codes, you may want to use an outline to build your project.

Building the WBS Codes Dictionary

After you establish the structure for WBS codes, you can begin adding the codes themselves. Each WBS code should have a title, or description, that describes what it represents in the project. SureTrak uses these titles when organizing and collapsing activities by WBS code. You can type the codes one at a time, or create one branch of codes and have SureTrak copy that structure to other branches.

To add WBS codes and titles Choose Define, WBS Codes. Specify the new code and the title. Do not include separator characters; SureTrak includes separators automatically. Continue adding codes or click Close.

Click to add a new WBS code and then type the WBS code using letters and numbers.

Specify titles for the codes you add.

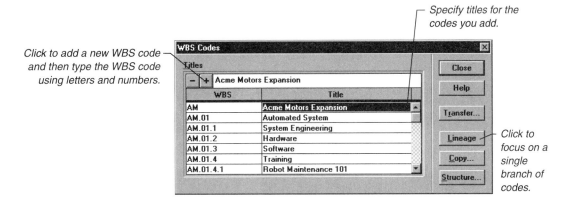

Click to focus on a single branch of codes.

 High-level codes roll up lower-level codes; a code such as AM.01.4.1 is a subdivision of the higher-level AM.01.4, which is a subdivision of the even higher-level AM.01, which is a subdivision of the highest level, AM. When you add a code such as PM.01.3.1, SureTrak automatically adds the codes PM.01.03, PM.01, and PM if they do not already exist.

To analyze a branch of WBS codes If the WBS becomes complex, with many levels and branches, use the Lineage button to focus on a single branch of codes.

Select a code for which you want to see all antecedents (higher-level codes) and descendants (lower-level codes). Click Lineage. Click Full to display the full list of codes.

Copying WBS Codes

You can copy a code and change letters or numbers by adding or replacing any of its characters. In addition, once you define a code branch from a higher level in the structure down to a lower level, you can copy that entire group of codes to a new branch with slightly different codes.

Consider a branch of WBS codes that includes the following: 1.1, 1.1.1, 1.1.2, 1.1.2.A, 1.1.2.B, 1.1.3, and 1.1.4. If you select the row containing 1.1 and click Copy, SureTrak prompts you to supply a unique WBS value for the highest level, such as 1.2 in this example. SureTrak then copies the remainder of the branch, resulting in codes 1.2.1, 1.2.2, 1.2.2.A, 1.2.2.B, 1.2.3, and 1.2.4. To copy a smaller branch, starting at a lower level, you might select the row containing 1.1.2. When you copy it, you might change the code to 1.1.5; SureTrak also creates 1.1.5.A and 1.1.5.B.

To preview the branch that will be copied, select the code you want to copy and click Lineage. SureTrak displays the selected code and all codes above and below it in the WBS. When you click Copy, SureTrak copies the highlighted code and those below it in the hierarchy.

To copy a branch of WBS codes Choose Define, WBS Codes.

Select the code you want to copy.

Click to copy the selected code.

When you copy a code, SureTrak copies the highlighted code and its descendants, down to the lowest level of that branch. Specify a new code name in the Define Unique WBS Value dialog box. Click OK.

Transferring WBS Codes from Another Project

If you use identical or similar work breakdown structures for several projects, you can transfer the WBS Dictionary from an existing SureTrak or P3 project to the current project.

For details on reviewing and editing WBS code assignments, see *Assigning WBS Codes* later in this chapter.

Transferring a WBS Dictionary completely overwrites the existing dictionary in the current project. Changing the dictionary this way has no effect on codes you've already assigned to activities, so their codes may no longer match the new WBS Dictionary.

To transfer WBS codes Choose Define, WBS Codes. Click Transfer. Specify the drive and directory of the project from which you want to transfer WBS codes. If the project you are looking for does not appear in the list below the Project Name field, make sure the drive and directory are correct and that you have specified the correct type of project.

Select the name of the project from which you want to transfer WBS codes.

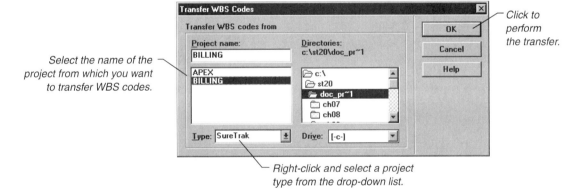

Click to perform the transfer.

Right-click and select a project type from the drop-down list.

SureTrak prompts you to confirm your decision to replace the current WBS Dictionary. Click OK to confirm, or Cancel to abort the transfer.

Creating a WBS Code Template

If you work with essentially the same WBS codes in each project, establish your own set of default codes so that you do not have to redefine or transfer them each time you create a new project.

To create a template Choose File, New. Choose Define, WBS Codes to open the WBS Codes dialog box. Define the WBS codes you want to use in the template. Click Close. Save the project and exit SureTrak.

Use Windows File Manager or Windows Explorer to locate the .TTL file for the newly created project. If you installed SureTrak according to its Setup defaults, the .TTL file is in the STWIN directory; SureTrak stores activity codes and WBS codes in this file.

Using File Manager or Explorer, rename this file TEMPLATE.TTL. Leave it in the STWIN directory or move it to the directory that contains STW.EXE.

If an existing project already contains the WBS codes you want to use as defaults, use File Manager or Explorer to copy the .TTL file for that project to the SureTrak program directory, renaming the copy TEMPLATE.TTL.

 If you create a project named TEMPLATE, do so in a directory other than the one where SureTrak is installed. If you create a project called TEMPLATE in the SureTrak directory (usually the STWIN directory), you may overwrite all the SureTrak defaults.

Assigning WBS Codes

You can assign one WBS code to each activity. These codes make it easy to organize activities according to the project's major and subordinate components. Your WBS codes will be more consistent, and therefore more useful for reports and graphics, if you define the WBS code structure and dictionary before you begin to add WBS codes to activities. Then you can select codes from the WBS drop-down list in the Activity form or on the WBS Activity column as you add or modify activities.

If the WBS code field is not visible when you open the Activity form, click More.

If you assign an undefined WBS code to an activity, SureTrak adds the new code to the dictionary and creates any antecedents for it. For example, if you assign an undefined WBS code of D.4.R to an activity, SureTrak adds D.4, and D to the WBS Code Dictionary as antecedents if they do not already exist. However, because SureTrak defined them, they will not have titles; if you organize activities by WBS code, their bands will be blank.

To assign WBS codes using the Activity form Select an activity and choose Edit, Edit Activity to open the Activity form. Assign a code in the WBS Code field then click OK.

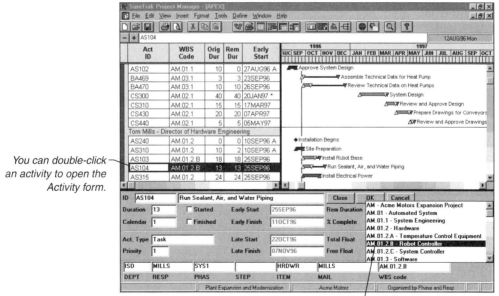

You can double-click an activity to open the Activity form.

Right-click in the WBS Code field and select the code you want to assign to the current activity.

Assigning WBS codes in the Codes form You can use the Codes form to review or assign all the codes associated with an activity. Choose View, Activity Detail, Codes to open the Codes form. Right-click in the WBS Code cell and select a code from the drop-down list. Click the up and down arrows to move to another activity, or close the form.

To assign WBS codes using the Activity columns Choose Format, Columns, and add a column for WBS codes.

Right-click in the edit bar and select a WBS code from the drop-down list. Click ✓ to confirm your choice.

Select the WBS code cell that you want to modify or assign a code to.

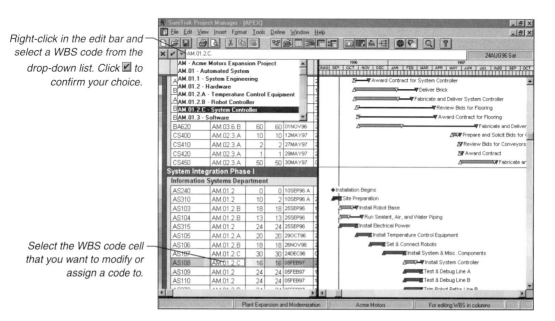

To assign a WBS code to several selected activities Select the cell in the Activity column containing the WBS code you want to copy; then choose Edit, Copy Cell. Select the activities to which you want to assign the WBS code. Be sure the WBS code is the focus cell. Choose Edit, Paste Cell. SureTrak assigns the WBS code to all the selected activities.

Changing Code Assignments

When you add an activity or drag an activity to a WBS-banded group, the activity inherits the WBS code of that banded group.

To add an activity with inherited codes

1 Organize the project by WBS code.

2 Select an activity row under the band or bands that represent the codes you want to assign to the new activity.

3 Add an activity and enter the new activity's data except for the codes by which the project is organized.

4 Click OK.

To change WBS codes by dragging activities

1 Organize your project by WBS codes.

2 Select the activity or activities whose WBS codes you want to change.

3 Point to the left edge of the activity (or one of the activities, if you've selected several) you want to change.

The mouse pointer changes to ⌧.

4 Drag the selected activities to the appropriate WBS band. SureTrak places the activity or activities below the activity row or band they are dragged to.

SureTrak displays a selected block that represents the activity or activities as you drag them.

For more information about organizing by WBS code, see the *Organizing and Summarizing Activities* chapter.

Organizing and Summarizing Activities

With SureTrak, you can control the order of activities and how to organize them into meaningful groups in the Bar chart and PERT views. Use these features to record project information from the top down in outline form, or hierarchically with work breakdown structure (WBS) codes.

Controlling information organization enables you to analyze different aspects of your project. For example, organizing the layout by resources is a quick way to see which team members and other resources are involved with each activity.

Once you organize activities into groups, you can summarize or "roll up" project data to simplify its presentation.

Organizing Project Data

In SureTrak, you can organize activities in the Bar chart view by activity data item, by work breakdown structure (WBS) code, or by outline code. You can organize activities in the PERT view by activity codes, project ID, calendar, or total float.

For more information about outlining activities, see Organizing an Outline *later in this chapter.*

Whether or not activities are grouped, you can specify their order in the Bar chart view by sorting them by any activity data item. If the order you want for activities doesn't coincide with any built-in grouping or sorting criteria, you can turn off automatic sorting and drag activities into any order.

This layout is grouped by activity data items: the department and responsibility activity codes.

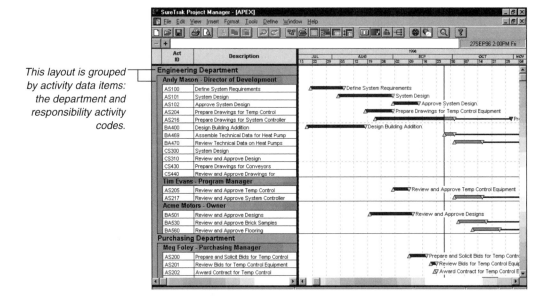

Organizing activities is useful while you are creating a project, as well as for later project analysis and reporting. By changing the way activities are grouped and sorted, you can focus on different but equally important aspects of a project. For example, by grouping activities by responsibility activity codes, you can focus on who is accountable for each activity. By sorting activities by early start, you can analyze their timing.

Use SureTrak's organizing options for any of these functions:

- *Sort activities by any SureTrak data item*—by code, numerically by any activity or resource value, or chronologically by date.

■ *Sort in ascending or descending order.* For example, sort dates in ascending order (earliest dates first), but costs in descending order (highest costs first).

■ *Group by several activity data items* with group headings in the font and color you choose. Use groups to make it easier to read a project report, and to keep similar activities close together.

■ *Show subtotals* at any grouping level.

■ *Assign activity codes, WBS codes, or resource codes* by dragging or copying and pasting.

■ *Group activities hierarchically* by the WBS code system you create to represent the scope of the project. Show up to 20 WBS levels, or hide the lower levels to focus on higher levels.

■ *Plan projects from the "top down"* by entering high-level outline topic activities, then filling in lower-level, more specific activities.

Sorting Activities

Sort activities into a specific order based on one or more SureTrak data items. A simple sort is based on one item; for example, sort by early start for chronological order, sort by total float to display the most critical activities at the top of the list, or sort by cost at completion to order activities by amount of expense.

You can also sort by more than one data item. For example, if you sort by early start and then total float, SureTrak displays activities in chronological order; if two or more activities are scheduled to start on the same day, SureTrak shows them in order of total float.

If you do not specify sorting criteria, or if all other sorting criteria are the same for two or more activities, SureTrak sorts by Activity ID.

Sorting in the Bar chart view Sorting a Bar chart view is independent of organizing activities into groups, but you can sort and organize simultaneously. If you sort activities while grouping them by activity data item, SureTrak sorts activities within each band. When grouping by WBS code, SureTrak sorts activities within each WBS level. When outlining, SureTrak sorts the activities at the lowest level of the outline (nontopic activities).

To sort activities Choose Format, Organize. In the Sort By section, click ⊞ to add a sorting criterion or select the row displaying the sorting criterion you want to change. Specify the data item you want to sort by and the order to sort in. Click OK.

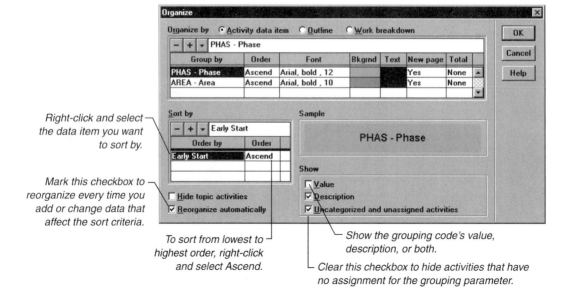

Right-click and select the data item you want to sort by.

Mark this checkbox to reorganize every time you add or change data that affect the sort criteria.

To sort from lowest to highest order, right-click and select Ascend.

Show the grouping code's value, description, or both.

Clear this checkbox to hide activities that have no assignment for the grouping parameter.

If you make changes in the Sort By section, those changes apply to the currently selected Organize By method: activity data item, outline, or work breakdown structure.

When you add an activity in the Bar chart view, SureTrak places it in the layout wherever it fits within the sorted activities. If you prefer to add activities in specific locations, choose Format, Organize and clear the Reorganize Automatically checkbox. Click OK.

To reorganize the displayed activities If you rearrange activities by dragging them when automatic sorting is turned off, SureTrak leaves the activities in the location they are dragged to. You can reorganize the activities on demand or turn on automatic sorting to reorder them in the sorting order currently defined.

Choose Format, Reorganize Now to sort activities based on their current information. Using this command does not turn Reorganize Automatically back on.

Grouping Activities in the Bar Chart View

Grouping (also called banding) enables you to focus on activities that have something in common. The activities in each group are clustered into a band, one band for each group. Group activities using broad categories, such as activity or resource codes. Then you can sort activities within each group.

To group activities by activity data items Choose Format, Organize. Choose the Activity Data Item option and group by activity codes, schedule dates, resource/cost data, float, relationships, variances, or other parameters.

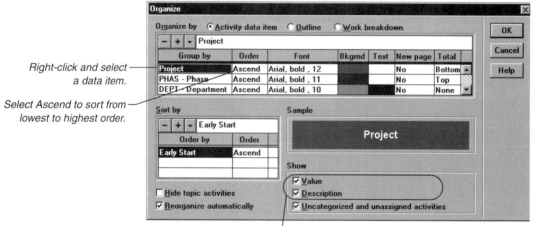

Right-click and select a data item.

Select Ascend to sort from lowest to highest order.

Mark these checkboxes to control the text that appears in the group bands.

Right-click in the Font, Bkgrnd (background), and Text columns to change the font and color of bands. Use the Sample section to preview the settings for each band.

To have SureTrak print each code value within a group on a separate page, specify Yes in the New Page column. To show subtotals above or below each group, specify Top or Bottom in the Total column.

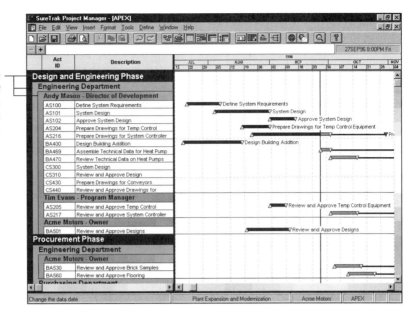

This layout is grouped by phase, department, and responsibility. You can group activities using up to 20 data items at a time.

Grouping and subtotals SureTrak calculates information for subtotals as follows:

Activity Column	Subtotal
Remaining duration	Elapsed worktime from the data date to the latest early finish among a group of activities.
Original duration	Elapsed worktime from the earliest early (or actual) start to the latest early (or actual) finish among a group of activities.
Cost, revenue, or net amount	Sum of a column of cost, revenue, or net amounts for a group of activities.
Start date	Earliest start date (earliest early start or earliest late start, depending on the column being subtotaled).
Finish date	Latest finish date (latest early finish or latest late finish, depending on the column being subtotaled).
Percent complete	Sum of the grouped activities' actual (accomplished) durations through the data date, divided by the sum of the grouped activities' original durations.

For more information about subtotals, see *Summarizing Activities* later in this chapter.

You can show subtotals within the band for the activities being subtotaled, or below the activities in the band. To display subtotals only, summarize the activities after grouping them.

Grouping Activities by WBS Levels

SureTrak's organizing features enable you to group activities in the layout based on their work breakdown structure (WBS) codes. You can use this arrangement while you build a project, and for analysis purposes later. Once activities are arranged in a WBS, you can summarize schedule, cost, and resource information by WBS code, and prepare reports arranged by WBS code.

For more information about work breakdown structures, see the Creating a Work Breakdown Structure *chapter.*

When you group activities by WBS code, specify the number of levels of the structure you want to include for grouping. For example, even if your WBS structure has five levels, you can group activities at the second or third level and have fewer groups with more activities per group.

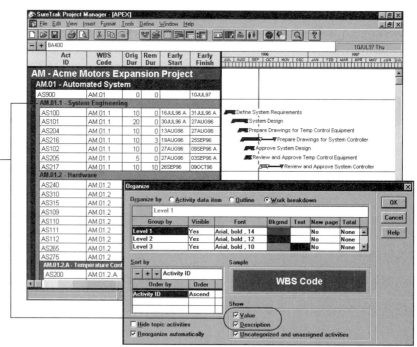

With these checkboxes marked, both the codes and their descriptions appear in the group bands.

 If you group by WBS code, you cannot group by other data items. You can, however, sort by other data items within each WBS group. Or, you can organize the layout by another data item, and sort activities within groups by WBS codes.

To organize by WBS code

1 Choose Format, Organize.

2 Choose the Work Breakdown option.

3 Right-click in the Visible cell for the structure level below the last one you want to use for grouping and select No from the drop-down list.

The Visible cell for all subsequent levels also changes to No, indicating that SureTrak will not use these levels for grouping.

4 Right-click in the Font cell and select a font for the WBS code text in the band for each level.

5 Right-click in the Bkgrnd (background) cell and select a band background color for each level.

6 Right-click in the Text cell and select a color for the WBS code and/or description in the bands.

7 Right-click in the New Page cell and select Yes or No.

Specify Yes for any level you want to separate from other sections of a printout.

8 Right-click in the Total cell and select Top, Bottom, or None.

Select Top or Bottom to include a subtotal row for that level and show a bar summarizing the group.

9 Click OK.

If you don't use all 20 levels of WBS codes—most work breakdown structures have five or fewer levels—hide the unused levels. For example, if the WBS has three levels, select Level 4 in the Organize By section and specify No in the Visible column.

Organizing an Outline

An outline is a noncoded hierarchical structure. In SureTrak, outlines subdivide a project into large work segments, and then into increasingly smaller amounts of work until you can assign each piece a duration.

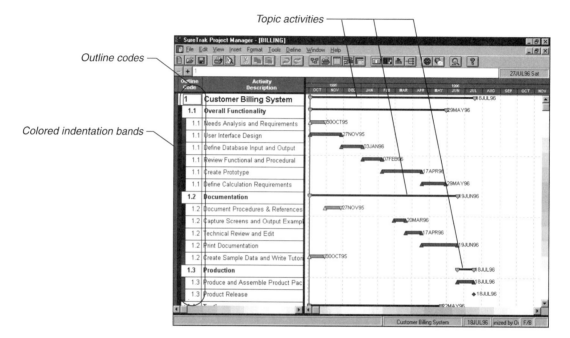

An outline looks similar to a work breakdown structure because it's hierarchical—made without subdividing. However, unlike a WBS, in an outline no codes are associated with titles or descriptions. Also, you don't specifically assign outline codes to activities in an outline; SureTrak assigns them according to each activity's location relative to other activities, and you move an activity to change its code.

SureTrak provides 10 outline levels. Use outlining to create projects from the top down, setting up topics (broad areas of work) and subtopics (more narrowly defined areas) with detailed activities at the bottom of the outline hierarchy.

To outline a project Choose Format, Organize. Choose the Outline option to organize the project into hierarchical levels of topics and tasks.

Most projects use three to five levels; SureTrak provides up to 10.

Specify Yes in all Visible cells; you can use this column later to specify the number of levels of the outline you want to show.

Only has effect when organized in Outline mode.

Organize					☒

Organize by ○ Activity data item   ● Outline   ○ Work breakdown

Level 2

Group by	Visible	Font	Indent	Text	New page
Level 1	Yes	Arial, bold , 12			No
Level 2	Yes	Arial, bold , 10			No
Level 3	Yes	Arial, regular, 10			No

Sort by

− + ▼ Early Start

Order by	Order
Early Start	Ascend

☐ Hide topic activities
☑ Reorganize automatically

Sample

Outline Code

Show
☑ Level Fonts
☑ Indent Colors
☑ Uncategorized and unassigned activities

OK **Cancel** **Help**

1 Use the Outline layout (choose View, Layouts), or add the Outline Code column to the current layout.

2 Add activities at the broadest work level (top level topics).

   You need not enter durations for topic activities; SureTrak calculates a topic's duration as the time elapsed over all the activities within that topic.

3 Select a topic activity that you want to position under a broader level and choose Insert, Indent.

   SureTrak adds a new activity (subtask) and indents it, numbering it using a decimal breakdown scheme. For example, if you add an indent below a topic activity numbered 2, SureTrak numbers the new activity 2.1.

4 To change the organization, choose Insert, Outdent to promote an activity one level in the hierarchy, making it a topic activity.

5 Repeat the process for all topics and subtopics.

   Some topics may have more subordinate levels than other topics. SureTrak treats any item with no further indented levels below it as a detailed activity.

For more information about adding new activities, see the *Adding Activities* chapter.

Alternatively, you can drag an activity to a specific place in the outline structure. If you drag it "on top of" another activity, SureTrak codes it at the same level, immediately above that activity.

Hiding Topic Activities

You can temporarily remove topic activities from view when your project is organized by outline by choosing View, Hide Topic Activities, by marking the Hide Topic Activities checkbox in the Organize dialog box, or by applying the XTOP filter.

The menu command changes to Show Topic Activities if all topics are hidden.

SureTrak hides all topic activities, while still displaying their detail-level components. To show topic activities again, choose View, Show Topic Activities or apply any filter or report, regardless of whether the filter or report actually specifies topic activities.

To hide topic activities using the XTOP filter Choose Format, Filter. Select the XTOP filter, which excludes all topic activities from the layout. Click Apply.

For more information about using filters, see the *Selecting Activities by Filter* chapter.

To show only topic activities Choose Format, Filter. Select the TOPX filter, which excludes all non-topic activities. Click Apply.

Summarizing Activities

In the Bar chart view, once you organize activities into groups you can summarize group information. Summarizing enables you to see large amounts of data condensed into an easy-to-read format. Summarizing is especially useful for presenting overviews to clients and management because it masks activity-level details.

SureTrak displays subtotaled information in the Activity columns for each group: summarized durations, dates, costs, and any other numeric or date items. In the Bar chart, you can specify that you want to see one summary bar per group; for each group, SureTrak displays one summary row of subtotals in the Activity columns and one matching summary bar in the Bar chart. Alternatively, you can specify that you want to display individual bars; for each group, SureTrak shows one summary row of subtotals in the Activity columns, and several bars, one for each activity in the summarized group.

For more information about subtotals, see Grouping Activities in the Bar Chart View *earlier in this chapter.*

SureTrak calculates summary totals for each kind of data (duration, dates, monetary values) using the same method as group subtotals. Remember that the summarized duration will probably differ from the actual total of the durations for a group of activities; if a gaps exists between the activities, the summarized duration may be longer than the sum of the durations, but if activities overlap, it may be shorter.

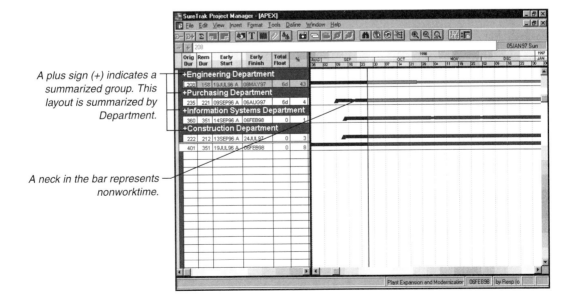

A plus sign (+) indicates a summarized group. This layout is summarized by Department.

A neck in the bar represents nonworktime.

To summarize all activities Choose Format, Summarization, Summarize All.

Choose this option. —

Right-click and select the level to summarize to. Select Project to summarize the entire project. —

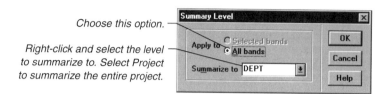

If you organize the layout by activity codes, SureTrak shows those activity codes in the Summarize To drop-down list. If you organize the layout by WBS codes or outline, SureTrak shows the WBS or outline levels in the Summarize To drop-down list.

To summarize one or several groups of activities Select the band that represents the group of activities you want to summarize, or press Ctrl and select several bands to summarize. Choose Format, Summarization, Summarize All. Choose Selected Bands and click OK.

To summarize activities directly in the layout In the Activity columns, double-click the band that represents the code you want to summarize. SureTrak displays a plus sign (+) on the left side of the band to denote that it is summarized.

Unsummarizing activities You can use the Summary Level dialog box to expand, or "unsummarize," all or selected summarized activities. You may want to summarize all groups, then expand one or a few groups of activities; you can focus on these individual activities while seeing their impacts on the other, summarized groups.

To expand summarized activities Choose Format, Summarization, Summarize All.

To display details for one summarized group Select the band for the summarized group of activities you want to expand. Choose Format, Summarization, Expand.

To expand summarized activities directly in the project window In the Activity columns, double-click the band for the summarized activity you want to expand.

Formatting Summary Bars

You can summarize activities using one bar to represent the summarized group, or using individual bars. When showing only one summary bar, SureTrak can indicate inactive time during a summarized period. The activity narrows to a "neck" for any period when no activities are scheduled.

To show one summarized bar in the Bar chart Choose Format, Summarization, Format Summary Bars.

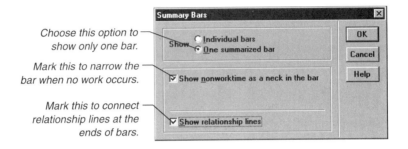

Choose this option to show only one bar.

Mark this to narrow the bar when no work occurs.

Mark this to connect relationship lines at the ends of bars.

SureTrak displays individual bars only for the key bar, which you designate in the Bars dialog box.

To show individual bars in the Bar chart You can also summarize activities in the Activity columns, yet see a bar or endpoint for each activity. SureTrak places as many individual bars as will fit on each row, end-to-end. If all the bars don't fit, some bars may move to another row; this occurs when there is not enough space to draw text next to bars, or when bars overlap in time.

Choose Format, Summarization, Format Summary Bars and choose the Individual Bars option.

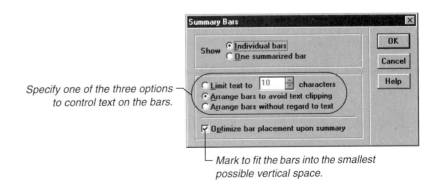

Specify one of the three options to control text on the bars.

Mark to fit the bars into the smallest possible vertical space.

If you do not want to show text on the bars, use the Bars dialog box to remove the label text.

Choose Limit Text To Characters to truncate the text at a specified number of characters. Choose Arrange Bars To Avoid Text Clipping to place bars so that text is not cut off by other bars. Choose Arrange Bars Without Regard To Text to place bars quickly, without regard for appearance of text.

For more information, see the *Customizing the Bar Chart View* chapter.

When you show individual bars for a summarized activity, you may need to increase the row height (choose Format, Row Height) and drag some activity bars up or down in order to fit all the bars neatly in an area of the Bar chart that corresponds to one group.

Adding and Editing Activities in an Organized Layout

When you add or drag an activity to a banded group, that activity inherits the information by which the group is banded. For example, if you organize activities by phase and base calendar, then drag an activity to a group with the Logistics phase code and Calendar 4, SureTrak assigns that phase and calendar to the moved activity. You can overwrite the inherited information in the Activity form, Codes form, or Activity columns.

To add activities using the Activity form while organized

Select an activity below the band or bands that represent the information you want to assign to the new activity. Add the activity. Complete the Activity form, then click OK.

Dragging activities When you drag an activity from one group to another, SureTrak changes the activity's data so that it matches the grouping data of the other activities in the group. For example, if activities are organized by responsibility and you drag an activity from Tom Mills' activities to a group of Andy Mason's activities, SureTrak changes the responsibility code for that activity from Mills to Mason.

Robotics Automation System		
Andy Mason - Director of Development		
AS100	Define System Requirements	10
AS101	System Design	20
AS204	Prepare Drawings for Temp Control Equipment	10
AS216	Prepare Drawings for System Controller	10
AS102	Approve System Design	10
Tom Mills - Director of Hardware Engineering		
AS240	Installation Begins	0
AS310	Site Preparation	10
AS103	Install Robot Base	18
AS104	Run Sealant, Air, and Water Piping	13
AS315	Install Electrical Power	24
AS105	Install Temperature Control Equipment	20
AS106	Set & Connect Robots	18
AS107	Install System & Misc. Components	30

Robotics Automation System		
Andy Mason - Director of Development		
AS100	Define System Requirements	10
AS101	System Design	20
AS204	Prepare Drawings for Temp Control Equipment	10
AS216	Prepare Drawings for System Controller	10
AS102	Approve System Design	10
AS106	Set & Connect Robots	18
Tom Mills - Director of Hardware Engineering		
AS240	Installation Begins	0
AS310	Site Preparation	10
AS103	Install Robot Base	18
AS104	Run Sealant, Air, and Water Piping	13
AS315	Install Electrical Power	24
AS105	Install Temperature Control Equipment	20
AS107	Install System & Misc. Components	30

SureTrak automatically changes an activity's data to match the data of the group when you drag the activity between bands.

1 In an organized project, select the activity(ies) that you want to move.

2 Position the mouse pointer at the left edge of the activities you want to move so that the mouse pointer changes to ⊕.

3 Drag the mouse to the appropriate band.

SureTrak places the activity(ies) below the activity row or band they are dragged to, and the moved activities inherit the data displayed in the band or bands.

Assigning predecessors or successors by dragging activities

If you organize by predecessor or successor, an activity can appear in the layout more than once; it appears once for each predecessor or successor assigned to it.

If you drag an activity to one of these groups, you're assigning that grouping item to the activity. Rather than changing information about the activity, you are assigning it a predecessor or successor in a finish to start relationship with no lag.

Assigning resources by dragging activities If you organize the layout by resource you can assign resources, or change existing resource assignments, by dragging activities from one group to another. Point to the left side of the activity row (in the Activity columns) whose resource you want to change. The cursor changes to ▣. Drag the activity up or down to the group band of the resource you want to apply.

If you drag the activity from the uncategorized band, SureTrak applies the resource. If you drag an activity from one resource band to another, SureTrak changes the resource assignment while leaving its budget, units per timeperiod, and quantity to complete unchanged. To apply an additional resource, rather than changing the resource, press Ctrl while pointing to the left edge of the activity row. When the cursor changes to a ▣ with a small plus sign next to it, drag the activity to a new group. Both the original and new resources are assigned to the activity.

Grouping Activities in the PERT View

You can arrange the PERT view so activities are grouped according to a common value. For example, group activities by activity code to focus on activities that are part of the same project, department, or phase.

To group activities in the PERT view Choose View, PERT, then choose Format, Organize. Use the Group By field to specify how to group activities.

Mark one or both checkboxes to display code values and/or descriptions in the band.

Clear to hide activities with no value for the grouping parameter.

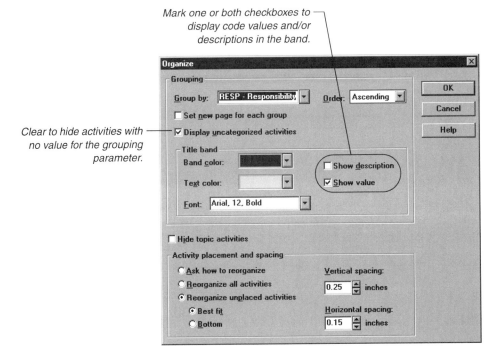

Organize activities by activity code, Activity ID code, calendar ID, or total float. SureTrak automatically positions groups in ascending order; to use a descending order, specify Descending in the Order field.

Use the Activity Placement and Spacing options at the bottom of the dialog box to control how SureTrak positions activities when moving from the Bar chart view after adding new activities.

Code grouping uses the order specified in the Activity Code Dictionary.

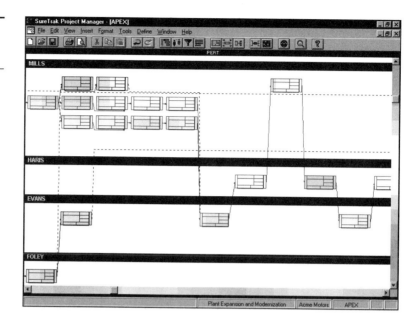

For information about grouping activities in PERT, see the *Customizing the PERT View* chapter.

To turn off grouping Choose Format, Organize. Select <None> in the Group By field, then click OK. SureTrak arranges activities based on schedule logic.

To reorganize activities at any time, choose Format, Reorganize Now.

Selecting Activities by Filter

Filters help you focus on specific areas of a project by displaying only activities that match criteria you specify. By using filters, you control the activities that appear in a layout. SureTrak temporarily hides activities that do not meet filter criteria.

You can use the filters SureTrak provides or create your own. Read this chapter to find out more about using and creating filters.

Using SureTrak Filters

You can use filters to analyze or report on activities that meet certain conditions. Use filters to limit the activities included in a layout or in a report; show activities that match one specification and another specification; or show activities that match one specification or another specification.

SureTrak provides predefined filters that you can use with your projects. For example, use a predefined filter to show only critical activities, or use one that shows only activities scheduled to start within 1 week, 4 weeks, or 3 months.

To cancel a filter, choose the All Activities filter at any time.

To apply a filter to the project Choose Format, Filter. Select the filter you want to apply from the list. Specify whether to replace the set of activities with only those that meet the criteria of the filter, to append to the current set of activities, or to remove activities from view if they meet the filter's criteria. Click Apply.

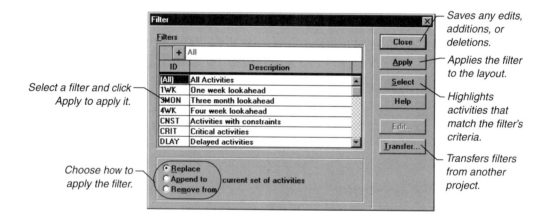

Select a filter and click Apply to apply it.

Choose how to apply the filter.

Saves any edits, additions, or deletions.

Applies the filter to the layout.

Highlights activities that match the filter's criteria.

Transfers filters from another project.

Although applying a filter temporarily removes certain activities from view, they remain part of the project and are included when you schedule or level the project.

Creating a New Filter

You can create your own filters. For example, create a filter to show activities with several responsibility codes that are scheduled to occur between two specific dates.

To create a filter Choose Format, Filter. As you add filters and assign IDs, SureTrak immediately sorts them alphabetically. Use the Filter Specification dialog box to define or add new filters. The logical statements on each row specify activities that you want to show in the layout. You can define filters on Level 1 only, or on Level 1 and Level 2. Click OK when you finish specifying selection criteria.

1 Adds a new filter; supply an ID and description.

2 Choose to replace the existing activities, append to them, or remove the selected activities from the layout.

3 Click to edit the currently selected filter specification.

4 Choose And if activities must meet both Level 1 and Level 2 criteria. Choose Or if activities can meet either Level 1 or Level 2 selection criteria to be included.

5 Right-click in any of these columns to select a value from a drop-down list.

6 Choose whether an activity must meet all the criteria at this level to be included in the layout, or whether meeting any of the criteria is sufficient.

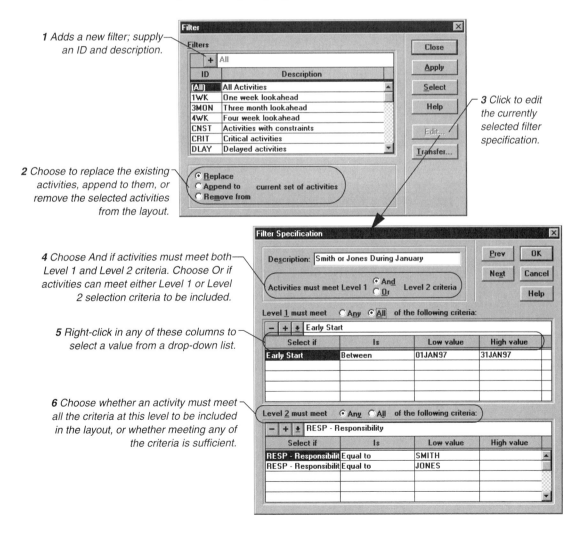

If you choose Between or Not Between as an operator, right-click in the High Value column and select a value.

 To filter using rolling dates in the specification, click the Cal button on the edit bar and select Start Date, Data Date, or Finish Date; then type a positive or negative number to specify the timespan of the filter in relation to the project's start date, data date, or finish date.

Click Close to save the filter without applying it. Click Apply to filter the activities in the layout. Click Select to highlight all activities that meet the filter's requirements. All other activities remain in the layout, but are not selected.

These are a few examples of the types of logical statements you can use as filter criteria:

- Select if the Activity ID is between 1000 (low value) and 5000 (high value)

- Select if the Phase code value is equal to LAUNCH (low value)

- Select if the early start date is between July 18, 1997 (low value) and July 31, 1997 (high value)

- Select if the WBS value is between 1.2.A (low value) and 1.4.* (high value)

Filtering by Codes

You can filter by codes, dates, float, activity type, relationship type, cost, budget, assigned resources, and other data items to see parts of the project from different perspectives.

Filtering by activity codes Use activity code values to find activities with filters. The following statement finds the activities in the preparation (PREP) phase of the project that are the responsibility of the office manager (OFFM).

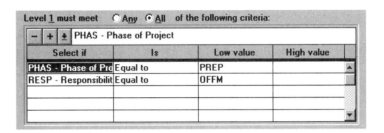

For more information about WBS codes, see the Creating a Work Breakdown Structure chapter.

Filtering by WBS codes You can filter activities based on WBS values by selecting activities in a specific branch within the work breakdown structure. The following example uses a wildcard to include part of a WBS branch; it includes activities with WBS codes of 1.1.2, 1.1.2.1, 1.1.2.2, and 1.1.2.3.

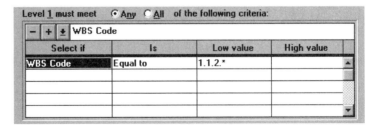

Filtering by Activity IDs and Descriptions

Filtering by Activity IDs If your Activity IDs contain meaningful information, use that information to filter activities. For example, the prefix HR in an Activity ID could stand for Human Resources. Combined with a wildcard character (*), this portion of this Activity ID produces a filter that shows all human resources activities.

Level 1 must meet   ● Any   ○ All   of the following criteria:

Select if	Is	Low value	High value
Activity ID	Equal to	HR*	

The Contains operator will not filter if the value contains an asterisk, which is a wildcard character.

Filtering by text in descriptions Add a new filter, or click Edit in the Filter dialog box to change an existing filter. Use the Contains operator in the Is column of the filter specification to filter activities based on partial or complete text strings. Type one or more words or a word fragment in the Low Value column; you need not match upper- or lowercase letters. This feature enables you to find activities with data items containing keywords; for example, filter for all activity descriptions that contain the word "deadline." Click OK.

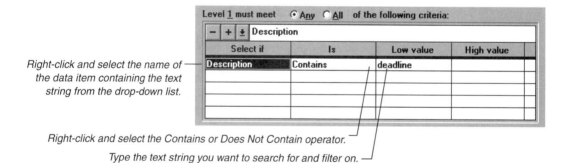

Right-click and select the name of the data item containing the text string from the drop-down list.

Level 1 must meet   ● Any   ○ All   of the following criteria:

Select if	Is	Low value	High value
Description	Contains	deadline	

Right-click and select the Contains or Does Not Contain operator.

Type the text string you want to search for and filter on.

Filtering by Dates

Combine some types of dates, such as early start or suspend dates, with a specific calendar date or a rolling date to create a filter that focuses on a specific period of time. The following filter specification displays activities that have an early start date between January 1, 1997, and January 31, 1997.

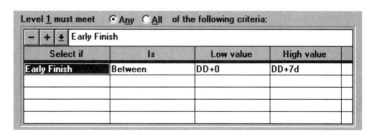

Filtering with rolling dates You can filter activities by their start or finish dates in relation to the project's start date, data date, or finish date, rather than by specific calendar dates. Rolling dates always use current project dates, so you needn't edit the filter to change a specific date each time the data date or other project dates change.

Rolling dates use continuous calendar days, whether or not those days are worktime on any project or base calendar.

For example, the following filter specification uses a rolling data date filter, to find activities scheduled to finish within 7 days of the data date. SureTrak looks at the current data date and filters activities finishing on that date through the next 7 days.

To designate a date in terms of a certain amount of time before the project start date, data date, or finish date, include a minus sign (–) before the number of hours, days, or weeks. For example, to filter activities that finish in the last 5 days of the project, choose FD for project finish date, choose Greater Than, and type –5 for the Low Value.

Filtering with Wildcards

You may sometimes want to show activities with data that matches a pattern. You can use the Equal To or Not Equal To operators with wildcard characters in the Low Value column. Wildcards "stand in" for one or more characters and show activities that have some characters in common. You can use wildcards with Activity IDs, activity codes, WBS codes, resources, predecessors, successors, and activity descriptions.

Use the question mark (?) wildcard to find a single character in the same position as the question mark. Use several question mark wildcards in a row to represent a specific number of characters. Use the asterisk (*) wildcard to find any number of characters in the same position as the asterisk.

The filter in the following example finds all activities with Activity IDs ending with HR that are the responsibility of Doug.

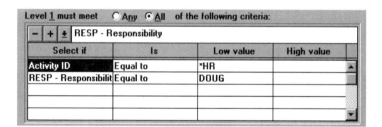

 You cannot use wildcards to filter by dates. However, you can use rolling dates to display activities within a given timespan, as described on the preceding page.

Finding Activities Without Using a Filter

Use SureTrak's Find feature to quickly find activities in the Bar chart or PERT views based on a search of any or all data items.

Finding items Use the Find feature to search any or all data items for the value you specify. SureTrak highlights activities containing or matching the search value. For example, SureTrak can find and highlight all occurrences of the word "technical" in any data item, whether it occurs in an activity description, a log entry, or any other data field.

To find an item

1 Choose Edit, Find to open the Find dialog box.

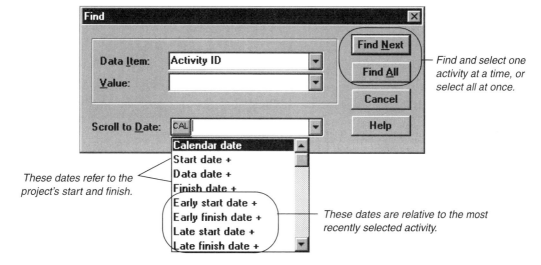

These dates refer to the project's start and finish.

Find and select one activity at a time, or select all at once.

These dates are relative to the most recently selected activity.

2 In the Data Item field, specify the data item in which to search. To search everywhere, select All Data Items from the drop-down list. To limit the search to a specific data item, such as the log lines or the activity descriptions, select that data item from the drop-down list.

3 In the Value field, type the value you seek. When the Data Item is an activity code, Activity ID, resource, or WBS value, you can select the value from a drop-down list. If the item is an activity description or a log record, type the string you are searching for in the Value field.

4 Click Find Next or Find All. Find Next highlights one occurrence of the search value; Find All highlights all occurrences.

*To find the next activity
without reopening the Find
dialog box, press Shift+F4.*

5 Click Cancel to close the Find dialog box. The selected activities remain highlighted.

 Find does not locate occurrences of the item in activities that are summarized, filtered, or hidden, unless it finds none in the visible layout. In this case, Find prompts you with the option of displaying filtered, hidden, or summarized activities that meet the Find criteria.

For added convenience, use the Scroll To Date field to scroll the timescale to a date you specify. Leave the field blank if you prefer not to scroll the view horizontally.

The following examples show the result of searching all data items in the sample project RADIO for the word "RECRUIT."

 Searches are not case-sensitive.

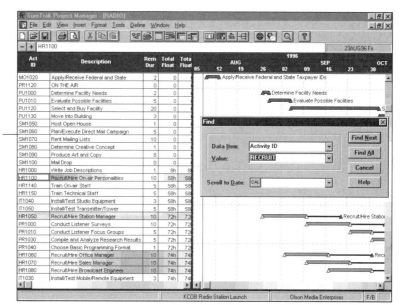

SureTrak highlights any or all activities that meet the Find parameter.

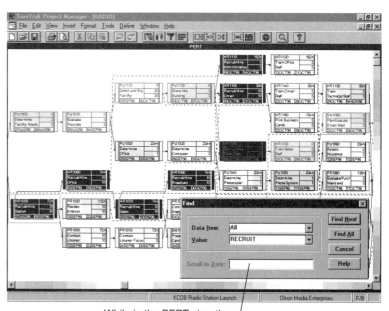

While in the PERT view the Date field is not available.

Hiding Activities Without Using a Filter

You may want to temporarily remove activities from your layout without creating a filter; perhaps the only thing the activities have in common is that you don't need to see them at the moment. The Hide command filters activities that may or may not have data items or codes in common.

To hide activities temporarily without using a filter Select the activities that you want to temporarily remove from the display. Choose View, Hide.

For more information about reports, see the *Creating SureTrak Reports* chapter.

SureTrak does not include hidden activities on printouts created using the File, Print command or the Print icon. However, if you print a report, the hidden activities may appear in the report because reports use their own filter specifications.

To show temporarily hidden activities Choose Format, Reapply Filter.

Part 4

Updating and Managing the Schedule

In this part:

Successful project management doesn't end after you develop a project plan. To accomplish the goals of the project, track daily events and update the schedule's activities, resources, and costs. First, create a baseline schedule that uses target dates to compare actual progress and current forecasts to the original schedule, then record progress by updating data in SureTrak. You can also use electronic mail (E-mail) to exchange and update project information quickly.

As your project progresses, concentrate on analyzing resource usage and adjusting it to ensure that resource demand does not exceed resource availability.

Read this part to learn how to update and manage your schedule in SureTrak.

Working with Target Dates

Target dates are the original plan for your project; define them before you update activity information the first time. As your project progresses, compare the current schedule and actual dates to the original plan.

Once you define target dates and update your project, you'll want to show early bars and target bars, so you can easily compare the current status of the project to the original plan and identify variances.

Assigning Target Dates

Creating a target, or baseline project, with target dates provides a way to compare actual progress and current forecasts to the original plan. You can include target dates on reports and the project window, but SureTrak does not use them to calculate early or late dates.

Use the Bar chart to compare the current schedule and actual dates to the target dates for a project.

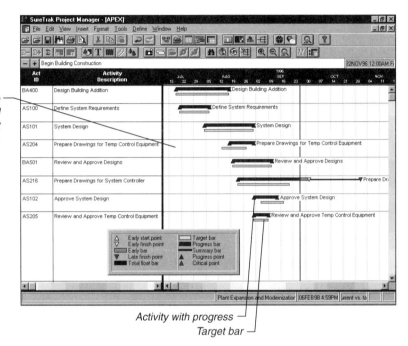

Activity with progress

Target bar

You can enter target dates or you can have SureTrak assign them. Once you enter or assign target dates, they do not change unless you edit them in the Dates detail form or in the Activity columns, or you reassign them to activities.

For information about layouts and target comparison reports, see the *Creating SureTrak Reports* and *Using SureTrak Layouts* chapters.

You can enter target dates in the Dates detail form one activity at a time, but it's faster to have SureTrak copy the early, late, or unleveled dates as the target dates. If you want SureTrak to assign target dates to only a few activities, select them first; otherwise, SureTrak assigns target dates to all activities in the project layout.

 SureTrak does not assign target dates to activities that are excluded from the project layout by a filter, even if you specify All Activities in the Target Dates dialog box.

To define target dates for all activities

1 Choose Define, Target Dates.

2 Select Early, Late, or Unleveled dates from the drop-down list in the Assign To Target Dates field.

3 Choose the All Activities option.

4 Click OK.

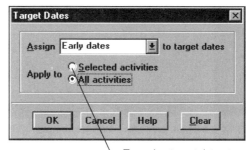

—To assign target dates to only specified activities, first select the activities, then choose this option.

Changing Target Dates

The easiest way to use target dates is to develop an achievable schedule, then define target dates. Once you assign target dates, review and edit them to keep your schedule current.

As portions of the project plan change, you can either select activities whose target dates have changed and redefine them, or use the Dates detail form or Target Date columns to change target dates for specific activities.

To modify target dates in the Dates detail form

1   Select the activities in the Activity columns for which you want to enter or change target dates.

2   Choose View, Activity Detail, Dates.

3   In the Target cell in the Start column, right-click and select the target start date from the pop-up calendar, or type the date in the correct format.

4   In the Target cell in the Finish column, right-click and select the target finish date from the pop-up calendar, or type the date in the correct format.

5   Click ⊠ to close the Dates form.

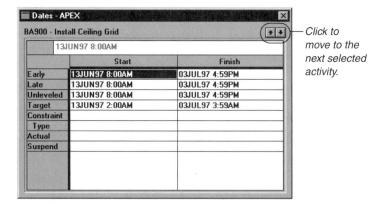

Click to move to the next selected activity.

To modify target dates in the Activity columns

1 Choose Format, Columns and add Target Start and Target Finish columns in the Columns dialog box.

2 In the Activity columns, select the cell containing the target date you want to change.

3 Select the new target date from the pop-up calendar, or type the date.

4 Click 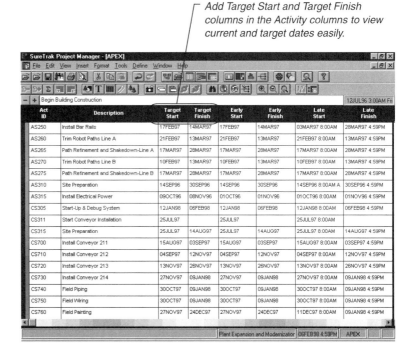.

Add Target Start and Target Finish columns in the Activity columns to view current and target dates easily.

For information about adding columns to the project layout, see the *Customizing the Bar Chart View* chapter.

Deleting Target Dates

Use the Target Dates dialog box to remove target dates for all or selected activities in the project.

To delete target dates for all activities

1 Choose Define, Target Dates.

   The Assign field can contain any date type.

2 Choose the All Activities option. If the project layout is filtered, the activities excluded from the layout by the filter are unaffected. Hidden activities are also unaffected.

3 Click Clear, then click OK.

To delete target dates for selected activities

1 Select the activities for which you want to clear target dates and choose Define, Target Dates.

2 Choose the Selected Activities option.

3 Click Clear, then click OK.

Showing Target Dates and Endpoints on the Bar Chart

For information on displaying target bars, endpoints, and labels on the Bar chart, see the *Customizing the Bar Chart View* chapter.

When activities have target dates, you can show these dates as bars or points on the Bar chart. Use the Bars dialog box (choose Format, Bars) to format the Bar chart so it includes the target bar and/or the target start or finish endpoints.

You can also include text on the Bar chart. For example, show the target start and finish dates as labels directly above, below, or next to the target graphic bar or endpoint(s).

Updating Activities

A primary benefit of critical-path-method (CPM) scheduling is the ability to recalculate the effects of surprise events, change requests, and shifting priorities to the rest of the project accurately and quickly.

Update your project regularly so that it reflects the current status. Depending on how quickly your projects change, you may want to update daily, weekly, monthly—perhaps even hourly. Analyze the updated project to identify areas where progress fails to match the original plan, and evaluate alternative courses of action that will meet project goals.

You can update individually in the Update Activity dialog box, Activity form, Activity columns, or the Bar chart.

Preparing to Update the Project

Before you begin updating a project, you'll need answers to these questions: Is it time to update the project? Which activities should be updated? What method is best for updating? As of what date should the updated project be current?

When should I update? Once a project is underway, you will need to update the schedule and resource use at regular intervals. Each project is different: you may need to update daily, weekly, or monthly, depending on the amount of time your project spans and how frequently you want to adjust your forecasts.

You also can update the project remotely using E-mail.

Although no set rules exist for update frequency, consider these general guidelines. If your project never seems to be accurate, you are not updating often enough, or the scope of your activities is too broad—you should divide activities into smaller ones. If you spend too much time updating, you're updating too often, or the scope of your activities is too narrow.

For more information about using E-mail, see the *Updating Project Data Remotely* chapter.

Which activities should I update? You should update any activity on which work has been performed—started, progressed, or finished—since the last update, or since the start date of the project.

Update activities that start and finish during the current update period; that start during a previous update period but finish during the current update period; that start during a previous update period and continue during the current update period, but are not finished; and that start during the current update period but are not finished.

If an activity hasn't started, even if it should have started, do not update it. SureTrak schedules activities that should have started, but have not, according to their predecessors; if their predecessors have completed, SureTrak schedules them as of the data date. Activities that should have started may also have negative float if their delay interferes with date constraints and must-finish deadlines.

If an activity finished during a previous update period, you've already updated it as complete; you needn't update it again. If an activity starts and/or finishes within the update period, enter actual start and/or finish dates for the activity. If an activity starts but has not yet finished, record actual start dates and remaining durations.

> *An activity is fully updated when you record actual start and finish dates, set remaining duration to zero, and set percent complete to 100.*

Milestone activities and updating A milestone resembles an activity, even though it represents only a point in time and therefore has no duration in the schedule. If you update activities individually, record an actual start date for a start milestone or an actual finish date for a finish milestone. If you have SureTrak estimate progress, it will update milestones appropriately.

Choosing a Method of Updating

SureTrak offers several ways of updating your schedule. You can update progress for all activities and resources as a whole; update activities and resources individually; or use a combination of the two methods.

If your project is progressing exactly as planned, you only need to estimate progress. Simply tell SureTrak the data date or "as-of" date, and have SureTrak determine which activities have progressed and how much, and calculate the remaining durations of activities that have started. SureTrak also notes which activities have completed and sets their remaining durations to zero.

If your project is not progressing as planned—many activities are starting out-of-sequence, activities are taking more or less time to complete than originally planned, actual resource use is exceeding planned use—update activities and resources individually. This will help you forecast the effects of this unpredicted progress or lack of progress, so that you can take appropriate corrective action wherever necessary.

Most projects progress somewhere between these two situations: some activities are progressing as planned and some are not. If this is the case, you'll want to combine the two updating methods. Let SureTrak calculate your project as if it is progressing exactly as planned, and then individually update those activities and resources that have deviated from the plan.

For information about target dates, see the *Working with Target Dates* chapter.

Before you update, define target dates so that you can later compare the updated project with the target (usually the original) project.

Understanding the Data Date

SureTrak uses the data date, or "as-of" date, when calculating the schedule. Before the first update, the project start date is the data date. As the project proceeds, move the data date forward, toward the end of the project. To update a project, you can change the data date by using the Progress Spotlight feature, dragging the data date line across the Bar chart, or entering the data date in the Progress dialog box.

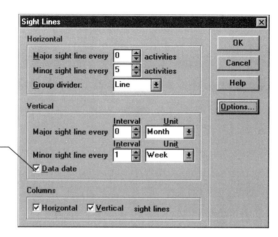

To display the data date line on the Bar chart, choose Format, Sight Lines and mark this checkbox.

 The data date may differ from the date on which you enter the update information. For example, you can enter update information on a Monday for a data date as of the previous Friday; the resulting project shows progress as of that Friday.

If you're working with a daily schedule, the data date is always in the morning. To update a project as of Tuesday night, make Wednesday morning the data date; since no work took place overnight, it's the same point in time as far as the schedule is concerned. If you're working with an hourly schedule, make sure the hour of the data date is appropriate; if you specify a data date of Friday at 3:00 p.m., SureTrak accepts progress up to that time—but not including it.

Highlighting Activities for Updating

The Progress Spotlight feature is SureTrak's updating tool; it shows the activities that should have been worked on during a specified timeperiod. You can also simply drag the data date line with the mouse until you reach the date you want. SureTrak spotlights the activities that fall between the last data date and the new data date. Once you spotlight activities, you can automatically status them, manually update them, or cut and copy them.

To use the Progress Spotlight feature

1 Click the Progress Spotlight icon to add a timeperiod equal to the smallest increment of the displayed timescale from the previous data date.

2 Click the Progress Spotlight icon again to increase the area between the previous data date and the new date by another timescale increment. To decrease the spotlighted area by one time increment, click the Progress Spotlight icon while pressing the Shift key.

3 Update activities as described later in this chapter, or reschedule the project according to the new data date immediately by pressing Ctrl+F9.

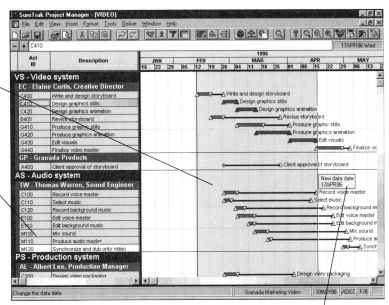

SureTrak spotlights activities that should have started, progressed, or finished between the previous data date and the new data date in the Activity columns.

SureTrak spotlights activities that fall between the previous data date and the new data date in the Activity columns.

When you drag the data-date line, a date window displays the new data date.

To drag the data date line

1 Position the mouse pointer at the data-date line; when it changes to ⟨⬦⟩, drag the line to the right until you reach the new data date.

For a daily project, position the data-date line on the morning after the evening through which you're recording progress; for an hourly project, position the data-date line on the hour after the time through which you're recording progress.

2 Release the mouse button. SureTrak spotlights the activities between the last data date and the new data date.

3 Update activities as described later in this chapter, or reschedule the project according to the new data date immediately by pressing Ctrl+F9.

For more information about the Progress dialog box, see Estimating Activity Progress Automatically *later in this chapter.*

Depending on the density of the timescale above your Bar chart, you may not be able to position the data-date line on the exact date and time you want to use. In this case, enter the data date in the Update Progress dialog box and have SureTrak estimate progress as of that date before you update individual activities.

 When you spotlight activities by dragging the data date line or by using the Progress Spotlight feature, SureTrak turns off automatic scheduling. Choose Tools, Schedule Now or press F9 to reschedule after you finish updating; SureTrak recalculates the schedule and turns automatic scheduling back on.

Estimating Activity Progress Automatically

If activities are progressing on schedule, you may want SureTrak to estimate progress for all activities as of the new data date you specify. SureTrak can quickly estimate their activity dates, percent complete amounts, and remaining durations when you use the Update Progress dialog box to update a project.

You can apply the PROG filter to display only activities that are underway.

Estimating activity progress is a quick and convenient way to update your project. SureTrak estimates progress only for those activities that were supposed to take place. Since progress can occur on activities out of sequence, you may need to update additional activities—especially if you selected activities by dragging the data-date line or by using the Progress Spotlight feature. You should also review all incomplete activities to make sure their remaining durations, actual dates, and percent complete amounts are realistic. Once you spotlight activities, you can quickly update the project as "on time."

Before you recalculate the schedule, you can adjust dates, percent complete amounts, and remaining durations for individual activities that aren't proceeding according to plan. SureTrak can also estimate the amount of resources expended for each activity during the update period.

For more information about spotlighting and dragging the data date, see *Preparing to Update the Project* earlier in this chapter.

If you spotlight activities or drag the data-date line to a new date before opening this dialog box, SureTrak turns off automatic scheduling.

To estimate progress for all spotlighted activities Spotlight the activities for which you want to estimate progress by dragging the data date line or by using the Progress Spotlight feature. Choose Tools, Update Progress.

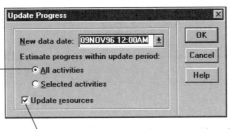

Choose to estimate progress within the update period for All Activities.

Depending on your Autocost settings in the Resource tab in the Options dialog box, mark to keep remaining durations of activities and resources in proportion and to estimate actual resource use, costs, and revenues to date.

If you spotlight activities, SureTrak displays the new data date in the Progress dialog box. If you enter a new data date in the Update Progress dialog box, the spotlighted area on the Bar chart does not change. However, SureTrak selects activities to update based on this date and on whether you choose All Activities or Selected Activities in this dialog box.

 Distinguish spotlighted activities from selected activities by assigning them different colors. If they are the same color, change one in the Screen Colors dialog box (choose Format, Screen Colors).

To estimate progress for selected spotlighted activities

1 Spotlight the activities for which you want to estimate progress by dragging the data-date line or by using the Progress Spotlight feature.

2 Select the spotlighted activities for which you want to estimate progress.

   The selected activities appear in the Activity columns in the column highlight color that normally designates selected activities.

3 Choose Tools, Update Progress to open the Update Progress dialog box.

4 Choose to estimate progress within the update period for Selected Activities, then click OK.

When you close the Progress dialog box, SureTrak updates the selected activities only: it estimates percent complete amounts as of the data date, sets dates to actual if they fall before the new data date, and estimates remaining durations for activities that are not finished as of the data date.

 If you estimate progress for selected activities that do not fall within the update period, those activities will show no progress. While spotlighting, you can only estimate progress—percent complete, remaining duration, and so on— for activities that are within the update period.

Updating Activities Manually

If you choose to update activities exactly, rather than estimate progress, update them individually by entering the actual start and/or finish date, percent complete, and remaining duration in the Update Activity dialog box (choose Tools, Update Activity).

If an activity has started but has not finished, the actual start date replaces the early and late start dates. If the activity has finished, the data contains an actual finish date instead of early and late finish dates.

To enter actual dates using the Update Activity dialog box

1 Choose Tools, Schedule to display the Schedule dialog box, choose Off in the Automatic Schedule Calculation section, and click OK. If you spotlight activities before beginning to update, SureTrak automatically turns off scheduling until you finish updating.

2 Select the activity you want to update in the Activity columns and choose Tools, Update Activity.

3 Mark the Started checkbox and change the actual start date.

4 Use the Progress scroll bar to automatically update remaining duration and percent complete. The scroll bar updates both remaining duration and percent complete if the Link Remaining Duration and Schedule Percent Complete checkbox is marked in the Options dialog box (choose Tools, Options, then click the Resource tab). Or, enter a specific number in the fields.

5 Click Update.

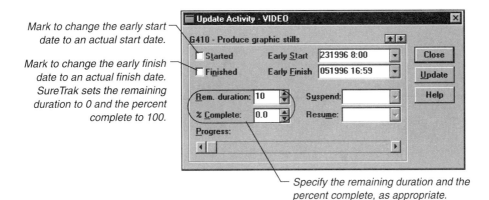

Mark to change the early start date to an actual start date.

Mark to change the early finish date to an actual finish date. SureTrak sets the remaining duration to 0 and the percent complete to 100.

Specify the remaining duration and the percent complete, as appropriate.

If you use the scroll bar to update an activity, or if you mark the Link Remaining Duration and Percent Complete checkbox in the Resource tab of the Options dialog box, SureTrak updates remaining duration and percent complete in proportion. If not, you should update both items. If these two items are linked in the Options dialog box and you want to update them out of proportion, update percent complete first, then update remaining duration to break the link.

The data date is the date up to which you're updating the project.

When you finish updating activities, choose Tools, Schedule. Enter a new data date, choose Forward And Backward in the Automatic Schedule Calculation section, and click OK. SureTrak recalculates the project based on the updates you've made.

Linking Remaining Duration and Percent Complete

When you update activities individually, choose whether you want SureTrak to link percent complete to remaining duration so that they are always proportionate. If you update one, SureTrak updates the other one accordingly, unless you specifically separate them by updating them both.

If you do not link remaining duration and percent complete, a change in either percent complete or remaining duration will not affect the other value.

By breaking the tie between remaining duration and percent complete, you can separate activity status (remaining duration) from activity performance (percent complete). For example, indicate that an activity with an original duration of 10 days is 50 percent complete, even though it still requires 8 days for completion, because it is going to take longer than originally planned.

For more information about Autocost rules, see the *Updating Resources and Costs* chapter.

Choose Tools, Options to display the Options dialog box and click the Resource tab to link remaining duration and percent complete.

Updating Activities Using the Activity Form

Use the Activity form to verify and modify an activity's actual start and finish dates, percent complete, and remaining duration. The main difference between updating in the Activity form and the Update Activity dialog box is that the Activity form does not have a scroll bar that you can use to update remaining duration and percent complete simultaneously, in direct proportion. However, if you link the two in the Options dialog box (choose Tools, Options, and click the Resource tab), you can update either of them (but not both) in the Activity form, and SureTrak immediately updates the other in direct proportion. To break the link to show out-of-proportion progress, update both percent complete and remaining duration.

To enter actual dates in the Activity form Choose Tools, Schedule to display the Schedule dialog box, choose Off in the Automatic Schedule Calculation section, then click OK. Follow the steps as shown.

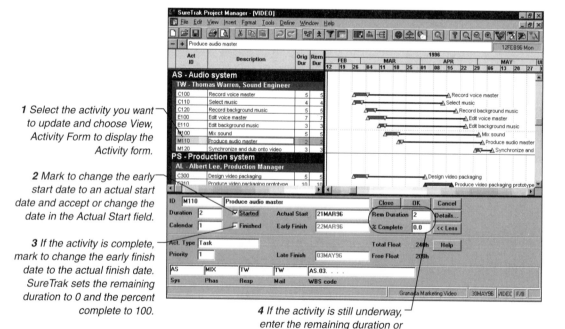

1 Select the activity you want to update and choose View, Activity Form to display the Activity form.

2 Mark to change the early start date to an actual start date and accept or change the date in the Actual Start field.

3 If the activity is complete, mark to change the early finish date to the actual finish date. SureTrak sets the remaining duration to 0 and the percent complete to 100.

4 If the activity is still underway, enter the remaining duration or percent complete. Click OK.

When you finish updating activities, choose Tools, Schedule. Enter a new data date, choose Forward And Backward in the Automatic Schedule Calculation section, and click OK. SureTrak recalculates the project based on the updates you've made.

Updating Activity Progress Using the Activity Columns

Use the Activity columns to verify and modify an activity's actual start and finish dates, and its percent complete and remaining duration. When you update in the Activity columns, you can also use the Copy Cell and Paste Cell commands if several activities have the same remaining duration, percent complete, or actual start and finish dates.

You can update an activity by entering an actual start date or actual finish date in the Activity columns.

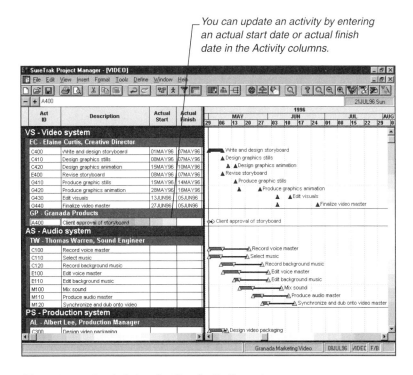

To enter actual dates in the Activity columns

For more information about adding columns, see the *Customizing the Bar Chart View* chapter.

1 Choose Format, Columns to display the Columns dialog box, add Actual Start and Actual Finish columns, then click OK.

2 In the Activity columns, click the Actual Start or Actual Finish cell for the activity you want to update and enter a date.

3 Click ☑.

Updating Activities Graphically on the Bar Chart

You can drag the ends of bars on the Bar chart to verify and modify actual start and finish dates, and percent complete and remaining duration.

For details on using the Update Activity dialog box, see *Updating Activities Manually* earlier in this chapter.

To update an activity on the Bar chart Point to the end of the activity bar you want to update and press the Shift key until the mouse pointer changes to ➘. Click the mouse to display the Update Activity dialog box for the activity and update the activity information.

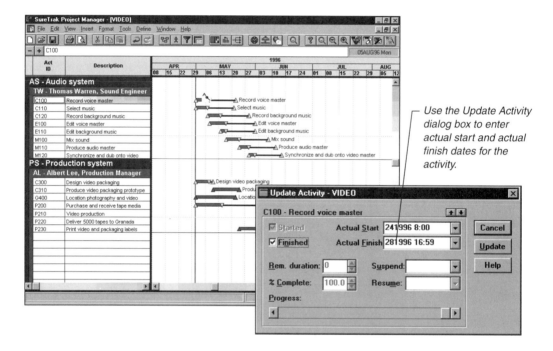

Use the Update Activity dialog box to enter actual start and actual finish dates for the activity.

SureTrak also displays the bar as completed, using the color specified in the Bar and Endpoint Options dialog box.

To apply actual start and finish dates on the Bar chart Point to the end of the activity bar you want to update and press the Shift key until the mouse pointer changes to ➘. Press the mouse button. The mouse pointer changes to ·**↟**· and a date box displays the date at the mouse pointer's location. Drag the mouse until the date you want appears in the date box. SureTrak opens the Update Activity dialog box and updates the activity with the specified Actual Start date. For example, if you drag the finish of the bar, SureTrak sets the Actual Finish to the displayed date and sets the activity percent complete to 100.

Suspending and Resuming Work on an Activity

Work on an activity may start, then stop, then resume. For example, inclement weather or employee reassignments may cause work to temporarily stop. You can model work interruption by entering the date work is suspended and the date work will resume in the Update Activity dialog box.

Specify the Suspend date as the end of the last day (and hour) work occurred for the selected activity. An activity must start in order to be interrupted, so you must enter an actual start date to enter a suspend date. For the Resume date, enter the date work resumed or the date you expect it to resume. SureTrak schedules the activity's remaining duration to start on the Resume date (and hour) you specify.

To suspend or resume an activity Select one or more activities on which work has suspended or resumed and choose Tools, Update Activity. The first selected activity appears in the Update Activity dialog box.

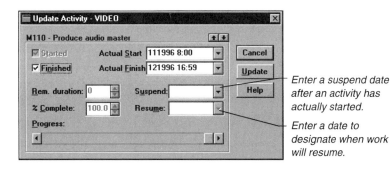

Enter a suspend date after an activity has actually started.

Enter a date to designate when work will resume.

To review suspend and resume dates with other activity dates, choose View, Activity Detail, Dates. SureTrak displays the suspend date in the Suspend Start cell and the resume date in the Suspend Finish cell.

The activity must have an Actual Start (AS) date for you to enter a Suspend date; the suspend date must occur on or before the data date.

The activity must have a suspend date for you to enter a Resume date. The Resume date is at least one hour or one day after the Suspend date, depending on how you're measuring activity duration. The resume date can occur before, on, or after the data date.

 You can suspend progress on an activity only once. If you need to suspend and resume progress on an activity more than once, divide the activity into two or more separate activities.

Updating Resources and Costs

Once work begins on your project, you should update the project to reflect any progress that is made. You can analyze resource usage and adjust it if you find over- or under-use, or if you find scheduling conflicts.

Read this chapter to learn how to update resource assignments, lump sum costs, and lump sum revenue.

Setting Autocost Rules for Automatic Updating

SureTrak's Autocost feature automatically updates resource and cost information based on the progress you report when you update activities. You can set these four Autocost options for the project by marking or clearing the checkboxes in the Options dialog box.

Choose Tools, Options, then click the Resource tab to set Autocost options.

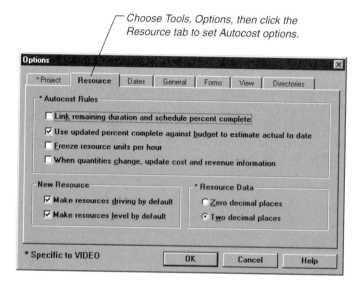

Linking remaining duration and percent complete When you mark this checkbox, each activity's remaining duration links to its percent complete, so that SureTrak updates percent complete when remaining duration changes; or SureTrak updates remaining duration when percent complete changes. If you do not link remaining duration and percent complete, a change in either percent complete or remaining duration will not affect the other value. By breaking the tie between remaining duration and percent complete, you can separate activity status (remaining duration) from activity performance (percent complete). For example, you can indicate that an activity with an original duration of 10 days is 50 percent complete, even though it requires 8 more days for completion.

If you use the Update Progress dialog box (choose Tools, Update Progress) to estimate progress on a project, specify whether SureTrak should estimate actual resource use, regardless of your choice in the Resource tab.

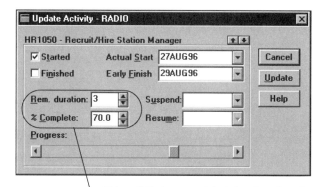

This activity has an original duration of 10 days. Its
remaining duration and percent complete are linked in the
Options dialog box in the Resource tab.

**Use updated percent complete against budget to estimate
actual to date** You can also have SureTrak multiply the updated
percent complete and the budget to estimate actual to date resource units,
costs, and revenue expended. Whenever the percent complete or budget
changes, SureTrak updates these resource values. SureTrak uses resource
percent complete for calculations. If no percent complete is entered in the
Resources detail form, SureTrak uses the percent complete for the activity.

 *Entering an actual value overrides the Actual To Date calcu-
lation only until the next time you change either the budget or
the percent complete.*

*To estimate progress for
activities and to estimate
resource use, mark both
Link Remaining Duration
And Schedule Percent
Complete and Use
Updated Percent Complete
Against Budget To
Estimate Actual To Date
checkboxes in the Options
dialog box.*

SureTrak estimates actual quantities and costs using these formulas:

Budgeted Quantity x Percent Complete = Actual Quantity To Date
Budgeted Cost x Percent Complete = Actual Cost To Date

If you always enter actual resource values directly, clear this checkbox.
For projects where tracking actual cost data is important, you should
always record the actual values rather than use the estimate based on
percent complete.

Resources - RADIO			
HR1040 - File Employment and Workers' Compensation			
	Resource 1	Resource 2	Resource 3
Resource	DOUG	LAWYER	TEMP
Driving	Yes	Yes	Yes
Units per hour	0.50	0.25	1.00
Budgeted quantity	8.00	4.00	16.00
Resource duration	2	2	2
Resource lag	0	0	0
Percent complete	60.0	25.0	0.0
Resource start	23AUG96	23AUG96	23AUG96
Resource finish	26AUG96	26AUG96	26AUG96
Actual to date	0.00	0.00	0.00
To complete	8.00	4.00	16.00
At completion	8.00	4.00	16.00
Completion variance	0.00	0.00	0.00

Doug's work on this activity is 60 percent complete, but the lawyer's work is only 25 percent complete.

Freeze resource units per hour SureTrak recalculates the quantity to complete when an activity's remaining duration or actual to date resource use changes. SureTrak multiplies quantity assigned by the remaining duration to calculate the quantity to complete. If your resource units per timeperiod are fixed, mark the Freeze Resource Units Per Hour checkbox in the Options dialog box to freeze the units.

For example, an activity originally estimated to require five, 8-hour days to complete, uses one resource, which is assigned at one unit per hour for a total of 40 hours. After the activity is underway, you realize it will take 1 day longer than expected, so you update the activity as having 3 days completed and 3 days of remaining duration.

By default, in the Options dialog box, SureTrak marks the Freeze Resource Units Per Hour checkbox, recalculating Quantity To Complete and keeping resources assigned at a constant number of units per hour.

If you freeze the resource's Units Per Hour, SureTrak updates 24 hours as completed; multiplies the remaining 3 days of duration by one unit per hour, resulting in a revised To Complete value of 24 hours; and updates the total resource At Completion to 48 hours (24 hours completed + 24 hours to complete).

If you do not freeze the resource quantity, SureTrak keeps the 40 total At Completion hours, updates 24 hours as completed, and calculates the remaining 16 hours over the 3 days (24 hours) of remaining duration at 0.67 Units Per Hour.

SureTrak recalculates the Quantity to Complete when an activity's Remaining Duration or Actual To Date resource use changes, but does not change the Units Per Hour. Resource quantities remain constant—the resource units assigned per hour remain unchanged.

When the Freeze Resource Units Per Hour checkbox is marked, SureTrak uses the equation:

Quantity To Complete = Units Per Hour x Remaining Duration

You can change the way SureTrak calculates resource use so that the total amount of the resource assigned remains constant, and SureTrak recalculates the Units Per Hour. Clear the Freeze Resource Units Per Hour checkbox if changing an activity's remaining duration after it is underway should increase or decrease the amount of each resource assigned per hour.

SureTrak recalculates Units Per Hour when the Remaining Duration or Actual To Date value changes: resource units depend on the amount of work to be performed in the allotted time. When the Freeze Resource Units Per Hour checkbox is cleared, SureTrak uses the equation:

Units Per Hour = Quantity To Complete ÷ Remaining Duration

When quantities change, update cost and revenue information SureTrak updates cost and revenue in proportion to changes in resource quantity, To Date, To Complete, or At Completion.

When you mark the When Quantities Change, Update Cost and Revenue Information checkbox, SureTrak updates costs and revenues proportionately each time you change a resource's Units Per Hour, To Date, To Complete, or At Completion value.

Mark the When Quantities Change, Update Cost and Revenue Information checkbox if you want SureTrak to recalculate a resource's costs and revenues proportionately each time you update its units per hour. Clear this checkbox if the resource costs the same regardless of the amount used, or if you want to enter cost and revenue values manually—leaving costs and revenues fixed, regardless of quantity re-estimates or updating.

Updating Resource Progress

In SureTrak, you can update resource use using either of two methods. You can let SureTrak estimate resource use and calculate costs and revenue for those resources based on percent complete; or you can enter specific amounts reflecting exact resource use, costs, and revenue.

Add a Resource Description column in the Bar chart (choose Format, Columns) to use as a reference when tracking resources.

Let SureTrak estimate resource use if you want to track approximate, rather than exact, amounts and if resources have been used in approximate proportion to progress on activities. If resource use differs significantly from activities' percent complete, enter exact resource quantities and amounts as described below.

If you update resources by entering exact amounts, be sure you also make all future updates by entering exact amounts. If you have SureTrak estimate resource use, it calculates updated amounts for all resources according to percent complete; SureTrak recalculates the resources you updated by entering exact amounts in proportion to percent complete.

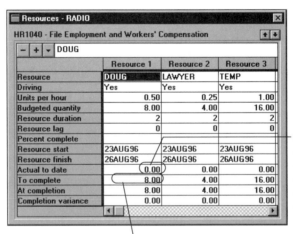

For a driving resource, enter the actual number of hours the resource has worked on the activity.

Enter the amount of the resource the activity is expected to require between the data date and the time the activity is complete.

To update a driving resource manually

1 Select the activity whose resources you want to update, then right-click and choose Activity Detail, Resources to display the Resources detail form.

2 In the Actual to Date cell, enter the amount of the resource that has been used.

SureTrak recalculates the To Complete amount so that Actual To Date + To Complete = At Completion.

You can also update the To Complete amount if it differs from the amount calculated. SureTrak then calculates a new At Completion and a variance. If the activity is finished, enter the total amount used for the completed activity. SureTrak also recalculates the resource's duration.

3 Click ▲ ▼ to move to the next activity or ⊠ to close the Resources form.

To update nondriving resources manually

1 Select the activity whose resources you want to update, then right-click and choose Activity Detail, Resources to display the Resources detail form.

2 In the Actual to Date cell, enter the amount of the resource that has been used.

3 In the To Complete field, enter the quantity of work to complete.

4 Click ▲ ▼ to move to the next activity or ⊠ to close the Resources form.

Analyzing Costs and Revenue

As your project progresses, you will need to review cost and revenue figures to keep them up to date. You can update costs and revenues using the Costs detail form and the Revenue detail form.

Update costs directly in the Costs form to maintain the budgeted and forecasted resource units and to show higher or lower than expected actual costs for resources.

Costs - APEX				
AS100 - Define System Requirements			+	↓
− + ↕ 1,150.00				
	Resource 1	**Resource 2**	**Resource 3**	
Resource	ANALYST	ATM ENG	MISC	
Budgeted cost	1,200.00	1,760.00	0.00	
Percent expended	98.7	98.7	0.0	
Percent complete				
Actual to date	1,184.40	1,737.12	0.00	
To complete	15.60	22.88	1,150.00	
At completion	1,200.00	1,760.00	1,150.00	
Scheduled budget	1,200.00	1,760.00	0.00	
Earned value	1,184.40	1,737.12	0.00	
Cost variance	0.00	0.00	0.00	
Schedule variance	-15.60	-22.88	0.00	
Completion variance	0.00	0.00	-1,150.00	

 To update costs SureTrak calculates costs when you enter or change resource quantities in the Resources detail form. However, you can override these calculations and make adjustments directly in the Costs detail form without affecting the resource quantities.

1 Select the activity that has a lump sum cost you want to update.

2 Choose View, Activity Detail, Costs to display the Costs form.

3 If the percent complete for this expenditure is not the same as the activity's percent complete, enter the percent complete for the cost.

   If you configured SureTrak to calculate Actual to Date based on Percent Complete in the Options dialog box, SureTrak updates the Actual to Date, To Complete, and At Completion cells in the Costs form.

4 If necessary, enter or edit the amounts in the Actual to Date, To Complete, and At Completion cells in the Costs form.

For information on how to assign lump sum costs to resources, see the Building a Resource Plan chapter.

   The At Completion amount should always be your current forecast of the total cost of the activity. If you change any of these three cells, SureTrak recalculates the others to show resource use according to the formula:

   Actual To Date + To Complete = At Completion

5 Click ▲ or ▼ to move to the next activity or click ✖ to close the Costs form.

To update revenue Use the Revenue detail form to see the amount of revenue each resource has earned and is forecasted to earn for the current activity. SureTrak lists all resources assigned to an activity in the Revenue form, whether or not they are defined as revenue-bearing. If they are revenue-bearing, the Revenue To Date and/or Revenue At Completion cells contain values.

1 Select the activity that has a lump sum revenue you want to update.

2 Choose View, Activity Detail, Revenue to display the Revenue form.

3 If the percent earned for this lump sum is not the same as the percent complete for the activity, enter the revenue's percent complete.

If you configured SureTrak to calculate Actual to Date based on Percent Complete in the Options dialog box, SureTrak updates the Revenue to date, Revenue at completion, and Net at completion cells in the Revenue form.

4 If necessary, enter the amounts in the Revenue to date and Revenue at completion cells in the Revenue form.

The Revenue at completion amount should always be your current forecast of the total revenue of the activity.

For information on how to assign lump sum revenue to resources, see the *Building a Resource Plan* chapter.

5 Click ▲ or ▼ to move to the next activity or click ☒ to close the Revenue form.

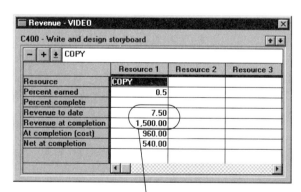

The values in the Revenue to date and Revenue at completion cells signify that the Copywriter is a revenue-bearing resource.

Analyzing Resource Use with Profiles and Tables

You can view and print resource information in either profile or table format. The profile is a graphical representation of resource information such as quantities, costs, revenues, net, budget, or budgeted cost for work scheduled (BCWS) over time, with optional cumulative curves. The table represents resource information in tabular format by timeperiod, like a spreadsheet.

Using the Resource Pane

You can view resource data for a specific resource, all resources, or any combination of resources. The profile and table can reflect this data for a selected activity, several selected activities, or all activities. Choose View, Resource Profile or View, Resource Table to display the Resource profile/table.

When you first open the resource pane, it shows resource information for all activities. The resource pane stays open until you close it or open the Activity form.

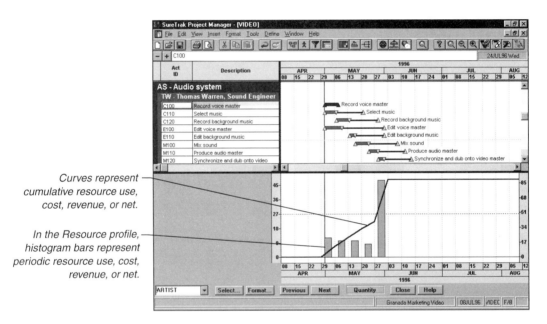

Curves represent cumulative resource use, cost, revenue, or net.

In the Resource profile, histogram bars represent periodic resource use, cost, revenue, or net.

Scrolling and resizing the profile or table Drag the scroll box along the horizontal scroll bar between the Bar chart and the profile until the resource pane displays the timespan you want to see. You can also click to the left or right of the scroll box on the scroll bar to move across half the visible timespan at a time.

Drag the vertical split bar to see more timeperiods.

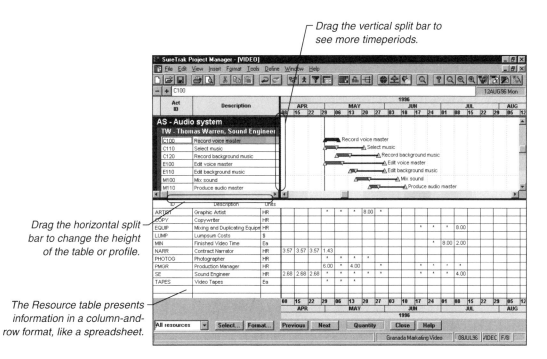

Drag the horizontal split bar to change the height of the table or profile.

The Resource table presents information in a column-and-row format, like a spreadsheet.

You can also use the PgUp and PgDn keys instead of Previous and Next.

In the resource pane, click Previous to show resource information for the selected activity above the current activity, or click Next to show resource information for the selected activity after the current activity.

Formatting the Resource Pane

To specify the appearance of the Resource profile or table, use the Format Resource Profile/Table dialog box; some general specifications apply to both the profile and the table, such as, whether to display resource quantities, costs, revenue, budget, earned value, budgeted cost for work scheduled, or net, and the length of the timeperiod, or interval.

SureTrak spreads units and monetary values over the dates the assigned resources are scheduled to work according to the activity type. For a task activity, resources are spread over workdays on the base calendar; for an independent activity, resources are spread over workdays on their own resource calendars; and for a meeting activity, resources are spread over workdays shared by their resource calendars in a combined calendar.

Specify the type of resource information to show in the resource pane.

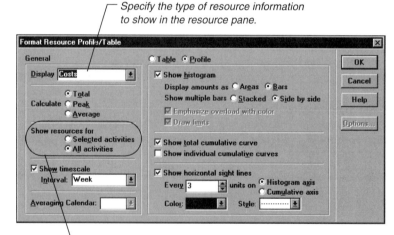

Choose Selected Activities to show resource information for one selected activity or subtotaled resource information for several activities. Choose All Activities to show totaled resource information for all activities in the project layout.

To specify resource data to view

1 Choose Format, Resource Profile/Table.

2 In the Display field, right-click and select the type of resource data you want to view in the resource pane.

3 Continue setting up other Resource profile/table specifications or click OK.

To specify resource calculations Use the Calculate section in the Format Resource Profile/Table dialog box to specify the method SureTrak uses to calculate the resource information in the profile or table.

1 Choose Format, Resource Profile/Table to display the Format Resource Table/Profile dialog box.

2 In the Calculate section, choose the type of calculation you want.

Choose Total to see the sum of use per timeperiod; Peak to see the greatest use for any hour in the timeperiod; or Average to see the sum of use per timeperiod divided by the number of hours in the timeperiod.

3 Continue setting up other Resource profile/table specifications, or click OK.

To set up the resource pane timescale You can show the timescale along the bottom of the Resource profile, or hide it so you have more room for the profile itself. Whether or not you display the timescale, choose a time interval—hour, day, week, month, quarter, or year. Each division of the timescale represents one time interval.

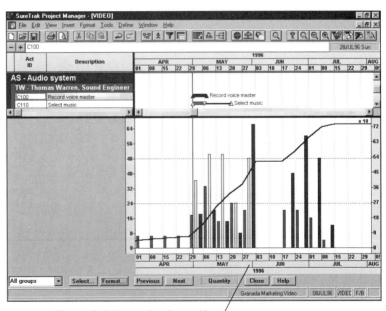

*The profile's timescale aligns with
the Bar chart's timescale, although
it can have a different interval.*

The timescale for the Resource profile and table covers the same timespan (begin date to end date) as the timescale above the Bar chart, although it can have its own time interval. For example, the bars show weekly timeperiods, but the Resource profile below the bars shows the corresponding monthly workload. When you adjust the Bar chart's timescale, perhaps by compressing it or changing the font, the timescale for the profile changes accordingly. If you adjust the timescale for the profile, the Bar chart timescale changes to match.

1 Choose Format, Resource Profile/Table to display the Format Resource Table/Profile dialog box.

2 Mark the Show Timescale checkbox.

3 In the Interval field, right-click and select an interval for the timescale from the drop-down list.

4 Continue setting up other Resource profile/table specifications or click OK.

Formatting the Resource Profile

You can customize the appearance of the Resource profile to show resource information in many different ways. For example, design a profile to show resource requirements and emphasize areas of resource overload. Another profile design can show costs per month or per week. Histograms for a particular timeperiod can appear side by side or stacked. You can also hide the histograms, drawing only cumulative curves that show the accumulation of money spent or earned, or resources used, over time.

Draw attention to resource overallocation with red.

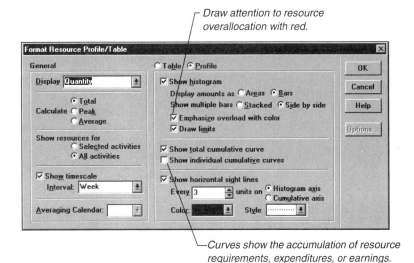

Curves show the accumulation of resource requirements, expenditures, or earnings.

To control the elements displayed on the Resource profile

1 Choose Format, Resource Profile/Table.

2 Choose the Profile option.

3 To display a histogram, mark the Show Histogram checkbox.

For more information about histograms or curves, see *Displaying Histograms* and *Displaying Curves* later in this chapter.

4 To display a cumulative curve, mark the Show Total Cumulative Curve or the Show Individual Cumulative Curves checkbox.

5 To display horizontal sight lines, mark the Show Horizontal Sight Lines checkbox.

6 In the General section, specify general resource pane display items.

7 Click OK.

Displaying Histograms

Histograms show periodic resource quantities, costs, or revenues per timeperiod: by hour, day, week, month, year, or quarter. You can show the histogram as an area chart or with individual bars; draw attention to timeperiods in which resources are overloaded; and show the limit of a resource as a line. You can display amounts as areas or as bars, and as stacked or side-by-side histograms.

Choose Stacked to show a vertical bar made up of several resources; choose Side By Side to show adjacent bars within a timeperiod for each resource.

Choose Areas to display a continuous profile across the timescale. Choose Bars to display a separate bar for each timeperiod.

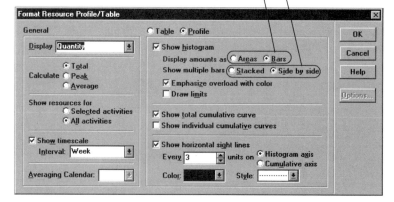

To display a histogram

1   Choose Format, Resource Profile/Table. First, choose the Profile option, then mark the Show Histogram checkbox.

2   Specify how you want amounts to display.

3   Specify how you want multiple bars to display.

If you choose not to show histograms, SureTrak disables all histogram options.

4   Specify whether to emphasize resource overload in red by marking the Emphasize Overload With Color checkbox.

5   Specify whether to display a red line to show resource availability limits by marking the Draw Limits checkbox.

6   Click OK.

Indicates overuse (displayed in red).

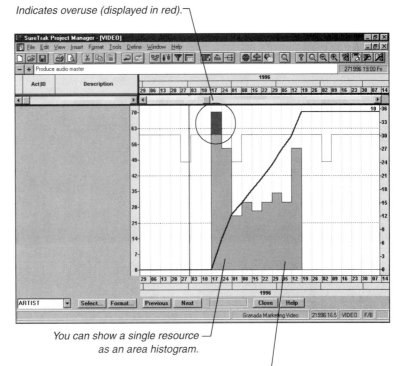

You can show a single resource as an area histogram.

To see which activities contribute to a histogram, press Ctrl and click a histogram bar; SureTrak selects the activities that contribute to that histogram's total in the Activity columns.

If you are showing several resources or resource groups, the stacked arrangement shows one bar for each timeperiod, with each resource depicted in a different color. Use this arrangement to analyze the combined resource requirements for a timeperiod, as well as the impact each resource has on the total amount. Stacked bars are most useful when the total resource amounts for a timeperiod are meaningful. For example, if each histogram represents an hourly resource, a timeperiod's stacked bar is the total labor hours for all resources; each vertical bar is divided into separate bars of different colors or fill patterns to represent individual resources.

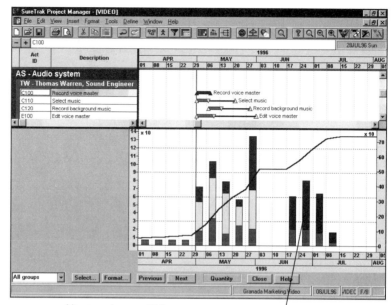

You can show multiple resources or resource
groups stacked in different colors.

Arranging bars side by side makes it easy to contrast resource amounts within each timeperiod. When you select several resources or resource groups for the profile, use this arrangement to compare the requirements for different resources to one another.

You can emphasize resource overload by filling in the over-limit areas of the histograms in red, or you can draw a red line that identifies limits, whether or not an overload exists. You can display overuse and limits for hourly, daily, and weekly time intervals, but for only one resource at a time.

For more information on resources, see the *Building a Resource Plan* chapter.

 To emphasize resource overloads, or to show resource limits on the histogram, define resource limits in the Define Resources dialog box.

Displaying Resource Values and Cumulative Use or Cost for a Timeperiod

You can show periodic values and cumulative use or cost by using the mouse. To see the specific resource values for any timeperiod, click any timeperiod in the Resource profile to see the periodic values, whether or not histograms are displayed.

To see cumulative use or cost for any timeperiod, right-click any timeperiod in the Resource profile to see the cumulative use or cost for the resource or group of resources—the values represented by curves. You can also right-click in any cell on the Resource table to see cumulative values.

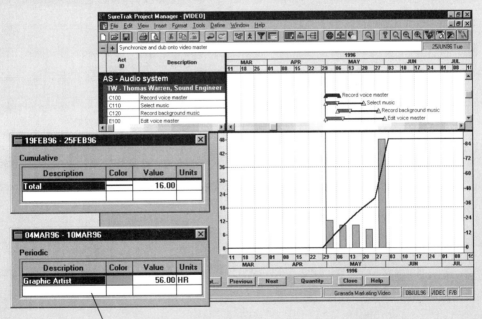

This resource shows periodic values. You specify whether to display periodic values or cumulative values on a histogram bar for a resource or resource group.

Displaying Curves

Cumulative curves show accumulated use, cost, revenue, net, budget, earned value, or budgeted cost for work scheduled (BCWS) for resources. A cumulative curve enables you to see resource quantities used to date and the forecasted amount of resource use. You can display a total cumulative curve, which represents all selected resources in one curve, or individual cumulative curves, each of which represents one of the selected resources.

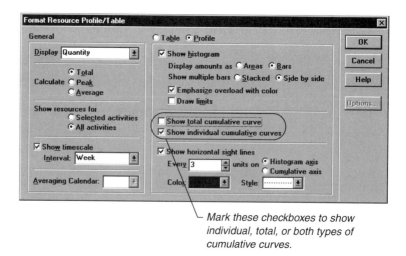

Mark these checkboxes to show individual, total, or both types of cumulative curves.

You can show a total cumulative curve and individual cumulative curves at the same time.

You can also combine a histogram with a cumulative curve. When the profile includes both curves and histograms, SureTrak displays two y-axes (vertical) with separate scales. The left y-axis displays amounts for the histogram bars; the right y-axis displays amounts of accumulated use or cost—the cumulative curve.

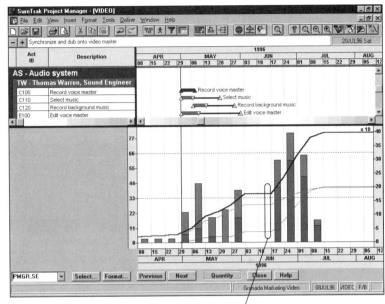

Display a cumulative curve for each resource or group
you select. If you select all resources or one resource,
the individual curve for the resource and the total
cumulative curve for the profile are the same.

Displaying Sight Lines

You can display both vertical and horizontal sight lines on a Resource profile. Vertical sight lines help you identify the timeperiod for a histogram or curve. Horizontal sight lines help you trace the divisions of the vertical axis (y-axis), showing quantities or monetary amounts across the profile; they're especially helpful for profiles that extend over several pages.

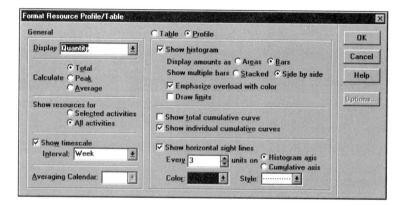

To use horizontal sight lines on a Resource profile Horizontal sight lines on the Resource profile correspond to the divisions of the profile's y-axes, so that you can gauge more precisely the numeric value of the bar or curve for any timeperiod. You can specify how often a horizontal line is drawn, such as at every division of a y-axis or every other division of a y-axis.

1   Choose Format, Resource Profile/Table and mark the Show Horizontal Sight Lines checkbox.

2   Enter a number to indicate the number of y-axis divisions between the horizontal sight lines.

   For example, 2 equals every other y-axis division, 5 equals every fifth division.

3   Choose Histogram Axis or Cumulative Axis to specify which scale the sight lines are based on.

4   In the Color field, right-click and select a color for the horizontal sight lines. If you specify a nonsolid color, SureTrak substitutes the closest solid color.

5   In the Style field, right-click and select a line type for the horizontal sight lines.

Using vertical sight lines Vertical sight lines correspond to the timescale interval. When you expand or compress the timescale, the vertical sight lines move with the intervals on the timescale. To control the appearance of vertical sight lines, use the Sight Lines dialog box (choose Format, Sight Lines).

For more information about defining vertical sight lines, see the *Customizing the Bar Chart View* chapter.

If a profile includes both histograms and cumulative curves, specify whether the sight lines match the y-axis for the histograms (on the left of the profile), or the y-axis for the curves (on the right of the profile). You can also specify a color and line type for the line.

Formatting the Resource Table

You can customize the appearance of the resource pane to display resource information in a tabular format, like a spreadsheet. The left side of the table includes resource names, descriptions, and units of measure. The right side shows resource values in columns, one for each timeperiod.

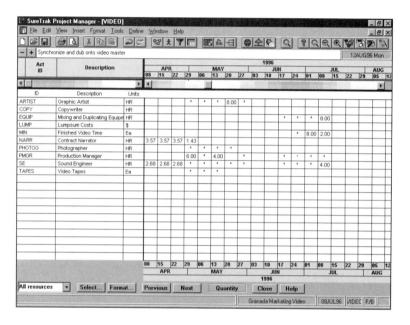

If you define limits for any finite resources, the table displays overallocated resources in red. For example, if you have two quality-control technicians and several of their activities are scheduled simultaneously so that three technicians will be required for a 2-week period, the resource units for the technicians displays in red for those 2 weeks.

The width of the cells depends on the interval and density of the timescale. If the value does not fit, SureTrak displays an asterisk rather than a partial value. Use a smaller font for data in the table cells, or expand the timescale's intervals by clicking its smallest-unit row and dragging the mouse to the right until the full values show.

To control the elements displayed on the Resource table

1 Choose Format, Resource Profile/Table.

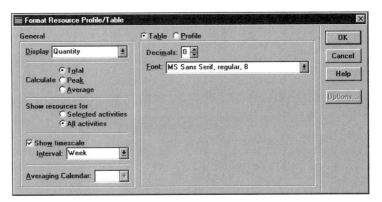

2 Choose the Table option to display specific options for formatting the Resource table.

3 In the Decimals field, specify 0 to show amounts as whole numbers; specify 1 to show amounts to one decimal place; specify 2 to show amounts to two decimal places.

4 In the Font field, right-click and select a font, font style, and size.

For details on displaying items in the resource pane, see *Formatting the Resource Pane* earlier in this chapter.

5 In the General section, specify general resource pane display items.

6 Click OK.

Selecting Resources

A Resource profile or table can show information for a single resource, several resources, or for a group or groups of resources.

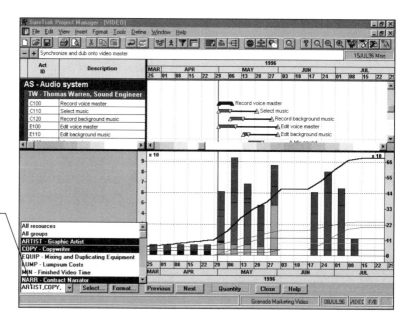

To display resources, right-click in this field to select one resource, several selected resources, a resource group, several resource groups, or all resources.

Selecting All Resources shows each resource individually. Selecting Total Resources shows one bar or row representing the sum of all resources.

You can display profile or table information for a combination of resources by selecting multiple resources or by defining groups of resources. Press Ctrl+click to select several resources or resource groups to feature in profiles and tables. If you plan to review a set of resources repeatedly, define that set as a resource group. After you define them, resource groups appear at the end of the drop-down list of individual resources.

You can select several consecutive resources by pressing Shift and clicking the first and last resource in the sequence.

You can use multiple selection to mix and match resources and resource groups. For example, if you will repeatedly review the information for data processors, medical secretaries, and nurse's assistants, create a resource group named DATA for these three resources.

Periodically, however, you may want to review information for the DATA resource group together with the information for other resources, such as doctors (DOC), nurse practitioners (NPRC), and nurses (NURS). To see the information for all these resources, select the resource group DATA, the individual resource DOC, the individual resource NPRC, and the individual resource NURSE. SureTrak will display four histograms or curves: one for the DATA group and one for each of the three individual resources.

For more information about defining resource groups, see *Creating Resource Groups* later in this chapter.

If you want subtotals only, create a resource group called Medical Professionals (MPRO) for the DOC, NPRC, and NURSE resources. Then choose DATA and MPRO from the resource list to display two histograms, or two individual curves, per timeperiod depicting the MPRO and DATA group subtotals.

Creating Resource Groups

Use the Select Resources dialog box to combine resources into groups so that you can display combined resource requirements, subtotaled costs, and so on for any set of resources you choose. You can create groups based on resource names, resource description, units of measure, unit cost, or revenue value, as well as whether resources are driving or subject to resource leveling.

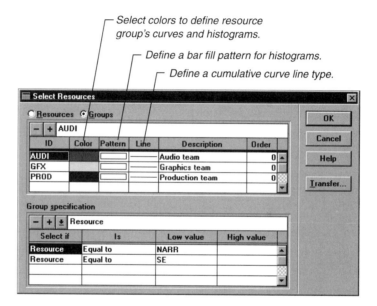

Select colors to define resource group's curves and histograms.

Define a bar fill pattern for histograms.

Define a cumulative curve line type.

For example, in a video production project, create a resource group for the graphics team with the description GRAPHIC, made up of a set designer, credits designer, and animators.

When you display a Resource profile or table for this resource group, SureTrak displays the combined totals of all these resources.

After you create resource groups, you can select a single resource group, several resource groups, or a resource group or groups in combination with individual resources.

To add a resource group

1 Click Select in the Resource profile/table pane to display the Select Resources dialog box.

2 Choose the Groups option.

3 Click ⊞ to add a row to the Groups section.

4 Select the ID cell, enter the ID, and click ☑.

5 In the Description cell, enter a description or name for the resource group.

6 In the Order cell, enter a number to specify the order in which the resource group will be listed on the Resource table, and its position among the bars on the profile.

For more information about specifying resources for a group, see the next section, *Selecting Resources for Groups*.

7 In the Group Specification section, specify the resources to include in the group.

8 Click OK.

To delete a resource group Choose the Groups option at the top of the Select Resources dialog box. Select the group you want to delete, then click ⊟.

Selecting Resources for Groups

Once you've added a resource group using the Groups option in the Select Resources dialog box, specify the resources to include in that resource group. You can include only those resources with a particular unit of measure, or with a unit cost within a specific range; or you can select resources based on an exact match (such as resource ID equal to CHRIS) or based on a range of values (such as unit cost greater than 500.00). In addition, you can specify patterns using the question mark or asterisk wildcard characters (such as MGR*).

Select a group name and define its members by listing group specification criteria in the section below.

Click to enter statements that control the resources the selected group above contains.

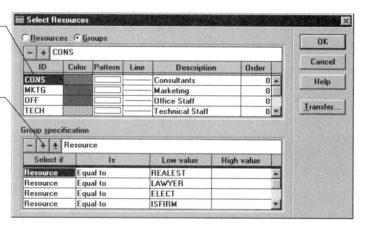

SureTrak uses logical operators, such as between, equal to, and greater than, in combination with resource data to determine which resources to include in the group. Specify the logical operator in the Is column in the Group Specification section.

As you enter criteria in the Group Specification section, you create logical statements that describe the conditions a resource must meet to be included in the group. For example, if your resource IDs are coded, create an engineering group with a statement like Select if the resource is between ENGR001 (low value) and ENGR099 (high value).

You can add several resource selection statements. When you enter more than one statement, SureTrak selects each resource that matches any selection criterion, even if it doesn't match any other criteria. For example, select several resources with unit costs greater than 40.00 whose resource IDs match MGR*.

You can type low and high values directly, using the edit bar in the selection table. However, if the value is the resource ID, you can click the down arrow in the edit bar to display a drop-down list of valid resources and select a resource.

 If the resources you want to include in a group have nothing in common, list each of them in the Low Value cells of the Group Specification section with the operator Equal To, such as Resource Equal To JOE, Resource Equal To JANE.

To specify resource group selection criteria

For more information about creating resource groups, see *Creating Resource Groups* earlier in this chapter.

1 Click Select in the Resource profile/table pane to display the Select Resources dialog box.

2 Choose the Groups option.

3 Create a resource group or select an existing resource group.

4 Click ⊞ to add a row to the Group Specification section.

5 In the Select If column, right-click and select a resource data item from the list.

6 Select a logical operator for the Is column.

7 Specify a low value to match. If you use the Between or Not Between operators, specify a high value as well.

8 Click OK.

To delete a group specification statement Choose the Groups option in the Select Resources dialog box. Select the Resource Group from the upper section to display its resources in the Group Specifications section. Select the group specification statement you want to delete and click ⊟.

Specifying an Average Calendar

You can specify which calendar SureTrak uses to calculate average worktime and resource limits when displaying an averaged profile or table for a resource group or the resource total. Choose Format, Resource Profile/Table to display the Format Resource Profile/Table dialog box and select the calendar to use for averaging.

Displaying Performance or Cash Flow

Resource profiles can show either of two sets of curves: cost/schedule performance or cash flow. You can display these curves for one resource or one resource group, or for the resource or group total by selecting Performance or Cash Flow in the Display field in the Format Resource Profile/Table dialog box. You can also display the first value from the Performance or Cash Flow curve on the Resource table (either Earned Value or Net).

The performance curve set includes earned value, BCWS, and costs. The cash flow curve set includes net, costs, and revenue.

To select specific line colors and types for the Performance and Cash Flow curves, click Options in the Format Resource Profile/Table dialog box. SureTrak displays the Curve Set Options dialog box, in which you can change the line colors and types for the three curves.

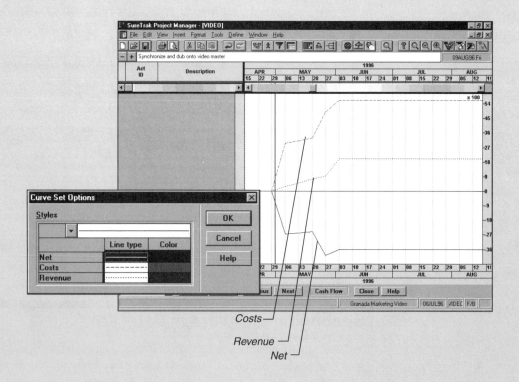

Costs

Revenue

Net

Using the Resource Legend

The resource legend identifies what the colors in a Resource profile represent. You can use it in the project layout as well as print it in a header or footer. Each resource and resource group you define has an associated color for the Resource profile. If you do not specify a color, SureTrak assigns a default color.

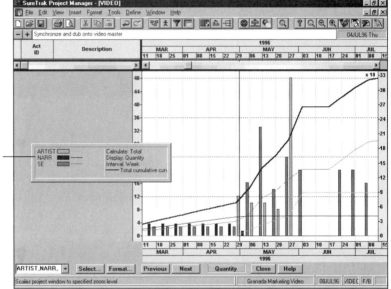

Choose View, Resource Legend to show or hide the resource legend. Double-click anywhere in the resource legend to close it.

For details on printing the resource legend in a header or footer, see the *Printing Project Information* chapter.

You can move the resource legend by dragging it to any location in the project layout. You can also change the size of the resource legend by positioning the mouse pointer over the border of the legend until it changes to ⊕ . Then drag the border to the size you want.

Leveling Resources

After you create a network of logically linked activities, define resources with their costs and limits, and allocate resources to the activities, you can compare resource demands for the project to the quantities available by leveling your resources.

If the demand for some resources exceeds the amount available, consider having SureTrak level the resources—resolving excess demands on resources by delaying lower-priority activities until the resources they require become available.

Understanding Resource Leveling

Resource leveling is an automated process SureTrak performs that delays the start of certain activities. SureTrak compares the requirements of all activities scheduled each hour to the maximum quantity available at each time. SureTrak delays an activity if resources are insufficient at any time during its duration. In SureTrak, you can select resources for leveling as well as specify the leveling priority for each activity.

Resource limit—

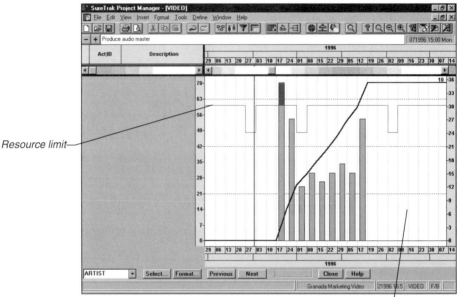

Use Resource profiles to compare resource use to the resource — limits specified for each resource. Determine whether remaining resources are sufficient to complete the scheduled work.

For details on using Resource profiles, see the *Analyzing Resource Use with Profiles and Tables* chapter.

During leveling, SureTrak reschedules activities whose combined, overlapping resource needs exceed the limit. SureTrak does not change resource durations or resource assignments. During leveling, SureTrak delays activities until resources are available.

 Leveling does not affect durations, which are controlled by the activity type and the driving resources assigned to the activities.

For information about displaying activity bars, see the *Customizing the Bar Chart View* chapter.

Use the Bar chart to review the results of leveling. You can set up the Bar chart to show activity early bars (when they are scheduled now), unleveled bars (when they were scheduled originally), and level delay bars and points (the amount of time they were delayed). SureTrak draws the level delay bar from the unleveled start date to the leveled start date, illustrating the amount of delay, and places the level delay point at the unleveled start.

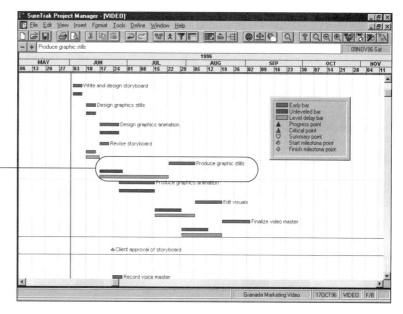

This level delay bar shows how many days this activity is delayed due to leveling.

If you turn on automatic resource leveling in the Level dialog box (choose Tools, Level), SureTrak levels resources each time you schedule your project or each time you change an activity's duration, relationship, or resource assignment. When you add a new resource, mark the Make Resources Level By Default checkbox in the Resource tab of the Options dialog box (choose Tools, Options) to make the resource level each time SureTrak schedules the project.

How does SureTrak level? SureTrak bases leveling on early schedule dates. It starts with the first activity in the network that has no predecessors and checks to see if its resource use is within the availability limits from its early start date to its early finish date. If sufficient resources are available, the activity is scheduled and its unleveled dates are the same as its early dates. SureTrak continues using this method until it reaches the last activity in the network. If sufficient resources are not available on the early start date based on the availability limits, SureTrak delays the activity until resources are available to complete it.

Before scheduling and leveling an activity, SureTrak schedules and/or levels all its predecessors. All the necessary resources to be leveled for an activity must also be available over the entire duration of the activity for SureTrak to schedule it; an activity will not be interrupted by leveling. If either of these two conditions is not met, SureTrak delays the activity until both requirements are satisfied, then schedules it on the first available date that both leveling conditions are met.

If resources are not available to complete the activity at any time during the project after its predecessors are scheduled, SureTrak uses whatever resources are required to complete the activity and schedules the activity according to its early dates (after all predecessors are completed), even though this overallocates resources. This remaining resource overallocation shows on a Resource profile.

If leveling delays the project's early finish date, SureTrak performs a backward pass to recalculate the late dates of the entire project based on the revised early dates of the activities.

Effect of Network Logic on Leveling

Before leveling resources, SureTrak determines the order in which activities should be considered. First, a topological sequence is created for all activities in the network, based on the logic of precedence relationships. If two or more activities have "equal" topological placement for leveling, SureTrak uses the prioritization settings in the Level dialog box.

In any sequential chain of activities, SureTrak levels resources on the first activity in the chain regardless of the prioritization criteria, since this activity is a predecessor to the remaining activities in the chain. Therefore, in a project that contains only one sequential chain of activities, the prioritization criteria have no effect. You can, however, prioritize activities in two or more parallel chains by assigning priorities.

In a project containing no relationships between activities, leveling prioritization settings completely dictate the leveling sequence of activities. However, resource leveling is not meant to be a substitute for entering relationships among activities to create a logical network.

Nearly all projects require that most activities be performed in a specific order, regardless of resource availability. Make sure those logical relationships exist before you reschedule activities using leveling.

If either activity 1010 or 1020 were a predecessor of the other, SureTrak would assign the resource to it, since SureTrak first considers network logic when leveling. However, in this example, no relationship exists between the activities. SureTrak therefore uses the prioritization criteria set in the Level dialog box to decide which activity gets resources first.

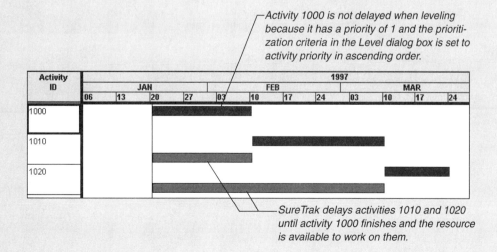

Activity 1000 is not delayed when leveling because it has a priority of 1 and the prioritization criteria in the Level dialog box is set to activity priority in ascending order.

SureTrak delays activities 1010 and 1020 until activity 1000 finishes and the resource is available to work on them.

Setting Up a Project for Leveling

To level a project, you must enter limits for resources by specifying the maximum limit available for each resource in the Resource Dictionary (choose Define, Resources). Without limits, SureTrak has no point of reference for determining whether or not a resource is overallocated.

A limit is an estimate of the maximum quantity you can assign at any one time, considering restraints such as limited storage space or the cost of retaining surplus skilled workers. These limits can change during the project; you can define up to six timeperiods with different limitations on a resource. Specify the number of resource units (according to the unit of measure for that resource) that are available per hour at the same time.

Specify Yes to designate a resource for leveling.

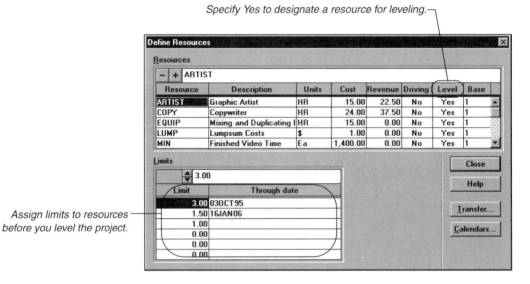

Assign limits to resources before you level the project.

For more information about Resource profiles, see the Analyzing Resource Use with Profiles and Tables chapter.

After you establish the resource requirements and limits, use a Resource profile to compare the demand for resources (all assignments to all activities, combined) to the supply (the limits). Look closely at periods where the demand exceeds supply. Designate overloaded resources for leveling.

To designate a resource for leveling Choose Define, Resources or click Resource in the Level dialog box. Select the Level cell of the resource whose leveling status you want to change and double-click to change No to Yes, then click Close.

You can have SureTrak automatically enter a resource to be leveled when resources are created. Choose Tools, Options, then click the Resource tab. Mark the Make Resources Level By Default checkbox. If you mark this checkbox, SureTrak sets the Level column in the Define Resources dialog box for the resource to Yes when you create a new resource.

For details about resource availability limits, see the *Building a Resource Plan* chapter.

Generally, you will level only time-constrained resources, such as labor or equipment. Limits on costs per timeperiod and quantities of materials per timeperiod rarely affect the times activities can be scheduled; when they do, control their scheduling by applying constraints.

Defining Activity Priority When Leveling

When leveling resources, SureTrak reschedules activities according to two sets of criteria. First, it schedules activities according to the relationships among the activities. Second, to resolve conflicts between activities that would be scheduled simultaneously except that, together, they require more of a resource(s) than the maximum available, SureTrak uses the Prioritization section in the Level dialog box to decide which activities receive resources first and are scheduled ahead of others.

Enter a number between 0 and 999 in the Priority field for each activity. Priorities from 1 through 999 indicate the leveling priority for an activity relative to other activities requiring the same resources. Use a low priority (such as 98, 99, or 100) on those activities that can be delayed; use a high priority (such as 1, 2, or 3) on activities that you prefer not to delay, or to delay less than others. The default activity priority is 1.

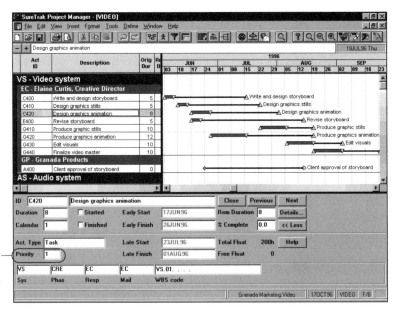

Open a full view of the Activity form (choose View, Activity Form) and enter the activity priority.

A priority of zero means that SureTrak schedules the activity according to network relationships, and the activity receives resources assigned to it, regardless of the resource demands and priorities of all other activities; as a result, this activity starts and finishes as early as possible. The activity may be indirectly delayed because some of its predecessors were delayed during leveling, but it will not be directly delayed during leveling; it will receive all the resources you've assigned to it, and SureTrak schedules it as early as possible.

You can specify the priority you assign in the Activity form as a leveling criterion in the Prioritization section of the Level dialog box; SureTrak considers it according to its placement in this section. If it appears first (the default), SureTrak considers it first. If it appears third, perhaps after total float and early start, SureTrak considers it after total float and early start.

 If priority is not a listed criterion in the Prioritization section in the Level dialog box, SureTrak ignores activity priority except for zero-priority activities. SureTrak schedules zero-priority activities according to their places in the project network rather than level them.

Setting Up Leveling Options

Use the Level dialog box to control when and how SureTrak levels resources. Choose Tools, Level to open the Level dialog box, then specify criteria that determine which of two simultaneous activities receive resources. You can also set SureTrak to level automatically each time the schedule is recalculated, and to level only to use current float or to extend the project's finish date.

Mark to level resources every time you schedule—whenever you change an activity's duration, resource assignments, or relationships (when automatic scheduling is on).

Mark to eliminate resource conflicts, even if it delays project completion.

Select a leveling prioritization criterion and click ▬ *to delete the criterion, then click* ✔ *to confirm the deletion.*

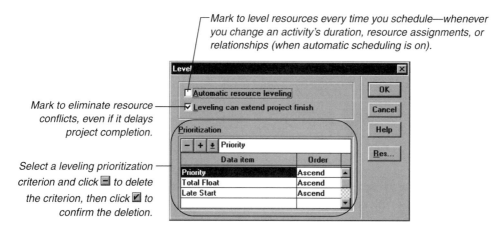

In the Level dialog box, mark the Automatic Resource Leveling checkbox to level resources each time SureTrak calculates the schedule; mark the Leveling Can Extend Project Finish checkbox to level resources without regard for the project finish date. If you do not want to level resources, clear both checkboxes. You can have SureTrak resolve resource overallocation completely, even if doing so delays the project as a whole. If you choose not to extend the project finish during leveling, SureTrak delays only those activities that have positive float—those that can slip without delaying the project's completion.

 If you do not choose to level resources automatically, you can force SureTrak to level resources at any time by choosing Tools, Level Now, pressing Shift+F9, or clicking the Level Now icon.

Defining leveling priority Use the Prioritization section in the Level dialog box to specify the criteria SureTrak uses to choose between two or more activities that simultaneously require the same limited resources. For example, you can assign the resources to the activity with the shorter duration, so that more activities complete earlier, or to the activity with the least total float, so that more critical activities complete earlier.

When prioritizing activities for resource leveling, SureTrak first determines the best order based on network logic. If two activities have simultaneous, equal claim to project resources, SureTrak refers to the settings in the Prioritization section in the Level dialog box.

To define leveling priority

1 Choose Tools, Level to display the Level dialog box.

2 Select a row in the Prioritization section. Right-click and select the data item you want to use as a leveling criterion from the drop-down list.

3 Right-click in the Order cell and select Ascend or Descend.

   Select Ascend to have SureTrak allocate resources to an activity with a lower duration, lower Activity ID, or earlier date before higher ones. Select Descend to have SureTrak allocate resources in the reverse sequence. For example, if you select Descend in the Order cell for Remaining Duration, SureTrak gives resources to an activity with a remaining duration of 10 before an activity with a remaining duration of 5.

4 Specify another leveling criterion or click OK.

SureTrak allows up to 10 prioritization criteria and comes with several default leveling prioritization criteria: activity priority (specified for each activity on the Activity form), total float, early start, remaining duration, and Activity ID. You can keep or change these default prioritization criteria.

If using the listed specifications in the Prioritization section results in a tie, SureTrak uses the Activity ID as the tie-breaker. No two activities can have the same ID; the activity with the lower Activity ID gets the resources before an activity with a higher ID.

 If you specify Activity ID as a criterion in the Prioritization section, SureTrak does not consider any of the criteria you list after the Activity ID; the Activity ID is always unique and will always determine which activity SureTrak schedules first.

If you assign more resources than are available to an activity, SureTrak cannot level resources for that activity; SureTrak schedules that activity according to its predecessors without regard to resource limits. For example, if two sound engineers are available throughout the entire project, and you assign four sound engineers to one activity, SureTrak overallocates that resource during the entire duration of that activity.

Using Mandatory Dates to Prevent Activity Delays During Leveling

To prevent an activity from being delayed during leveling or any other scheduling change, use a mandatory start or finish date. When you assign a mandatory start date, SureTrak sets both the early and late start dates equal to the mandatory start date you specify. When you assign a mandatory finish date, SureTrak sets both the early and late finish dates equal to the mandatory finish date you specify.

When you apply mandatory start and finish dates, SureTrak uses those dates for scheduling whether or not they are consistent with network logic. If the mandatory dates are set earlier than the calculated early dates, SureTrak may schedule an activity earlier than its predecessor(s). Review any activities with mandatory dates when you update or modify the project to ensure that the dates used as constraints are still appropriate. Since SureTrak never moves activities with mandatory constraints during scheduling or leveling, if two or more of these activities have overlapping dates, their combined resource use may exceed the availability limits.

During scheduling, SureTrak schedules an activity with a mandatory date constraint to start or finish on the specified date. If you level resources, an activity with a mandatory date receives its resources first.

If one or more activities with mandatory dates compete for the same resources, SureTrak assigns them all the resources needed—regardless of the criteria set up on the Prioritization section, and even if resource demands exceed the resources available. SureTrak schedules and levels other activities requiring resources around the activities with mandatory dates.

Assign mandatory dates in the Constraints detail form.

Other constraints will not affect leveling. For example, you can impose a deadline on an activity's start or finish with a start no later than or finish no later than constraint; the activity may be delayed during leveling, but you can still see its logical place in the schedule.

Another alternative to using mandatory constraints to control delays in leveling is to use activity priority as the first criterion in the Prioritization section in the Level dialog box. Then assign a priority of 0 to activities that should not be delayed by leveling; SureTrak delays these activities if their predecessors are delayed, but not because of their own resource conflicts.

For more information about assigning constraints, see the *Creating and Fine-Tuning the Project Schedule* chapter.

Interpreting Dates After Leveling Resources

When you level resources, SureTrak stores the original early start and finish dates from the forward and backward passes as unleveled dates. Immediately following these forward and backward passes, SureTrak performs the leveling pass and records the new, leveled early and late start and finish dates in the early and late start and finish fields. This enables you to compare the dates for activities before leveling (unleveled) with those resulting from leveling (early and late).

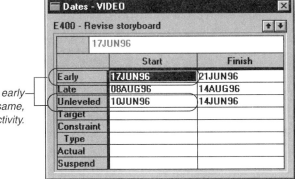

Since the unleveled and early dates are not the same, leveling delayed this activity.

For details on showing the amount of time activities have been delayed by leveling, see the *Customizing the Bar Chart View* chapter.

Comparing leveling dates To compare activities' leveled dates to original preleveled dates on the Bar chart, add two bars to the Bar chart—the early bar and the unleveled bar. The early bar represents the early dates based on the newly leveled schedule; the unleveled bar represents the times an activity would have been scheduled if resources had not been leveled.

The Bar chart also includes bar and endpoint options for the level delay.

To compare the dates directly, add columns to a layout that show early, late, and unleveled dates. You can also add the Level Delay column, which shows the variance, or difference, between the unleveled date and the early start date—the number of days or hours by which each activity was delayed.

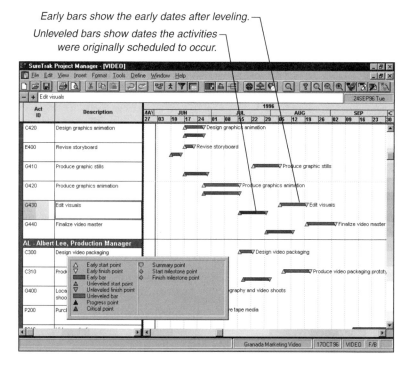

Early bars show the early dates after leveling.
Unleveled bars show dates the activities were originally scheduled to occur.

Unleveling a Project

If you level resources and decide that you prefer to use the unleveled schedule, schedule the project again without leveling. SureTrak recalculates the project without considering resource demands.

To unlevel a project, choose Tools, Level to display the Level dialog box. Clear the Automatic Resource Leveling checkbox and click OK, then click the Schedule Now icon or press F9.

Effects of Leveling on Activity Types

SureTrak levels different types of activities differently. The three main activities—task, independent, and meeting—are leveled. Milestones are leveled as though they were task activities, except that they have no duration. Hammock, WBS, and topic activities are not leveled. Driving and nondriving resources also affect leveling.

For more information about driving resources, see the *Building a Resource Plan* chapter.

Leveling and task activities SureTrak always schedules a task activity according to the activity's base calendar, which you assign in the Activity form; all resources must work concurrently on the activity. If several resources that can be leveled are assigned to a task activity, leveling will reschedule the activity when all the resources are available in sufficient quantities under their limits.

Task Activity	Calendar Used When Leveling
With only nondriving resources	Activities and resources use the base calendar and duration assigned in Activity form.
With driving resources	Uses activity's base calendar; activity duration is determined by the duration of the single longest driving resource.
Effects of leveling on activity with only nondriving resources	SureTrak schedules the activity and all its resources according to the activity's base calendar when the necessary quantities of resources are available simultaneously for the activity's entire duration, which is assigned in the Activity form.
Effects of leveling on driving resources	SureTrak schedules the activity and its resources according to the activity's base calendar when the necessary quantities of resources are available simultaneously for the activity's entire duration, which is equal to the duration of the single longest-duration driving resource.

Leveling and independent activities SureTrak schedules each resource for independent activities according to its individual calendar. When you level an independent activity, SureTrak considers each resource individually and schedules that resource when sufficient quantities are available. It then schedules the activity from the earliest start of any driving resource through the latest early finish of any driving resource.

Since driving resources determine the dates an activity is scheduled, any nondriving resources assigned to an independent activity in conjunction with driving resources can work according to their own resource calendars. Such nondriving resources work outside the duration of the activity and can possibly overlap other activities.

After leveling, the duration of an independent activity that has been assigned driving resources can be different than it was before leveling. Differences may result from scheduling the driving resources at different times with more overlap, or with smaller or larger gaps reflected in the duration of the activity. The amount of effort for each resource, however, is the same. The duration of an independent activity is the elapsed time between the start and finish of all driving resources.

For example, before leveling, an engineer driving resource has 25 days of continuous work, starting May 1 and ending May 25. A data entry driving resource has 5 days of continuous work, starting May 23 and ending May 27. The duration of the activity extends from May 1—the start of the first driving resource—to May 27—the end of the last driving resource.

When SureTrak levels resources for this activity, it may reschedule them at different times. For example, the engineer resource may not be available for 25 consecutive days until May 5, and the data entry resource may not be available for 3 consecutive days until June 3. In this case, the engineer resource starts on May 5 and works through May 29 (assuming that the workweek is 7 days per week); the data entry resource starts on June 3 and works through June 6. Because these resources are driving, the activity's duration now extends from May 5 through June 6; its duration and dates have changed, although the amount of work involved remains the same.

Any additional nondriving resources that are also assigned to this activity, such as a secretary and a programmer, will work according to their own calendars and durations, just as they would with an independent activity.

Independent Activity	Calendar Used When Leveling
With only nondriving resources	Activity uses the base calendar and duration assigned in the Activity form; resources use their resource calendars and their own durations, assigned in the Resources detail form.
With driving resources	Resources use their resource calendars and their own durations, assigned in the Resources detail form; activity duration equals the elapsed time between the start of the first driving resource and the finish of the last driving resource.
Effects of leveling on activity with only nondriving resources	SureTrak considers each assigned resource individually and schedules it when sufficient quantity is available; resources are scheduled according to their own calendars, possibly causing resources to work outside the duration of the activity or other resources.
Effects of leveling on driving resources	Same as above, except the duration of the activity may change if the driving resources' schedules, whose combined elapsed time determines the activity duration, are rescheduled closer together or farther apart.

Leveling and meeting activities Meeting activities with nondriving resources are identical to task activities with nondriving resources. Like a task activity, SureTrak schedules a meeting activity with nondriving resources according to the duration and calendar specified in the Activity form.

However, SureTrak calculates the durations of meeting activities with driving resources based on the driving resource with the longest duration. A meeting activity with driving resources uses a calendar that is a conglomerate of all driving resources' calendars. SureTrak schedules a meeting activity like a task activity during leveling, except that it uses the conglomerate calendar for all assigned driving resources instead of using the activity's base calendar.

Meeting Activity	Calendar Used When Leveling
With only nondriving resources	Activities and resources use the base calendar and duration assigned in Activity form.
With driving resources	Activity uses a conglomerate calendar of its assigned driving resources' calendars; the activity's duration is determined by the duration of the longest driving resource, assigned in the Resources detail form.
Effects of leveling on activity with only nondriving resources	SureTrak schedules the activity and all of its resources according to the activity's base calendar when the necessary quantities of resources are available simultaneously for the activity's entire duration, which is assigned in the Activity form.
Effects of leveling on driving resources	SureTrak schedules the activity and all its resources according to a conglomerate calendar of its assigned driving resources that determines when the necessary quantities of resources are available simultaneously for the activity duration, which is based on the duration of the single longest-duration driving resource.

For more information about types of activities, see the *Adding Activities* chapter.

You can repeat leveling using different resource limits, different activity priorities, or different leveling prioritization options until you are satisfied with the results. Never assume, however, that a leveled schedule is an optimal solution to a scheduling problem. Once you complete the leveling process, you may want to adjust the resource assignments on key activities or adjust the scheduling of specific activities by applying date constraints.

Updating Project Data Remotely

Electronic mail (E-mail) is an easy way to distribute lists of activities, entire projects and project groups, and messages to others in your workgroup. SureTrak and your E-mail system work together to help you share project information with others, whether or not they have SureTrak.

Use SureTrak's E-mail feature as a tool for updating project progress. The project manager can send activities to multiple recipients, who can then update the activities and return them, again via E-mail, to the manager.

This chapter describes how to send and receive project information using SureTrak's Send Mail and Receive Mail features.

Mailing Projects and Activities

To facilitate the communication of vital project data in the corporate office or between offices worldwide, use SureTrak's E-mail capabilities to send and receive project information. You can send or collect update information and merge it into your project, keeping the project as current as possible.

Sending E-mail from SureTrak Use SureTrak to create a mail message with one or more attachments, such as a backup of your project, a picture of the project window, or selected activities. SureTrak uses your mail system to address the message, specify the attachments, enter message text, and send the message. You can send mail messages to one or more persons either as a group or individually, using unique codes to address each activity.

SureTrak's Send Mail feature enables you to

- Send a project backup through E-mail. The recipient can restore and use the project with SureTrak or P3.

- Send a snapshot of the SureTrak window through E-mail. The recipient can view the bitmap using Microsoft Paint or any other program that can open and display bitmaps.

- Send a Clipboard (.CLP) file that contains activity data for the activities you copy to the Clipboard. The recipient can paste the activities into a SureTrak project, or into another application such as a spreadsheet.

- Send activity information as an attachment to a message.

Logging into mail When you finish selecting project elements to send by E-mail, you will be prompted to log into your mail system. Enter your login name and password and, if necessary, specify the storage location for your post office information. When the message appears, you can review its contents before sending it. SureTrak automatically fills in the subject of the message with "Primavera update:" followed by the name of the project. Address the message and send it.

Receiving E-mail in SureTrak   You can also receive messages through E-mail that contain SureTrak attachments, and merge an attached project or activities into a project on your computer.

SureTrak's Receive Mail feature enables you to

■   Merge activities into a project. You can edit the activities before merging them into your project, or simply merge activities that have been returned, updated, to you.

■   Reply to an E-mail message. Update the activities sent to you in a mail message and return the message to its originator without affecting the activities in your project.

Using Primavera Post Office   You can also use Primavera Post Office, which is included with SureTrak, to edit Primavera updates and return them to the message's originator without opening SureTrak.

Primavera Post Office enables you to

■   Update activities and reply to the mail message. Whether or not the recipients have SureTrak, they can edit the information in the Primavera attachment and return it via E-mail so the message's originator can merge the changes into the project.

 SureTrak's mail features and Primavera Post Office work with Lotus cc:Mail and other mail systems compliant with Vendor Independent Messaging (VIM), as well as Microsoft Mail and other mail systems compliant with Messaging Application Programming Interface (MAPI).

Setting Up E-Mail for Sending Status Sheets

SureTrak sends activity and resource information as status sheets which users of P3 or Primavera Post Office can recognize; however, SureTrak does not distinguish between different status sheets when receiving mail. If you plan to send activity and resource information rather than a complete backup of a project, set up mail to send status sheets which include only the activity and resource information you want to send.

For more information on Primavera Post Office, see Receiving an Activity Status Sheet in Primavera Post Office later in this chapter.

For example, if you use mail to request update information, you'll want to send the data items that you want updated with new information, such as remaining duration, percent complete, actual start date, actual finish date, and resource quantities used to date. Use the preformatted Standard status sheet, or define a Custom status sheet, to gather the information you need.

Once you set up mail for sending status sheets, choose the Send Data For All/Selected Activities option in the Send Mail dialog box to send the activity and resource information.

 Mail Setup applies only to mail containing SureTrak activity and resource data. You do not need to set up mail for sending bitmaps, projects, or the Clipboard contents.

Sending Standard status sheets Standard status sheets offer a standardized method for updating activity information. Standard status sheets always send the same activity information; you determine only how progress is recorded, either using remaining duration or percent complete.

Determine how progress is collected, as remaining duration or percent complete.

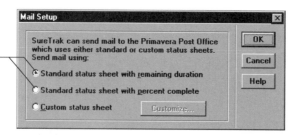

The data items contained in the Standard status sheets are received differently in SureTrak than in the Primavera Post Office:

■ SureTrak users receive: Activity ID, Description, Actual Start, Actual Finish, Early Start, Early Finish, and either Remaining Duration or Percent Complete.

■ P3 and Primavera Post Office users receive: Activity ID, Description, Started? (to indicate if an activity has started), Start Date, Finished? (to indicated if an activity has finished), and either Remaining Duration or Percent Complete.

When you send a Standard status sheet, SureTrak asks you to indicate which date you want the activities progressed through. This date is included on the Standard status sheet for P3 and Primavera Post Office users.

To set up mail to send a Standard status sheet

1 Choose File, Mail, Setup to open the Mail Setup dialog box.

2 Choose Standard Status Sheet With Remaining Duration or Standard Status Sheet With Percent Complete.

3 Click OK.

Sending Custom status sheets Standard status sheets send only activity information. If you want to send activity and resource information, or if you want to send additional or alternate data items in an E-mail message, use the Custom status sheet to specify the activity and/or resource data items to send.

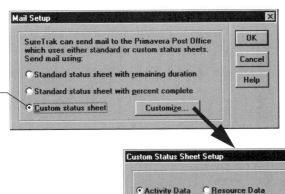

Choose to include both activity and resource information in a mail message.

P3 users can determine if a particular data item in a Custom status sheet can be edited by the recipient. Items flagged as non-editable cannot be altered. By default, SureTrak also sends non-editable data items, such as Activity ID, though you cannot change a data item's status from non-editable to editable in SureTrak. In general, items whose values you cannot alter in the Activity columns cannot be edited in a mail message.

To set up mail to send a Custom status sheet

1 Choose File, Mail, Setup to open the Mail Setup dialog box.

2 Choose Custom Status Sheet and click Customize.

3 Choose the Activity Data option to select the activity data items you want to send.

4 Click ▣ to add a data item above the selected row.

5 Click ▣ and select any activity data item from the drop-down list.

6 Use the default title, or type a title for the activity data that corresponds to the terminology used in your organization in the Title column. SureTrak includes these titles in the message as column headings for the data.

7 Continue adding activity data items until you have included all the activity information you want in the message.

8 Choose the Resource Data option and repeat steps 4 through 7 for resource data. If you aren't sending resource data, leave the Resource Data table blank.

9 Mark the Include Relationships checkbox if you want SureTrak to include predecessor/successor information for the activities sent.

10 Click OK.

 SureTrak always includes the resource and Activity IDs, so you do not need to add them as rows in the Custom Status Sheet Setup dialog box.

Sending an Entire Project

Use SureTrak to send a backup of an entire project or project group to another member of your workgroup using your E-mail system. SureTrak backs up the open project into one file with the project name and the extension .PRX. If the project hasn't been saved since the last change made to it, SureTrak saves it first.

Mark to send a compressed backup of the current project.

Before sending mail, open the project containing the information you want to send.

To send a backup of an entire project to a SureTrak or P3 user

1   Choose File, Mail, Send to open the Send Mail dialog box.

2   Mark the Send Project checkbox to attach a copy of a project to the mail message.

For more information about file types, see the Creating SureTrak Projects chapter.

If you send an entire SureTrak-format project, the recipient of the message will need SureTrak to restore and open the project. If you send an entire P3 (Concentric)-format project, the recipient of the message can use either SureTrak or P3 to restore and open the project.

3   Click OK. SureTrak backs up the open file and attaches it to a new E-mail message.

For more information about sending P3 and SureTrak projects, see the Concentric Project Management Handbook, available from Primavera Systems, Inc.

4   Address and send the message using your E-mail system.

Sending a Picture of a Project

To present project information, as perhaps a quick summary or print out, use Send Mail to send a picture of the project window using your E-mail system. The bitmap SureTrak sends can be opened, viewed, and printed with Microsoft Paint or with any Windows program that opens bitmaps.

Mark to send a picture of the current project window, then specify the type of image to send.

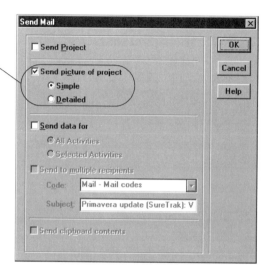

To send a picture of a project

1 Open the project containing the information you want to send and compose the project window to contain the necessary information.

2 Choose File, Mail, Send to open the Send Mail dialog box.

3 Mark the Send Picture Of Project checkbox to include a bitmap of the current SureTrak window.

The recipient must have compatible video hardware and drivers to view the bitmap; most systems can read simple captures, but not necessarily detailed pictures.

SureTrak captures all the information onscreen, including the edit bar, visible activity columns, bar chart, Activity form, Resource profile or table, and any open detail forms or dialog boxes (except the Send Mail dialog box).

4 Specify the size and complexity of the screen capture by choosing Simple to create a bitmap using only 16 colors, or Detailed to create a bitmap using the current resolution setting for your system. The Detailed option results in a much larger bitmap that has greater color variations.

5 Click OK, then address the message using your E-mail system.

Sending a Portion of a Project

Instead of sending an entire project or project group through E-mail, you can send a status sheet containing specified activity and resource data as a Primavera attachment to a mail message. You can send information for all activities in a project, or for only selected activities.

 Before sending activity information you must determine which status sheet to include in the mail message. Choose File, Mail, Setup to specify which status sheet and data items to include in the mail message.

For more information about updating project information, see Updating Project Data Received Through E-Mail later in this chapter.

You can send activity and resource information to participants who do not have SureTrak or P3 if they have the Primavera Post Office application, which is available from Primavera Systems. The recipient can change the data using Primavera Post Office, and then return the message by E-mail. After receiving this reply, the original sender can update the project by merging the updated information.

Mark to send activity and resource data as a status sheet, then specify which activities to send.

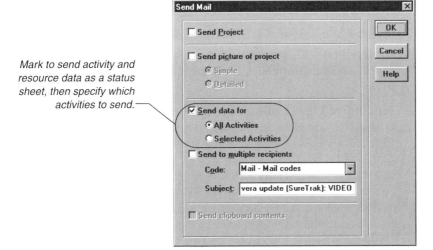

To send all activities in the current project

1 Open the project containing the activities you want to send.

2 Choose File, Mail, Send to open the Send Mail dialog box.

For details on sending individual E-mail messages in SureTrak, see *Assigning Addresses to Activity Codes* later in this chapter.

3 Mark the Send Data For checkbox and choose All Activities.

The specifications you set in the Mail Setup dialog box determine the activity and resource data items included in the mail message.

4 Click OK, then address the mail message using your E-mail system.

If you are sending a Standard status sheet, SureTrak asks you to indicate the date through which recipients should update their activities.

Instead of sending all activities in the current project as an E-mail attachment, you can restrict the number of activities included in the mail message.

To send selected activities from the current project

1 Open the project containing the activities you want to send and select the activities to include in the mail message.

2 Choose File, Mail, Send to open the Send Mail dialog box.

3 Mark the Send Data For checkbox and choose Selected Activities.

The specifications you set up in the Mail Setup dialog box determine the activity and resource data items included in the mail message.

For more information about how to select activities, see the *Adding Activities* chapter.

4 Click OK, then address the mail message using your E-mail system.

If you are sending a Standard status sheet, SureTrak asks you to indicate the date through which recipients should update their activities.

Sending activity relationships data If you mark the Include Relationships checkbox in the Mail Setup dialog box, SureTrak includes predecessor/successor relationship information among activities selected for the mail message. You cannot view relationship information from SureTrak, though this information is merged into your project if the Update Relationships checkbox in the Receive Mail dialog box is marked. To view relationship information included in a mail message, open the Primavera attachment from your E-mail system, then choose View, Relationship Data in Primavera Post Office.

Sending a Clipboard File

If you have copied activities to the Clipboard, mark the Send Clipboard Contents checkbox to attach a .CLP file containing those activities to the mail message. The recipient need not have any software other than a compatible mail system to receive this kind of SureTrak attachment. The recipient of the message can save the .CLP file to their hard disk, open it in the Clipboard, and then paste the activities from the Clipboard into SureTrak, P3, or other Windows programs such as Microsoft Excel.

Mark to attach the contents of the Clipboard as a .CLP file.

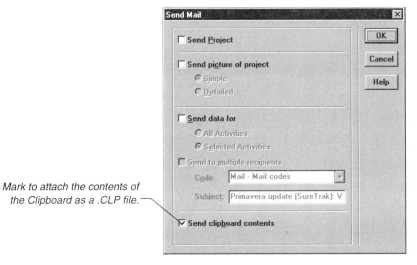

If no activities have been copied to the Clipboard, this checkbox will be disabled in the Send Mail dialog box.

Assigning Addresses to Activity Codes

With SureTrak, you can assign E-mail addresses in the Activity Codes Dictionary. Instead of creating a separate E-mail message for each person to whom you want to send project information, you can assign each activity an activity code that contains an E-mail address. Then, when you send E-mail, SureTrak automatically sends all coded activities to the mail addresses assigned to them.

For example, define the RESP code to contain each person who will be responsible for activities in your project. In the Values section, add the E-mail address of the person represented by the code.

 SureTrak provides a MAIL activity code, but you can define mail-address codes in any code you find convenient.

To set up mail addresses for activity codes

1 Choose Define, Activity Codes to open the Activity Codes dialog box.

2 In the Codes section, select or create the code that will contain the E-mail addresses.

3 In the Values section, define values for the people to whom you will send E-mail updates.

4 In the Description column, type the appropriate E-mail addresses.

5 In the Order column, enter a number that specifies where this code value should appear among other values. The sequence of numbers in this column controls the sorting order of the code values. If you do not enter numbers in this column, or if you enter values with the same order numbers, SureTrak sorts them in alphabetical order.

6 After you define all the necessary values, click Close.

 You can also assign E-mail addresses using the MAILRES script included with SureTrak. Run this script, select each resource from the list of those defined for your project, and assign an E-mail address to the resource. The script writes the E-mail addresses to your STWIN.INI file, making them available for all projects in which the resources are defined; however, these codes are nontransferable and must be set up for each copy of SureTrak used.

Once you define the mail address code values, assign them to the appropriate activities. SureTrak sends a message to each E-mail recipient associated with project activities by an activity code. Each recipient receives only the activities that are coded as pertaining to him or her.

Mark to automatically address each mail message based on the E-mail activity codes you assigned and include only the project data you specify.

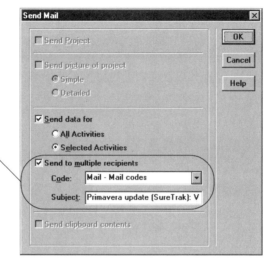

To send E-mail messages using activity code mail addressing

1 Choose File, Mail, Send to open the Send Mail dialog box.

To send only specific activities to be updated, select the activities you want to send before opening the Send Mail dialog box.

2 Mark the Send Data For checkbox and choose the appropriate option.

3 Mark the Send to Multiple Recipients checkbox.

4 In the Code field, select the code that contains the E-mail addresses you want to use.

5 As appropriate, edit the Subject field to change the E-mail title.

6 Click OK and when SureTrak displays the Mail Login dialog box, log into your E-mail system as you normally do.

For more information about default activity codes, see the *Creating Activity Codes* chapter.

 If SureTrak encounters an invalid E-mail address, it will ask whether you want to send the remaining messages. Click Yes if you want to send those messages with valid addresses.

Adding E-Mail Addresses to Templates

For more information about templates, see the *Creating SureTrak Projects* chapter.

If you plan to use activity code mail addresses in future projects, open the TEMPLATE project located in \STWIN\TEMPLATE (or the project you use as your template project) and follow the previous steps to enter E-mail addresses into the template project. Each new project you create will include the E-mail activity codes from the template project.

Receiving Projects Through E-Mail

In SureTrak, you can receive an E-mail message without switching to your E-mail system and review and modify any SureTrak data included with those messages. If this message contains a backup of an entire SureTrak project, restore that backup from your E-mail system.

A backup of an entire project or project group has "Primavera project" in the Subject line and a .PRX extension.

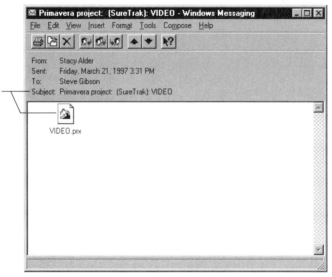

To restore a backup of a project or project group

1 Open the mail message containing the backup file in your E-mail system.

2 Open the backup file attached to the E-mail message. In many E-mail systems, this is done by double-clicking the attachment.

The backup file will have a .PRX extension.

3 SureTrak opens the Restore dialog box. Select the drive and directory where you want to restore the project.

4 Click OK.

If you restore the project to a directory that contains another version of the project, or a different project with the same name, you must choose whether to overwrite the existing project.

For more information about how SureTrak backs up projects, see the *Creating SureTrak Projects* chapter.

 SureTrak cannot restore a project if that project is currently open. Close the project before restoring it.

Updating Project Data Received Through E-Mail

You can open any SureTrak message directly from your E-mail system. Use your E-mail software to save a copy of the backup project, the project snapshot, or the Clipboard file to your hard disk. You can also use your E-mail software to review and even edit messages that contain activity and resource data as an attachment, or you can review and edit update messages from within SureTrak.

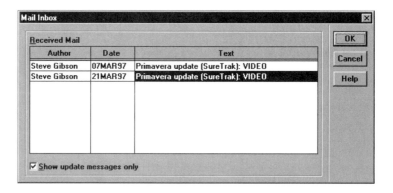

To receive E-mail in SureTrak

1 Choose File, Mail, Receive Mail to open the Mail Inbox dialog box. SureTrak lists all messages that contain "Primavera update" in the subject.

2 If the message you want to use doesn't have these words in the subject, clear the Show Update Messages Only checkbox and SureTrak will list all the messages in your Inbox; however, it can only access messages that contain SureTrak information.

To merge activity and resource data from a mail message into a new or existing project, use SureTrak's Receive Mail feature. When you merge activities into a project, SureTrak opens the Receive Mail dialog box, where you can review incoming activity, resource, and relationship data. This dialog includes columns for each data item the mail message contains.

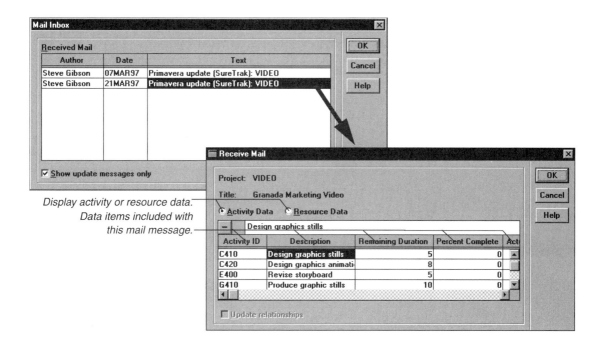

Display activity or resource data. Data items included with this mail message.

Scroll through the activity/ resource data items table horizontally to see more activity or resource data items; scroll vertically to see more activities or resource assignments.

To merge activity and resource data

1 Choose File, Mail, Receive Mail to open the Mail Inbox dialog box.

2 Login and double-click a SureTrak Update mail message in the Received Mail table, or select a message and click OK.

3 SureTrak asks you to pick a project to merge the activities into. Click OK to merge the activities into the default project, or click Browse to open a new project to merge the activities into. If the default project is not currently open, clicking OK will open the project.

4 In the Receive Mail dialog box, review incoming activity and resource information, making changes if necessary.

   Switch between activity and resource information by choosing the Activity Data or Resource Data option.

5 Clear the Update Relationships checkbox if you don't want to merge any relationships into the project.

6 Click OK.

When you receive replies from people to whom you have sent activities by E-mail, you can compare the data in your project with the updated data that has been returned to you.

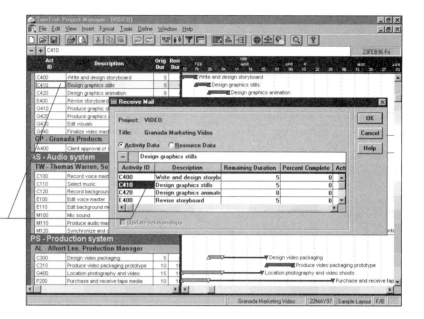

Select activity C410 in the Receive Mail dialog box and SureTrak selects the corresponding activity in your project.

To compare activities in your project with an E-mail reply

1 Choose File, Mail, Receive to open the Mail Inbox dialog box.

2 Open the mail message with the Primavera update attachment containing the activities you want to compare.

3 Select an activity in the Receive Mail dialog box. SureTrak selects the corresponding activity in the project window.

4 If you do not want to update the activity in the project with the activity data in the message, delete it from the message.

Deleting Activities and Data Items in Mail Messages

If you receive information that you do not want to merge into your project, such as activity descriptions, delete this information from the mail message before merging it into your project. Select any cell and edit its contents in the edit bar, or click ▇ to delete activities or resource assignments. You can also delete individual cells or columns containing information you don't want to merge into the project; when you click ▇ to delete, SureTrak asks whether you are deleting the activity (row), data item (column), or cell.

Receiving an Activity Status Sheet in Primavera Post Office

Primavera Post Office enables you to receive and edit activity and resource information without opening SureTrak. Primavera Post Office receives activity information in one of two formats: the Standard status sheet or the Custom status sheet. The author of the message determines the status sheet used to view an attachment.

Primavera Post Office is fully compatible with Excel's copy and paste features; you can copy all fields in Primavera Post Office as text fields.

Starting Primavera Post Office Use Primavera Post Office to update or edit project information attached to a mail message. You can access Primavera Post Office using either an external E-mail system, or independently.

■ To launch Primavera Post Office from your mail system, open the SureTrak attachment.

■ To launch Primavera Post Office independently, access PRMMAIL.EXE. Once you start the program, you can open any mail text or attachment that has been copied to a local or network drive. From Primavera Post Office, choose File, Open, then select any file with a .PRD extension.

For more information about merging updated activities into your project, see *How To Receive Information Through E-Mail* in SureTrak Help.

Updating activity data in the Standard status sheet Use the Standard status sheet to update activity information and return it to the person who sent the mail message. In the status sheet, you cannot edit columns that appear gray. Once an activity starts, you can edit the Start Date and Finished? columns for that activity; when an activity is marked finished, you can edit the Finish Date column. If an activity is marked finished, Primavera Post Office automatically enters a value of 0 for the activity's remaining duration, or 100 for percent complete.

 You cannot merge updated information into your project from Primavera Post Office. To merge updated information, open the mail attachment in SureTrak.

Enter the date the activity started.

Mark to indicate that an activity has started.

Indicates the date through which activities should be updated.

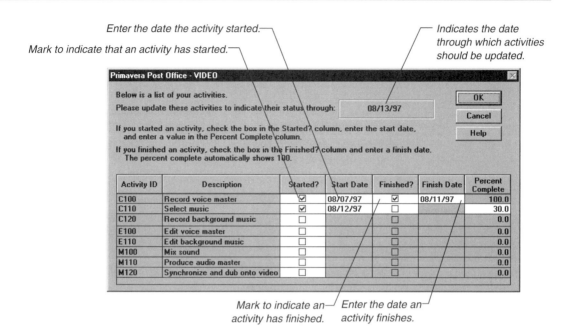

Mark to indicate an activity has finished.

Enter the date an activity finishes.

Updating a Custom status sheet This status sheet enables you to view and edit more data items than the Standard status sheet. You can view the information contained in the Custom status sheet as either activity or resource data. Any data item can be included in the Custom status sheet, it is not limited to the data items sent with the Standard status sheet. If the person who composes the mail message uses P3, he/she can determine the data items presented in the Custom status sheet, and specify whether the recipients can edit the items.

The originator of this message made this column noneditable.

Activity ID	Description	Original Duration	Remaining Duration	Per
A400	Client approval of storyboard	0	0	
C100	Record voice master	5d	5d	
C110	Select music	4d	4d	
C120	Record background music	5d	5d	
C300	Design video packaging	5d	5d	
C310	Produce video packaging prototype	10d	10d	
C400	Write and design storyboard	5d	5d	
C410	Design graphics stills	5d	5d	
C420	Design graphics animation	8d	8d	
E100	Edit voice master	7d	7d	
E110	Edit background music	3d	3d	
E400	Revise storyboard	5d	5d	
G400	Location photography and video shoots	15d	15d	
G410	Produce graphic stills	10d	10d	
G420	Produce graphics animation	12d	12d	
G430	Edit visuals	10d	10d	
G440	Finalize video master	10d	10d	

Recipients can update information in these columns.

Adding activities to the Custom status sheet If you want to add an activity from your project to the Custom status sheet, choose Insert, Activity and type the Activity ID for the activity you want to include. Fill in the appropriate activity information, then exit the Custom status sheet. You can then forward the information in a new mail message to be merged into the project.

Viewing resource information in the Custom status sheet
Choose View, Resource to view resource data contained in the Custom status sheet. When viewing resource data, organize the activities in the Custom status sheet by Activity ID, resource, or cost account. To sort the activities, choose View, Organize and select the option you want to use.

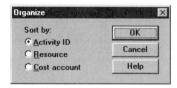

Viewing relationships and logs in the Custom status sheet If the person who sent the mail message included relationship or log information for the activities, you can view that information in separate dialog boxes.

■ Choose View, Relationships to view an activity's predecessors or successors separately. To view the relationships for a different activity, select it in the Custom status sheet and Primavera Post Office automatically shows the selected activity's information in the Relationships dialog box.

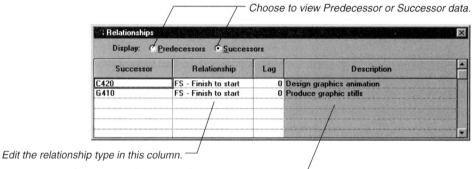

Choose to view Predecessor or Successor data.

Edit the relationship type in this column.

A description is available for each predecessor or successor activity only if the data file contains both relationship and activity description information.

■ Choose View, Logs to review log information for an activity. This option is not available if log information was not sent with the activities, or if the mail message originated in SureTrak. SureTrak log messages display as columns in Primavera Post Office.

Viewing the text sent with the mail message In Primavera Post Office, choose View, Message to display any text message included in the main body of the mail item; you cannot edit this message.

For more information about using Primavera Post Office, access the Primavera Post Office Help system (PRMMAIL.HLP).

Viewing data copied into the body of the mail message Some Internet gateways copy attachments to the body of the mail message. To update activities sent in attachments that were moved into the body of the message, copy the mail message to your local or network drive and give the new file a .PRD extension, then run Primavera Post Office and update the activities.

Customizing Project Information

In this part: *Customizing the Bar Chart View*

Customizing the PERT View

Customizing SureTrak's Default Options

This part describes how to present, format, and organize project data onscreen in concise, attractive, informative ways. You can create Bar charts and customize activity columns to spotlight specific aspects of the project. You can create PERT charts to illustrate the logic of the project network while still presenting detailed data about each activity.

Tailor each type of presentation by customizing the columns, bars, dates, colors, and shapes used to identify various parts of the project.

Part 5 also discusses how to customize many preset options in SureTrak, such as default fonts, tabors, and how often to save projects.

Customizing the Bar Chart View

The Bar chart enables you to show some or all project information graphically. If you prefer to work in a graphic environment, you can display more of the Bar chart and fewer Activity columns. If you like to work in a more spreadsheet-like environment, you can choose to display only a small portion or none of the Bar chart while you work with your project.

Formatting Activity Columns and Data

The Activity columns make it easy to view or update activity information in a tabular format, similar to a spreadsheet. After you format the Activity columns so that they contain the information you want, browse through the activity information using the arrow keys or the mouse. You can easily change information in specific cells without opening the Activity form or a detail form. Enter text, dates, codes, or numbers in an Activity column cell using the edit bar. Select the cell and type the information, or select a date from a pop-up calendar or a code from a drop-down list. You can also use special techniques to copy information from cell to cell in the same column.

Double-click a column title to open the Columns dialog box for adding, deleting, and modifying columns.

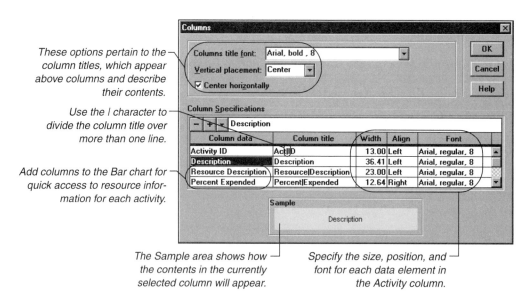

These options pertain to the column titles, which appear above columns and describe their contents.

Use the I character to divide the column title over more than one line.

Add columns to the Bar chart for quick access to resource information for each activity.

The Sample area shows how the contents in the currently selected column will appear.

Specify the size, position, and font for each data element in the Activity column.

To add an Activity column

Select Blank from the drop-down list to create an empty column to print a report and then have other team members fill in the blank column.

1 Choose Format, Columns. Select a row in the Column data column.

2 Insert a row above the selected row by pressing Insert or add a row at the bottom of the list by clicking below the last item in the table.

3 Right-click in the new row and select the column contents from the drop-down list.

4 Use the default column title or select the Column Title cell and type a different title in the edit bar, then press Enter.

5 Click ▣ to confirm the new column title.

6 Use the default width, text alignment, and font, or change them as described later in this chapter. Click OK.

To delete an Activity column, in the Column Specifications section, select the column data item you want to delete, then press Delete or click ▣.

To specify column title placement

1 Choose Format, Columns.

2 Right-click in the Vertical Placement field and select Center, Bottom, or Top.

   The Vertical Placement setting specifies whether SureTrak aligns the rows of text with the top or bottom of the title area, or centers the rows between them. Select Center if your column titles have different numbers of rows of text.

3 Mark the Center Horizontally checkbox to center column title text horizontally within the column title cell, or align each column's title with its contents.

To change a column quickly, double-click the column title in the Bar chart.

   For example, if you select left justification for the column data in the Column Specifications section, the column title is also left-justified.

4 Click OK.

Displaying Activity Code Descriptions in Columns and Bars

SureTrak enables you to display activity codes you defined in the Activity Codes Dictionary as either descriptions or names in the Activity columns and Bar chart.

Define the project's activity codes in the Activity Codes dialog box (choose Define, Activity Codes). Then, Choose Tools, Options, and click the View tab. In the Activity Codes section, mark Show As Values to show activity codes as names or mark Show As Descriptions to show activity codes as descriptions in bars and columns.

To view activity code descriptions or values in the Activity columns, choose Format, Columns and add an activity code column, such as Area, Phase, Responsibility, or System. To view descriptions or values on the Bar chart, choose Format, Bars and add Area, Phase, Responsibility, or System as a description on the bar. SureTrak displays activity codes values or descriptions depending on the option you selected in the Options dialog box.

 If you add an Activity column to display activity code descriptions, it is non-editable.

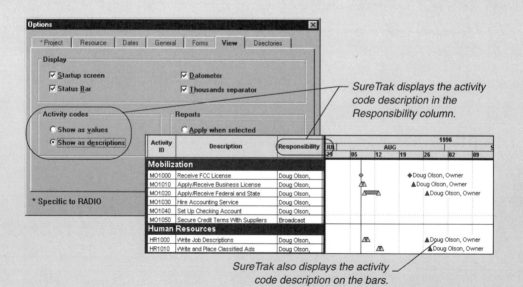

SureTrak displays the activity code description in the Responsibility column.

SureTrak also displays the activity code description on the bars.

Sizing Columns and Rows

SureTrak automatically sizes columns and rows based on the data items you select and how you format them. However, you can override automatic sizing by adjusting columns or rows directly in the Bar chart or by choosing Format, Columns or Format, Row Height.

To size columns using the mouse Point to the vertical line on the right side of the column title. When the mouse pointer changes to ⇼, drag the line to the left or right to adjust the width.

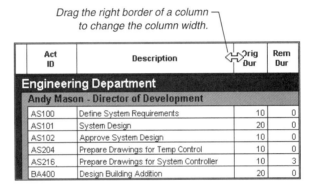

Drag the right border of a column to change the column width.

You can hide a column by dragging the vertical line all the way to the left, which sets the width to zero. To redisplay the column, choose Format, Columns and change the width.

To size columns using the Columns dialog box Choose Format, Columns and specify an exact width for columns.

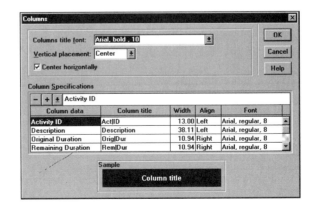

Sizing rows Row height is the amount of vertical space you want to allocate for text in the Activity columns and the corresponding graphic elements on the Bar chart. Use the Row Height dialog box to enter an exact row height or to have SureTrak automatically calculate row height.

SureTrak bases automatic sizing of row height on the larger of two values: the text in Activity columns; or the height of all activity bars, endpoints, and label text for an activity on the Bar chart.

To apply automatic row height to only a few activity rows, select those activities before opening the Row Height dialog box. When you apply a row height to all activities, it applies to all activities, whether or not they match the current filter. When you apply a row height to selected activities, it applies only to the selected activities; those rows keep the specified row height until you change it or apply automatic row sizing again.

 To have SureTrak automatically determine row height Choose Format, Row Height.

Mark to have SureTrak determine row height.

To control the exact height of rows, clear the Automatic Size checkbox and specify a number in points.

Choose to apply the row height to all activities or only to the selected activities.

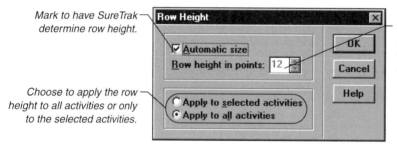

If you assign a specific row height or resize rows by dragging row borders instead of using Automatic Row Height, you may limit the "rows" so that not all bars are visible. For example, if you define row height as 10 points, and you define three bars as 5 points each at positions 1, 2, and 3 so they do not overlap vertically; SureTrak hides the last bar. Likewise, text in the Activity columns can be cut off if the font size is larger than the row height allows.

To size rows using the mouse Point to the horizontal grid line between two activities. When the pointer changes to a ⇕ , drag the line up or down until the row reaches the size you want. If you are not displaying sight lines between the columns, point to the empty space between rows to display the pointer.

Act ID	Description	Orig Dur	Rem Dur
Design and Engineering Phase			
AS100	Define System Requirements	10	0
AS101	System Design	20	0
AS102	Approve System Design	10	0
AS204	Prepare Drawings for Temp Control	10	0
AS205	Review and Approve Temp Control	5	0
AS216	Prepare Drawings for System Controller	10	3

Adjust the height of a specific row by dragging its lower sight line.

Adjusting the Timescale

The timescale is the calendar heading that appears above the Bar chart. You can control the timescale from the Timescale dialog box, or by clicking directly on the timescale. Changing the timescale density only affects the amount of information displayed on the Bar chart; it does not affect the schedule or activity durations.

You can set up the general appearance of the timescale from the Timescale dialog box when you start planning your project. Then, after you enter project data, you can adjust the timescale directly on the Bar chart.

Drag the scroll bar to the left to compress the timescale density; drag it to the right to expand it.

Mark to format the timescale to match a fiscal year then specify the start month for the year.

Choose to show ordinal dates (such as Day 1 or Month 1) instead of calendar dates.

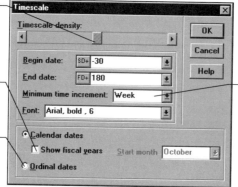

Specify the smallest time increment to show on the timescale. SureTrak divides the bottom row of the timescale into increments of this size.

To set up the timescale using the Timescale dialog box

1 Choose Format, Timescale or double-click anywhere in the top two rows of the timescale.

2 Click the button to the left of the Begin Date field and select a date type.

3 Right-click in the Begin Date field and select a date when the timescale should begin from the pop-up calendar.

4 Click the button to the left of the End Date field and select a date type.

5 Right-click in the End Date field and select a date when the timescale should end from the pop-up calendar.

6 Right-click in the Font field and select a font.

7 Click OK.

If you drag the timescale density scroll bar in the Timescale dialog box to adjust the timescale and click OK, when you reopen the Timescale dialog box, the scroll bar automatically sets itself back to the middle of the bar.

Setting the timescale on the Bar chart You can also adjust the timescale while viewing the Bar chart, so that you can see the effects on bars and visible timespan immediately. Click the bottom row of the timescale and drag the mouse to the left to compress or to the right to expand timescale density.

To change the time interval directly on the timescale Double-click the left mouse button on the bottom row of the timescale to change the interval from years to months to weeks to days to hours. Double-click the right mouse button on the bottom row of the timescale to change the interval from hours to days to weeks to months to years.

Defining Bars and Endpoints

 Use the Bars dialog box to choose the bars and endpoints you want to show, and to customize their size, style, and color.

You can show each activity as one or more bars and/or one or more endpoints. A bar represents a pair of dates and the time elapsed between them, and an endpoint represents a specific date. Use any combination of bars and endpoints to convey the information you want to present.

Choose Yes in the Visible column in the Bars dialog box to show the early bar and late bar on the Bar chart.

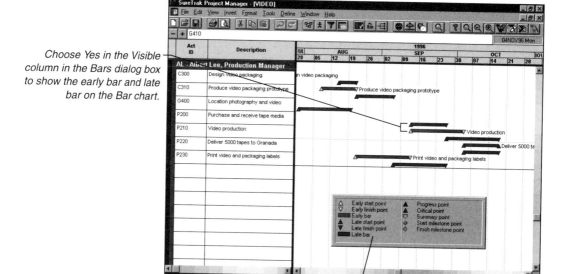

Choose View, Bar Chart Legend to identify what each bar and endpoint represents. Resize the legend by dragging the box's border.

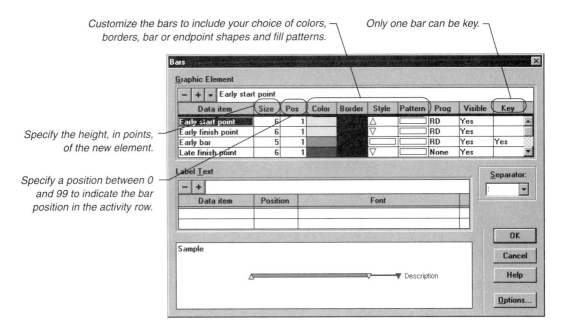

Customize the bars to include your choice of colors, borders, bar or endpoint shapes and fill patterns.

Only one bar can be key.

Specify the height, in points, of the new element.

Specify a position between 0 and 99 to indicate the bar position in the activity row.

To add a bar or endpoint

1 Choose Format, Bars.

2 In the Graphic Element section, click ⊞ to insert a row, or click an empty row at the bottom of the table.

3 Add a bar or endpoint at the top of the Graphic Element section if you want to superimpose it on any bars or endpoints it overlaps.

For example, if two bars have the same position number and their dates overlap, SureTrak displays the one listed higher in this table "on top," or completely visible, obscuring part or all of the one it overlaps.

To control the appearance of progress bars or points, click the Options button, and specify Yes in the Visible cell of the progress bar and/or progress point cells.

4 Right-click in the Data Item section and select a bar or endpoint.

5 Right-click in the Prog (Progress) cell and select RD (remaining duration), Pct (percent complete), or None as the basis for showing progress.

6 Right-click in the Key cell and select Yes to designate a bar as the key bar. Only one bar can be designated as the key bar. Endpoints are blank.

You can draw relationship lines to and from only the key bar, and you can change an activity's duration by dragging the edges only of the key bar. A key bar can be the early bar, late bar, target bar, or unleveled bar.

Adding Labels to Bars and Endpoints

You can associate a label with a bar or endpoint. For example, you can show activity descriptions on the Bar chart next to the bars they describe, instead of in the Activity columns; for a long report, you can put them in both the Activity columns and the Bar chart. If your Bar chart has endpoints that represent early finish dates, include finish date labels next to the endpoint symbols so you can see the date each activity finishes.

To add a label Choose Format, Bars to display the Bars dialog box.

1 Select the bar or endpoint to which you want to add a label.

2 Click to insert a row.

3 Right-click to select the data item to use as a label.

4 SureTrak displays how the bar, endpoint, and label will look on the Bar chart. Click OK to apply your specifications.

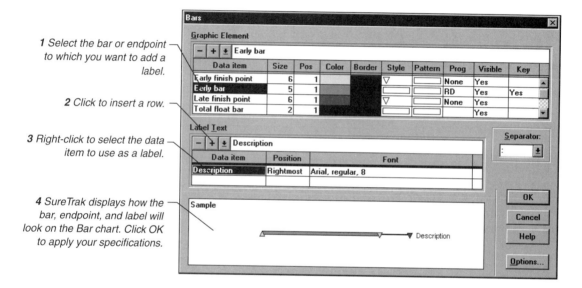

Labels are not visible if they are assigned to bars that are not visible. In the Bars dialog box, specify Yes in the Visible cell of a graphic element to display it and its associated label on the Bar chart.

Positioning the label Choose a position for the label relative to the graphic element: Left, Right, Top, Bottom, Leftmost, or Rightmost. If you display several graphic elements in the same position, label text displayed to the right or left of a graphic element can appear over or under some of these graphic elements. To avoid this problem, choose Rightmost or Leftmost, which places label text to the right or left of all graphic elements in the same position.

Separating multiple labels In the Separator field, choose a separator character if you want to add more than one label in the same position to the same graphic element. For example, if you add Activity ID and Description labels to the early bar and use a slash (/) as a separator, the label text might look like this: HR1150 / Train Technical Staff.

Customizing Summary, Critical, and Progress Bars and Endpoints

You can define special bars and endpoints to look different from standard bars as defined in the Bars dialog box. For example, if you show early bars for your activities, you may want to distinguish between critical and noncritical activities. SureTrak formats noncritical activities using the color and style you establish for early bars in the Bars dialog box. SureTrak formats critical activities using the color and style you select in the Bar and Endpoint Options dialog box.

Select a style, pattern, and color that differs from your standard bars and endpoints.

Showing an early bar, a late bar, and a late start point emphasizes criticality and slack time for each activity.

Bar and Endpoint Options

Bars/Endpoints

	Style	Pattern	Color	Visible
Progress bar				Yes
Critical bar				Yes
Summary bar				Yes
Progress point	△			Yes
Critical point	△			Yes
Summary point	▽			Yes
Start milestone point	◇			Yes
Finish milestone point	◇			Yes

OK

Cancel

Help

Specify Yes or No to show or hide each bar or endpoint.

Formatting Sight Lines

Sight lines are vertical and horizontal lines that help you visually trace a bar or endpoint to its date on the timescale, or to its row in the Activity columns. You can choose which sight lines SureTrak displays, the interval at which they are displayed, and their line types and colors. You can also specify the style of the data date line, and whether a line or band extends across the Bar chart to visually separate one group of activities from another.

By default, SureTrak separates Activity columns and rows with vertical and horizontal lines.

Choose a sight line interval that is the same as or greater than the minimum time interval defined in the Timescale dialog box. SureTrak does not draw sight lines smaller than the timescale's smallest interval; for example, if the timescale's smallest interval is months, sight lines can be drawn for months, quarters, or years, but not for weeks or days.

SureTrak draws weekly sight lines on the first day of the global calendar's workweek. Monthly vertical sight lines are drawn according to calendar dates, starting on the first calendar day of the first month shown on the timescale. Quarterly sight lines are placed at the beginning of January, April, July, and October.

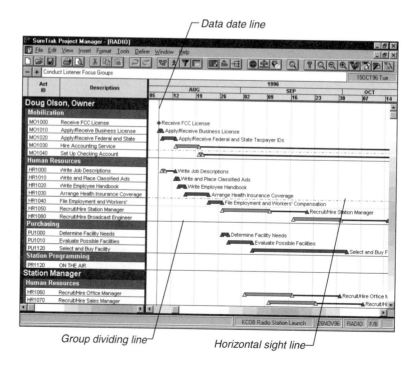

Group dividing line — Horizontal sight line —

You can choose to have one or two sets of sight lines, and you can choose any available line type and thickness for either set. If you use both major and minor sight lines, the minor sight lines must be at a smaller interval than the major sight lines. For example, create yearly major sight lines and monthly minor sight lines, or monthly major sight lines and weekly minor sight lines.

To adjust the spacing between sight lines, change the Horizontal and Vertical sections in the Sight Lines dialog box.

To show sight lines between Activity columns and rows

1 Choose Format, Sight Lines.

2 Enter the number of activities (between 0 and 99) you want between each horizontal sight line.

3 Enter a number to indicate the interval at which vertical sight lines should occur, then select a unit of time from the drop-down list. The interval combined with the unit tells SureTrak exactly where the sight line should appear.

For example, if you specify 2 as the interval and Week as the unit, SureTrak draws a sight line at 2-week intervals.

4 Right-click in the Group Divider field and select None, Line, or Band.

Select None if you do not want to separate organized groups of activities. Select Line if you want to separate organized groups with a horizontal line across the Bar chart. Select Band if you want to extend the colored band of an organized group across the Bar chart.

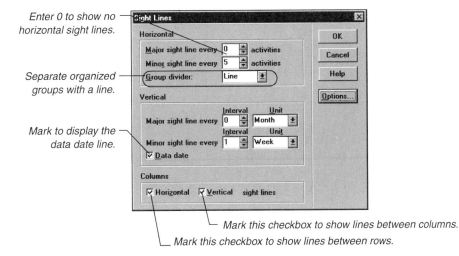

Enter 0 to show no horizontal sight lines.

Separate organized groups with a line.

Mark to display the data date line.

Mark this checkbox to show lines between columns.

Mark this checkbox to show lines between rows.

To control the appearance of sight lines Choose Format, Sight
Lines, then click Options.

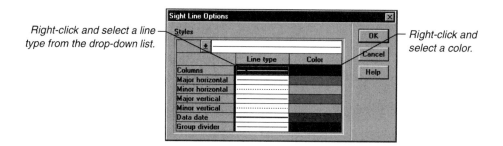

*Right-click and select a line
type from the drop-down list.*

*Right-click and
select a color.*

Formatting Relationship Lines

You can customize your Bar chart presentation by changing the line types and colors for driving and nondriving relationships. You can also choose to hide or show relationships that drive the schedule.

Specify whether you want SureTrak to display critical, driving, and nondriving relationships on the Bar chart.

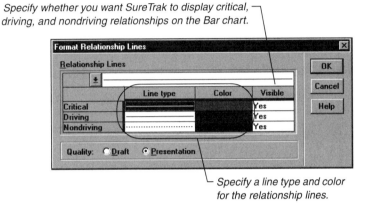

Specify a line type and color for the relationship lines.

For information on formatting relationship lines in PERT, see the *Customizing the PERT View* chapter.

Finding Dates on the Bar Chart

You can move across the Bar chart by dragging the horizontal scroll bar along the bottom of the project window, or by using SureTrak's Find feature to search for a specific date. Use the Find dialog box to automatically move the timescale to a date you specify.

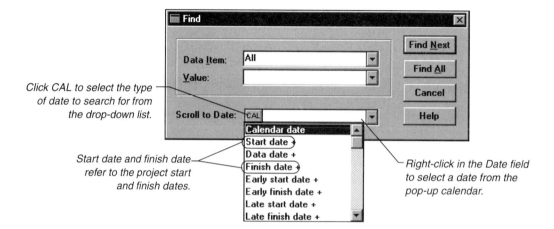

Click CAL to select the type of date to search for from the drop-down list.

Start date and finish date refer to the project start and finish dates.

Right-click in the Date field to select a date from the pop-up calendar.

To search for a date using the Find dialog box Choose Edit, Find to display the Find dialog box. In the Scroll To Date field, select Calendar Date to select a specific date from the pop-up calendar. Or, you can select rolling dates. Rolling dates, such as Start date + and Data date + are based on their relationship to the data date or the project start date or the finish date, rather than by specific calendar dates, plus or minus a specified number of days. For example, if the project start date is February 10, 1997 and you enter SD + 10, SureTrak scrolls to February 20, 1997.

If you select early start, early finish, late start, or late finish dates, SureTrak scrolls to the early start or finish, or late start or finish of the selected activity. If SureTrak finds multiple activities, click Find Next or Find All to go to the next activity.

To review dates on the activity bar Position the mouse pointer over a bar until the pointer shape changes to +; this shape appears only when the bar is designated as a key bar (choose Format, Bars). Click the left mouse button to display the start and finish dates for that bar.

The Datometer contains the exact date represented by the location of the mouse pointer as you move the mouse over the Bar chart.

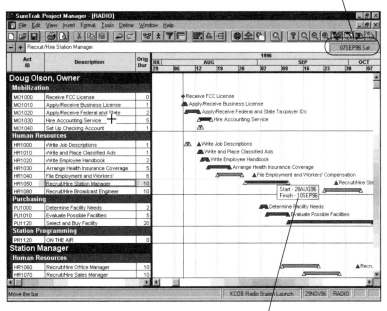

Drag an activity bar to change its dates temporarily.

Adding a Picture to the Bar Chart

SureTrak provides a clip-art library that contains pictures in the Windows metafile (.WMF) format. You can insert any of these graphics or a bitmap or metafile you've created in another Windows application, such as Microsoft Paint, on the Bar chart.

When you first insert a picture, SureTrak displays it at the top left corner of the Bar chart; you can then drag it anywhere on the Bar chart, or you can attach it to a specific activity, band, or date so that it remains associated with that row or date as you scroll around the Bar chart.

Select any bitmap or metafile and click OK to insert it on the Bar chart.

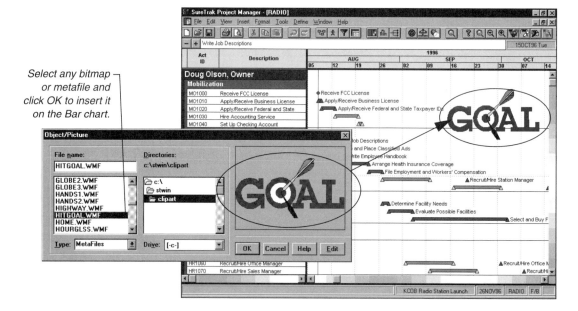

To add a picture to the Bar chart

1 Choose Insert, Object/Picture.

2 Specify the drive and directory of the graphic you want to attach.

3 Preview the picture in the box on the right side of the dialog box. Click OK to insert it, or click Edit to edit the picture in its associated application. When you close the application associated with the graphic, SureTrak redisplays the Object/Picture dialog box.

4 Click OK.

5 Position the mouse pointer over the graphic. When the pointer changes to ⊕, drag the graphic anywhere on the Bar chart. SureTrak attaches the graphic to a specific location on the Bar chart.

Adding Text to the Bar Chart

In addition to displaying labels associated with bars and milestones as described earlier in this chapter, you can add annotations—such as messages or in-depth descriptions of activities or delays—by attaching text. You can specify the font and color of the text you attach to emphasize it.

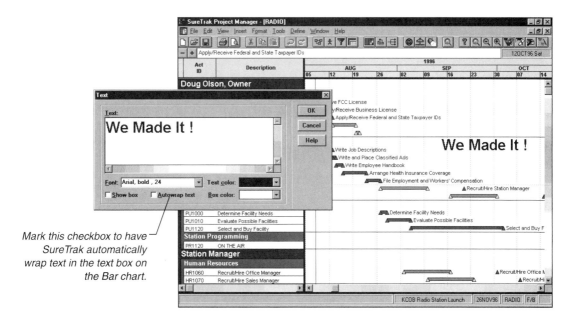

Mark this checkbox to have SureTrak automatically wrap text in the text box on the Bar chart.

To add text to the Bar chart

1 Choose Insert, Text/Hyperlink.

2 In the Text section, type the text you want to attach to the Bar chart.

3 Right-click in the Font field and select a font, font style, and size.

4 Right-click in the Text Color field and select a color.

5 Mark the Show Box checkbox if you want to surround the text you are displaying with a frame, then right-click in the Box Color field and select a background color for the frame.

6 Click OK.

7 Position the mouse pointer over the text. When the pointer changes to ✛, drag the text anywhere on the Bar chart. SureTrak attaches the text block to a specific location on the Bar chart.

Linking to Documents and the World Wide Web

SureTrak enables you to create hot links, or shortcuts, from activities, bars, or dates in the Bar chart to a document or a World Wide Web page. You can link to actual reports or pictures, rather than embed them in your project, to decrease the size of the project and provide more details about an activity.

For example, you can insert a file hot link that points to an HTML report on the Web, then launch directly to that report from the shortcut in the Bar chart. Or, you can create a hot link that points to a document written in Microsoft Word.

If you mark the Autowrap Text checkbox and use the handles to resize the text box, SureTrak automatically wraps the text to fit the size of the box.

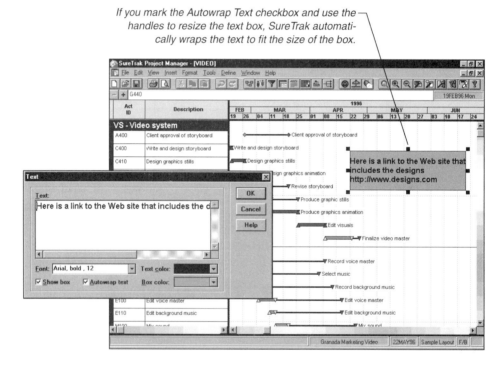

To create a link to other documents

1 Choose Insert, Text/Hyperlink.

For information on creating reports on the World Wide Web, see the *Publishing Reports on the World Wide Web* chapter.

2 In the Text dialog box, type the address of the Web page to which you want to jump. For example, type **http://www.primavera.com**. Or, type a valid file path for the document to which you want to link. For example, type **file:\c:\msoffice\access\bitmaps\resource.bmp**. SureTrak also supports links to ftp:// addresses.

You can include only one link per item. For example, if you create a link with both http://www.primavera.com and http://www.microsoft.com, SureTrak launches the first item, primavera.com only.

3 Right-click in the Font field and select a font, font style, and size.

4 Right-click in the Text Color field and select a color.

5 Mark the Show Box checkbox if you want to surround the text with a frame, then right-click in the Box Color field and select a background color for the frame.

If you mark the Autowrap Text checkbox, the text wraps in the Bar chart, not in the Text dialog box.

6 Mark the Autowrap Text checkbox to have SureTrak automatically wrap the text in the text box when you resize the text box. If you do not mark this checkbox, SureTrak displays the text in the Bar chart in a straight line.

7 Click OK.

8 Position the mouse pointer over the text. When the pointer changes to ✛, drag the text anywhere on the Bar chart. SureTrak attaches the text block to a specific location on the Bar chart.

To attach links to activities, bars, or dates

1 After you have created a link, choose Insert, Attach Object.

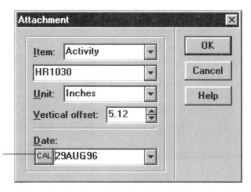

Click CAL to attach the link to a changing date.

You can also access the Attachment dialog box by right-clicking on the link and choosing Attach.

2 In the Attachment dialog box, right-click in the Item field and select an item such as an activity or band to which to attach the link.

To attach the link to a date, select None in the Item field.

3 To move the link up or down the Bar chart, specify the amount of distance in the Vertical Offset field and the unit of measure for the offset in the Unit field.

4 To move the graphic horizontally, specify the date for its horizontal position in the Date field.

5 Click OK. SureTrak saves the link with the layout.

To edit a link After you have created a link, choose Insert, List Objects to edit the text, link, and text properties in the List Objects dialog box. Or, right-click on the link and choose List.

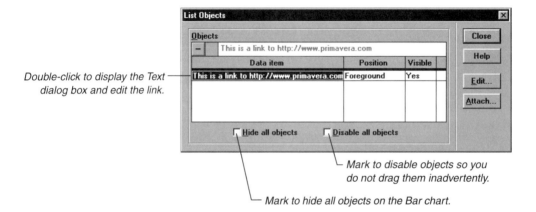

Double-click to display the Text dialog box and edit the link.

Mark to disable objects so you do not drag them inadvertently.

Mark to hide all objects on the Bar chart.

To access the document or Web page After you have created a hot link, double-click any portion of the link in the Bar chart to access the document or launch the Web page. Or, right-click on the link and choose Open.

To delete the link Right-click on the link and choose Delete from the pop-up menu.

Shading a Timeperiod on the Bar Chart

 To focus attention on a specific timeperiod, you can add a curtain of color to shade a portion of the Bar chart. You can specify the duration (width) of the curtain and the colors for its border and interior, as well as a fill pattern such as stripes or crosshatch.

Drag either border of the curtain to change its duration.

Right-click in these fields to select a color or pattern.

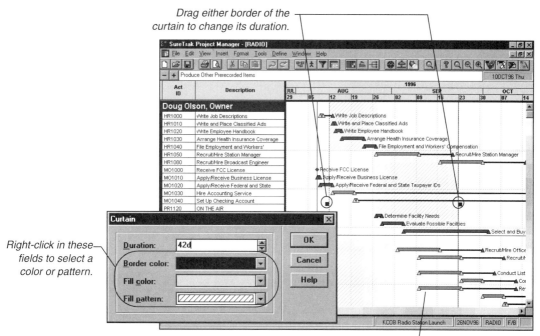

Drag the curtain to change its location on the Bar chart.

To add a curtain over a timeperiod in the Bar chart

1 Choose Insert, Curtain.

2 In the Duration field, type a duration for the curtain, followed by a duration abbreviation (h, d, or w).

3 Right-click in the color fields and select a border and fill color.

4 Right-click in the Fill Pattern field and select a pattern.

5 Click OK.

SureTrak inserts the curtain next to the left border of the Bar chart.

6 Position the pointer over the curtain. When the pointer changes to ✛, drag the curtain anywhere on the Bar chart.

Positioning a curtain When you add a curtain, SureTrak places it in the background and draws graphic elements such as bars and labels over it. You can move it from the background to the foreground in the List Objects dialog box (choose Insert, List Object); the curtain then hides everything it overlaps.

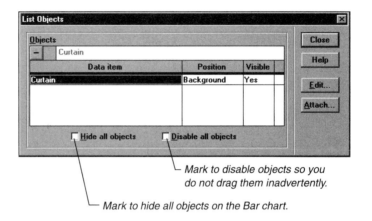

Mark to disable objects so you do not drag them inadvertently.

Mark to hide all objects on the Bar chart.

Inserting Objects Using OLE

 Object Linking and Embedding (OLE) is a Windows data-sharing technique that enables you to insert data from other applications into SureTrak. For example, include a portion of a spreadsheet or a graphic object in a SureTrak project by inserting it on the Bar chart. To change the object, you can edit it directly in SureTrak.

To use OLE, an application must be an OLE server, an OLE client, or both. An OLE server is a Windows application that can share data with OLE clients. An OLE client is a Windows application that can use data from OLE servers. SureTrak is an OLE client.

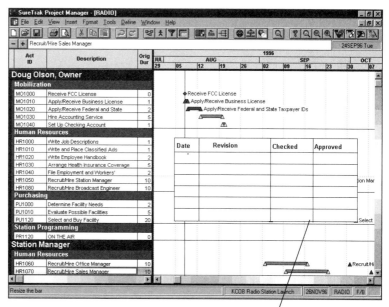

Use OLE to embed a revision worksheet in the project.

You can use OLE to place a logo in a header or footer, enabling you to insert graphics created in other applications, such as CorelDRAW or Visio.

To link an object to a SureTrak project

1 Choose Insert, Object/Picture.

2 Change the Type to All Files, then select the file you want to link from the file list.

You can also specify the exact file type you want to use: metafiles, bitmaps, .PMT, Microsoft Word, Microsoft Excel, CorelDRAW, or Visio Files.

3 Click OK.

Customizing the PERT View

The PERT view displays your project as a diagram of activities and relationships. Use the PERT view to examine the relationships among activities and the flow of work through a project.

You can also use the PERT view to create a new project based on existing activity templates, add and delete activities, change relationships, and edit activity data.

What Is the PERT View?

The PERT view displays your project as a diagram of activities and relationships. Use the PERT view whenever you need to focus on the logical sequence of relationships among activities, rather than on the schedule dates. Choose View, PERT to display project activities beginning with the first activity that has no predecessors and ending with the last activity that has no successors.

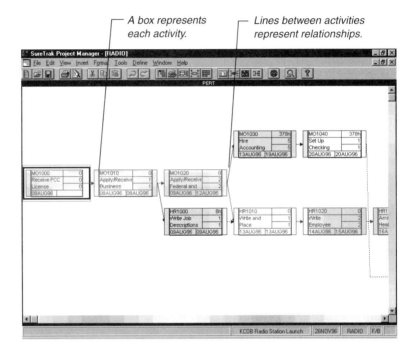

A box represents each activity.

Lines between activities represent relationships.

Customizing the PERT view In each activity box, SureTrak shows the Activity ID, activity description, early start, early finish, original and remaining durations, and total float. You can customize the activity boxes to show only the information you want. For example, instead of showing early start and finish dates, show WBS codes and calendar IDs. You can adjust the font type, size, and style for the data items in the activity boxes. You can also modify the ends and colors for specific activities so they stand out from the rest of the project.

The PERT view provides many options for customizing your presentations, as illustrated by the following examples.

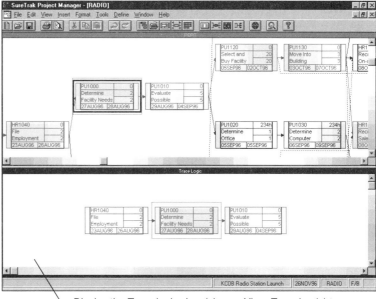

Display the Trace logic view (choose View, Trace Logic) to
focus on an activity's predecessors and successors.

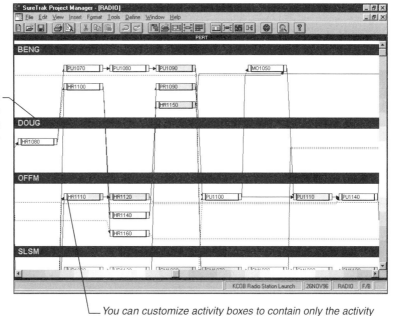

Organize activities into
groups to focus on
specific areas of the
project, such as responsibility or department.

You can customize activity boxes to contain only the activity
information you want by choosing Format, Activity Box
Configuration, and selecting an activity box template.

Moving Around the PERT View

SureTrak provides several ways for you to move around a project. Use the scroll bars to move vertically and horizontally.

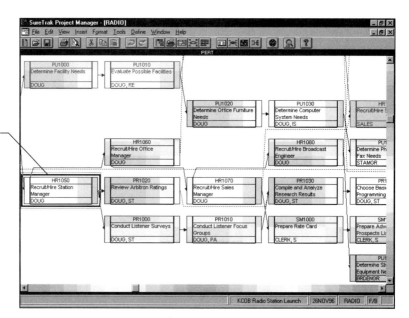

When you select an activity, SureTrak displays a black outline around it. Use the mouse or arrow keys to move between activities.

You can also use the keyboard to move around the window. The following table describes the keys for moving around the PERT view.

Choose	To
PgUp	Scroll one page up.
PgDn	Scroll one page down.
Ctrl+PgUp	Scroll one page left.
Ctrl+PgDn	Scroll one page right.
Home	Move to and select the first activity in the current row.
End	Move to and select the last activity in the current row.
Ctrl+Home	Move to the top left portion of the network. SureTrak unselects any previously selected activities and selects the cell in the top left-most position in the network.
Ctrl+End	Move to the bottom right portion of the network. SureTrak unselects any previously selected activities and selects the cell in the bottom right-most position in the network.

To access menu commands quickly Instead of navigating the menu bar to access PERT commands, right-click in an open area in the PERT view to access a menu of common PERT functions. If you right-click on an activity, you can quickly access activity commands, including cut, copy, paste, insert, delete, and update.

Right-click in an open area in PERT to quickly access commands.

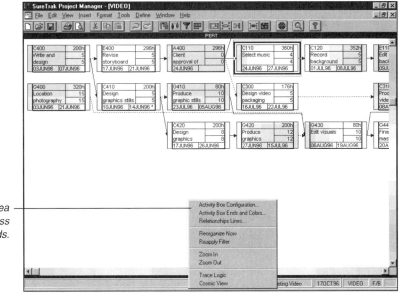

Keeping Track of Your Place in PERT

The Cosmic view enables you to navigate the PERT view while keeping track of your position in relation to the entire project. The Cosmic view displays your project at a reduced magnification so you can see almost the entire project on one page.

To display the Cosmic view Choose View, Cosmic View, or right-click in an empty area of the project window and choose Cosmic View. SureTrak displays the Cosmic view to the right of the PERT view, by default. The Cosmic view shows only activities; relationships and text are not visible.

The shaded box represents the portion ⌐ *Cosmic view*
of the project in the PERT view.

To view the entire project in the Cosmic view at the smallest magnification, right-click in the Cosmic view and choose Zoom Out.

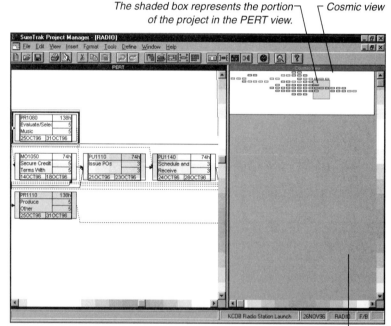

To close the Cosmic view window, right-click anywhere ⌐
in the Cosmic view and choose Hide Cosmic View.

To move around the network You can drag the shaded box to the portion of the project you want to view. The PERT view changes to display that portion of the project.

*Move the shaded box around the network
to see a specific portion of the project.*

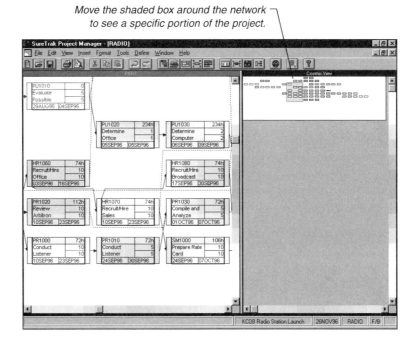

*To change the Cosmic
view window to a docked
window, right-click in the
Cosmic view and choose
Dock Cosmic View.*

To move the Cosmic view window

1 Right-click anywhere in the Cosmic view, then choose Undock Cosmic View. SureTrak reduces the Cosmic view window and places it in the upper right corner of your window.

2 Drag the Cosmic view title bar anywhere in the project window.

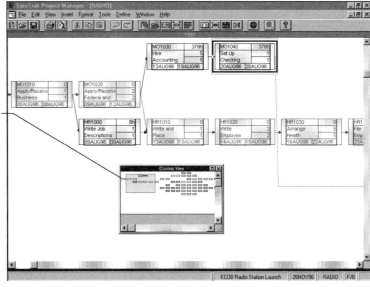

*You can undock the Cosmic
view and place it anywhere in
the project window.*

Displaying Activity Predecessors and Successors

 The Trace logic view enables you to focus on an activity's predecessors and successors, one at a time, while also displaying the entire network. SureTrak displays the Trace logic information below the PERT view, by default.

To display predeccesors and successors

1 Select an activity for which you want to see its predecessors and successors.

2 Choose View, Trace Logic, or right-click in an empty area of the project window and choose Trace Logic. SureTrak displays the predecessors and successors of the selected activity.

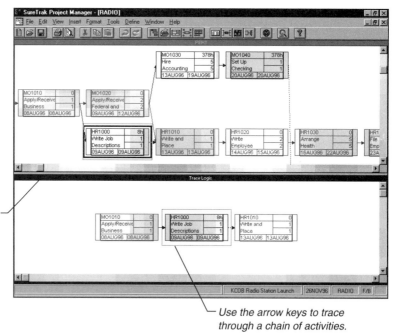

Drag the horizontal split bar up or down to adjust the size of the PERT and Trace logic views.

Use the arrow keys to trace through a chain of activities.

If you don't select any activity and choose the Trace logic view, SureTrak informs you that no activity has been selected. Once the Trace logic view window is open, move around the project by selecting different activities.

To change the Trace logic view to a docked window, right-click in the Trace logic view and choose Dock Trace Logic.

To move the Trace logic view

1 Right-click anywhere in the Trace logic view, then choose Undock Trace Logic. SureTrak reduces the Trace logic view and places it in the upper left corner of your window.

2 Drag the Trace logic view title bar anywhere in the project window.

To define options for viewing logic

1 Right-click anywhere in the Trace logic view, then choose Trace Logic Options.

2 In the Trace Logic Options dialog box, specify whether SureTrak displays all levels of predecessors and successors or only specific levels.

If you choose not to display all levels, specify the number of levels or generations of predecessors and successors to display.

3 Mark the Show Activities With Driving Relationships Only checkbox if you want to display activities with driving relationships only.

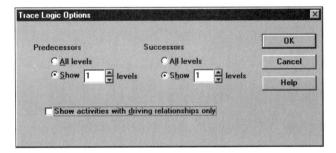

To close the Trace logic view Right-click anywhere in the Trace logic view, then choose Hide Trace Logic.

Hiding Activities in the View

You can hide activities and topic activities in the PERT view without deleting them from the project. To hide activities, select the activity or activities to hide, then choose View, Hide. The activities disappear from the view. To hide topic activities, choose View, Hide Topic Activities. SureTrak hides the topic activities in the view.

To view the activities again, choose Format, Reapply Filter. The activities that were hidden and those that were filtered are brought back into the view. To show topic activities again, choose View, Show Topic Activities.

Reducing or Enlarging the View

  You can enlarge the PERT view of your project to focus on details, or reduce the size of the view to show the big picture.

Choose View, Zoom Out to make activity boxes smaller so you can see more activities.

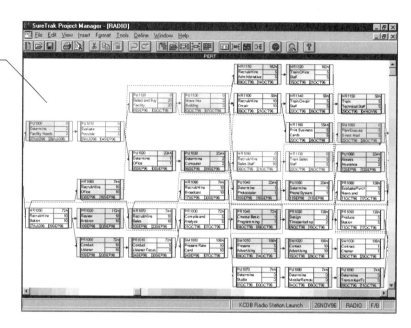

Choose View, Zoom In to magnify activity boxes so you can focus on a selected group of activities.

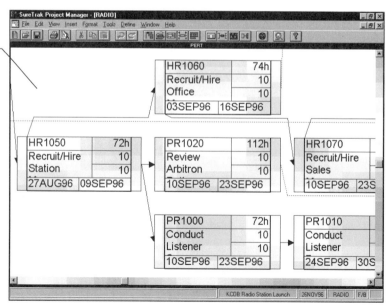

You also can use Zoom In the Cosmic view and Trace logic view.

To customize a zoom level Choose View, Zoom, then choose the Custom option to display the view at a specific percentage.

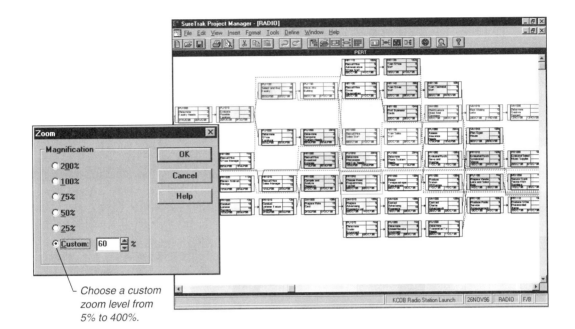

Choose a custom zoom level from 5% to 400%.

 The number of activities that fit onscreen also depends on the activity box configuration and size. Choose Format, Activity Box Configuration to change the size of activity boxes.

Modifying Activity Box Ends and Colors

You can change the appearance of specific activities so they stand out from the rest of the project. For example, configure all engineering activities as yellow ovals and purchasing activities as blue squares. You can also assign different patterns to the ends and change the color of text in the activity box.

To customize activity box ends and colors

1   Select the activities that you want to change. To select one activity, click the activity box. To select several activities, click the first activity box, then press Ctrl while clicking the other activities you want to select. Or, press Shift and click the first and last activities, and SureTrak automatically selects all activities in between.

2   Choose Format, Activity Box Ends and Colors or right-click anywhere in the project window and choose Activity Box Ends and Colors.

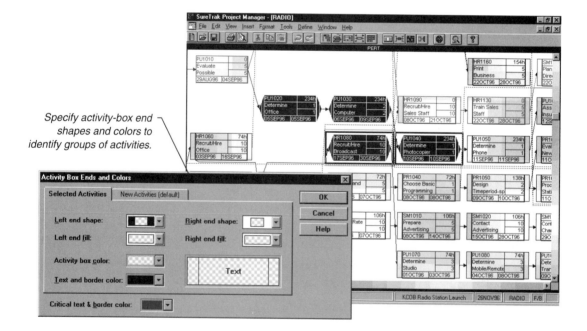

Specify activity-box end shapes and colors to identify groups of activities.

To customize the appearance of new activities You can change
the shapes and colors of activities that are new to the project or view. Click
the New Activities tab in the Activity Box Ends and Colors dialog box and
specify end shapes and colors for new activities.

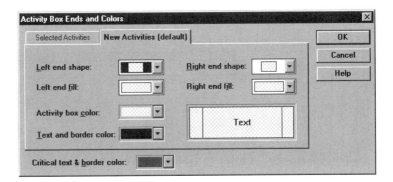

To customize critical activities SureTrak identifies critical activities
by using red as the activity box border, text color, and relationship line
color. If you want to use a different color for critical activities, select a
color in the Critical Text & Border Color field. Make sure the critical color
you choose will be visible with the current fill colors for activity boxes.

Formatting Relationship Lines

You can customize your PERT presentation by changing the line types and colors for driving and nondriving relationships. You can also choose to hide or show relationships that drive the schedule. To format relationship lines, choose Format, Relationship Lines.

Mark one or both check-boxes to display relation-ships in the PERT view.

You can also specify a line style and color for relationship lines.

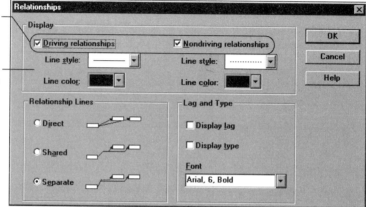

For more information about driving and critical relationship lines, see the *Linking Activities with Relationships* chapter.

If you have driving relationships that are critical, SureTrak displays the color for the relationship lines as critical. Choose Format, Activity Box Ends and Colors to define the relationship line color for critical activities.

To format the angle of relationship lines between activities
Choose Direct, Shared, or Separate in the Relationship Lines section in the Relationships dialog box.

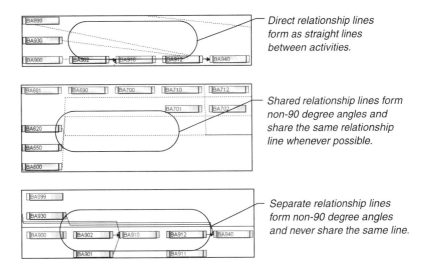

Direct relationship lines
form as straight lines
between activities.

Shared relationship lines form
non-90 degree angles and
share the same relationship
line whenever possible.

Separate relationship lines
form non-90 degree angles
and never share the same line.

To show relationship types and lag amounts Choose whether to
display lag and type in the PERT view by marking the checkboxes in the
Lag and Type section in the Relationships dialog box. SureTrak indicates
the relationship type and lag amount by displaying abbreviations and
values next to the relationship line. You can also adjust the font type, size,
and style in the Font field.

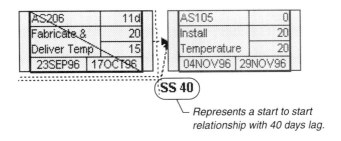

Represents a start to start
relationship with 40 days lag.

Changing the Content and Appearance of Activities

 You can customize your PERT presentation by changing the type and amount of data that appears for activities. SureTrak provides a set of activity templates that display activity data in various levels of detail. Choose Format, Activity Box Configuration to customize the appearance of activities.

To choose an activity-box template

For more information about templates, see Creating Your Own Activity Template later in this chapter.

1   Click the scroll arrows in the Activity Box Templates section in the Activity Box Configuration dialog box and select the template you want to use.

2   Click OK.

SureTrak applies this template to all activities in the project.

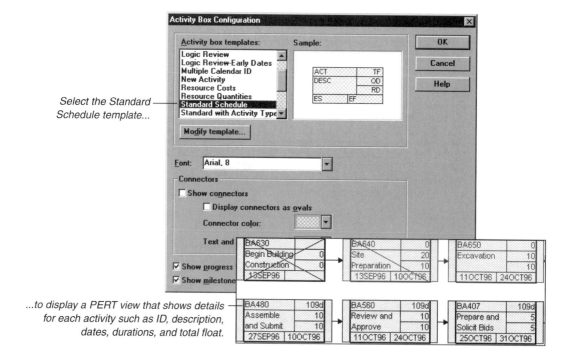

Select the Standard Schedule template...

...to display a PERT view that shows details for each activity such as ID, description, dates, durations, and total float.

Resource/cost templates SureTrak provides templates that display resource/cost data for each activity. For activities with multiple resource assignments, the resource names and descriptions are separated by commas and quantity and cost values are totaled.

For more information about log text data items, see the Adding Activities *chapter.*

Log templates The Log Text1 template shows any text notes that you recorded in the Log Text 1 column in the Bar chart. You can customize a template to show any or all logs (1-10). The Log Record Content item automatically combines all 10 logs in one cell.

To show or hide progress Mark the Show Progress checkbox in the Activity Box Configuration dialog box to display progress in the PERT view. SureTrak indicates progress by drawing an X on a complete activity or a slash on an activity in progress. To hide the progress indicators, clear the Show Progress checkbox.

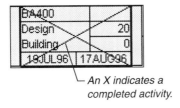

An X indicates a completed activity.   *A slash indicates an activity has started.*

To show milestones

1 Mark the Show Milestone checkbox in the Activity Box Configuration dialog box to display milestone activities with only one end, depending on whether the activity is a start or a finish milestone.

   Milestones are activities with no duration that indicate the beginning or end of a major event or group of activities.

2 Clear the Show Milestone checkbox if you want SureTrak to display milestones with both ends, that is, milestone activities appear as regular activities with both ends showing.

If you mark the Show Milestone checkbox, SureTrak displays a start milestone activity with only a left end, indicating that it has no finish date.

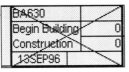

You can change the appearance of milestones. For example, use a pattern for the activity ends so the milestones stand out from the rest of the activities. Select the appropriate milestone activities, then choose Format, Activity Box Ends and Colors.

Displaying Activity Code Descriptions in PERT

In SureTrak, you can display activity codes that you defined in the Activity Codes Dictionary as either descriptions or names in the activity box. Define the project's activity codes in the Activity Codes dialog box (choose Define, Activity Codes). Then, choose Tools, Options, and click the View tab. In the Activity Codes section, choose Show As Values to show activity codes as names or Show As Descriptions to show activity codes as descriptions in the PERT activity box.

To view activity code descriptions or values in PERT, choose Format, Activity Box Configuration. Select an available template and click Modify Template. In the Activity Box Cells section, insert a row and add an activity code box, such as Area, Phase, Responsibility, or System, as the cell content. SureTrak displays activity code values or descriptions depending on the option you selected in the Options dialog box.

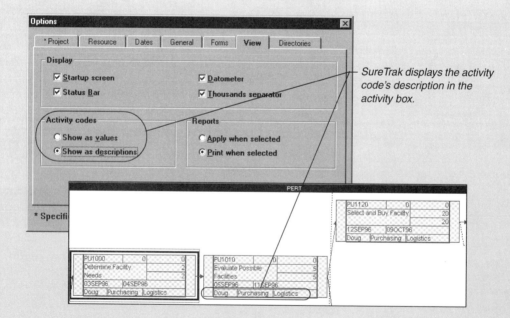

SureTrak displays the activity code's description in the activity box.

Displaying Connector Blocks

Sometimes the predecessor or successor of an activity does not appear in the layout because a filter selects only certain activities. As a result, some activities may seem to be missing relationships. You can display connectors to represent activities excluded from the current view. Connector blocks appear either as ovals, containing only the Activity ID, or as activity boxes, containing activity box information.

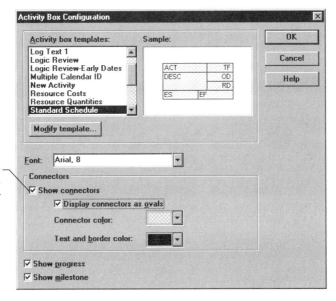

To show connectors, mark this checkbox. Choose whether to show connectors as ovals or as activity boxes.

To display connector blocks containing only Activity IDs
Choose Format, Activity Box Configuration. Mark the Show Connectors checkbox. Then, mark the Display Connectors As Ovals checkbox. Specify the background, text, and border color for the connector blocks.

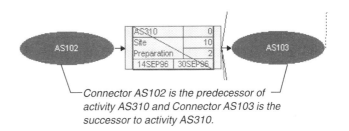

Connector AS102 is the predecessor of activity AS310 and Connector AS103 is the successor to activity AS310.

To display connector blocks as activity boxes Choose Format, Activity Box Configuration. Mark the Show Connectors checkbox. SureTrak displays activities not included in the current view as activity boxes with circles as endpoints. Specify the background, text, and border color for the connector blocks.

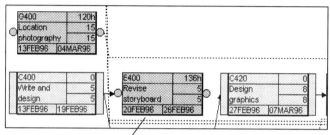

You can display connector blocks to contain activity information specified in the activity box template.

For more information about grouping activities, see *Organizing Activities in PERT* later in this chapter.

 SureTrak does not group or organize connector blocks (unless they have relationships with more than one activity in different bands). If you organize or group activities in PERT, SureTrak displays the connector blocks with the activities to which they are connected by relationships.

Creating Your Own Activity Template

SureTrak provides 17 templates with different activity box formats. If none of these templates contain the configuration you want, modify one or create your own. Start with one of the defined templates, then modify it by adding and deleting rows and choosing the data items each cell contains. You can save up to 25 templates for each layout. You must save the layout to save changes to templates.

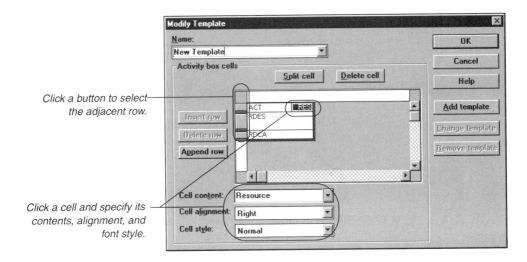

Click a button to select the adjacent row.

Click a cell and specify its contents, alignment, and font style.

To create your own template

1 Choose Format, Activity Box Configuration.

2 Click Modify Template.

3 In the Name field, select a template that is similar to the one you want to create, then enter a new name for your template.

4 Modify the template by changing cell contents, splitting cells, or deleting cells, and inserting or deleting rows as described in the following set of steps.

5 Click Add Template when you complete your changes.

 The Add Template button is only active when you enter a new name in the Name field. If you keep the same name and modify a template, the Change Template button becomes active.

To delete rows, select a row, then click Delete Row.

To add rows to the template

1 Click the button to the left of a row, then click Insert Row.

SureTrak adds the new row above the selected row.

2 Click Append Row to add a row to the bottom of the activity box.

To delete cells, select the cell you want to delete, then click Delete Cell, or press the Delete key.

To add cells

1 Select the cell next to where you want to place the new cell.

2 Click Split Cell.

SureTrak divides the selected cell into two cells.

To resize cells Drag a row or cell separator until the cell reaches the size you want.

To resize the activity box Choose Format, Activity Box Configuration, then click Modify Template. In the Modify Template dialog box, point to the bottom right corner of the activity box, then drag the mouse until the box reaches the size you want. You can also extend the right of the box to widen it, or the bottom to lengthen it.

To modify an existing template Choose Format, Activity Box Configuration and select the template you want to modify. Click Modify Template. Make the changes, then click Change Template.

Remember to save the layout to save any changes to templates for the current layout.

To transfer templates SureTrak stores up to 25 activity box templates for each layout. You can use templates stored in another layout by copying and pasting them to and from the Clipboard. You must save the layout to save the transferred template.

1 Select the template you want to copy in the Modify Template dialog box, then press Ctrl+C to copy it to the Clipboard.

2 Close the current layout and open the layout where you want to paste the template.

3 Open the Modify Template dialog box and click in the template area. Press Ctrl+V to paste the template. SureTrak does not overwrite the displayed template.

4 Specify a name in the Name field, then click Add Template to add the template to the current layout.

Choosing Resource/Cost and Log Content Items

You can choose from several resource/cost data items to display for each activity, such as resource name, description, actuals to date, units per hour, and quantity to complete. For activities with multiple resource assignments, the resource names and descriptions are separated by commas and quantity and cost values are totaled.

For more information about log text data items, see the *Adding Activities* chapter.

Log text data items are cells that contain free-form text notes about activities that you record in the Activity columns of the Bar chart. These notes can also be displayed in PERT activity boxes. Select Log Text (1-10) to show individual log text cells or select Log Record to combine all 10 logs stacked in one cell. Be sure to size the cell so that it's long enough to fit all log records.

Organizing Activities in PERT

 You can arrange activities in the PERT view so they are grouped according to a common value, such as department, responsibility, or phase. Choose Format, Organize in the PERT view to specify grouping options.

Use these fields to organize activities in PERT.

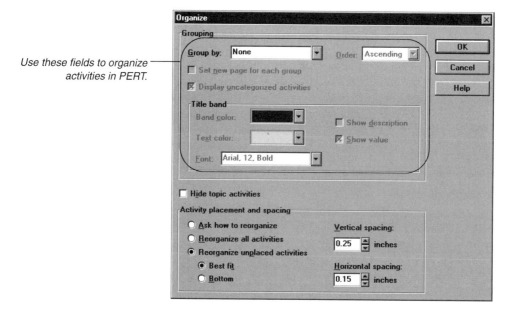

To group activities

1 Click ▼ in the Group By field in the Organize dialog box and select how you want to group the activities from the drop-down list.

You can organize by activity code, Activity ID code, calendar ID, or total float.

2 In the Order field, specify whether the activities should be in ascending or descending order.

The default sort order is ascending.

3 Mark the Set New Page For Each Group checkbox to print each group of activities on a separate page.

4 To display uncategorized activities, mark the Display Uncategorized Activities checkbox.

To customize group title bands

1 In the Title Band section, specify the band color, text color, and font.

2 In the Show Description and Show Value fields, mark the checkboxes to show activity code descriptions, values, or both in the title band.

To reorganize activities at any time, choose Format, Reorganize Now.

To turn off grouping

1 Select <None> in the Group By field.

2 Click OK.

SureTrak arranges activities based on schedule logic.

Choose to group by system in the Organize dialog box.

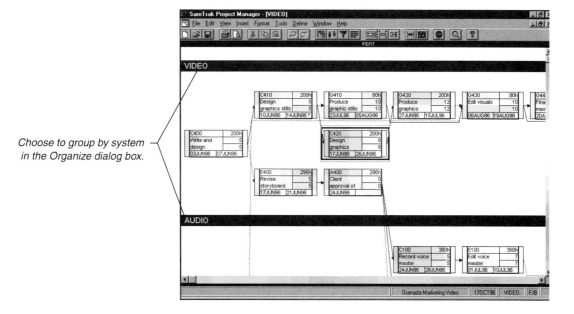

For details on grouping, see the *Organizing and Summarizing Activities* chapter.

Controlling Activity Placement and Spacing

You can add space between activities to widen the network, or reduce space to see more activities per page.

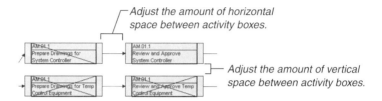

Adjust the amount of horizontal space between activity boxes.

Adjust the amount of vertical space between activity boxes.

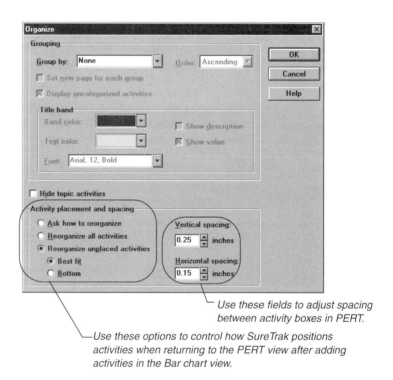

Use these fields to adjust spacing between activity boxes in PERT.

Use these options to control how SureTrak positions activities when returning to the PERT view after adding activities in the Bar chart view.

To adjust space between activity boxes Type new measurements in the Vertical and Horizontal Spacing fields. Adding space between activities widens the network; reducing space shows more activities per page. Click OK.

Placing new activities When you add activities in the PERT view and switch to the Bar chart view, SureTrak places the activities in the appropriate rows, based on the current sort and group settings defined in the Organize dialog box.

If the Bar chart view is set to reorganize automatically, SureTrak reorganizes the Bar chart view when you switch from the PERT view after adding activities. SureTrak positions new activities in the appropriate rows, based on the current sort and group criteria.

When you add activities in the Bar chart view, then switch to the PERT view, SureTrak rearranges all activities in the PERT view and places the new activities based on their relationships. SureTrak positions activities without relationships at the bottom of the network. If activities are organized into groups in the PERT view, SureTrak places the new activities within the appropriate group.

If you do not want SureTrak to rearrange all activities when moving to the PERT view, you can have SureTrak place only the new activities, or ask how to rearrange activities. Choose Format, Organize to set the arrangement options for the PERT view.

Choose Reorganize Unplaced Activities to have SureTrak position only new activities. Choose Best Fit to have SureTrak place new activities to the right (or in the first empty spot) of the right-most predecessor. If a new activity has no predecessor, SureTrak places it to the left of the leftmost successor. Choose Bottom to have SureTrak place new activities at the bottom of the network.

Choose Ask How To Reorganize to have SureTrak ask you to choose a method for arranging activities when moving to the PERT view.

Customizing SureTrak's Default Options

When you install SureTrak, the Setup program establishes a number of defaults that affect the appearance and function of the project window. You can change these defaults so that SureTrak operates the way you want it to. For example, specify the date format you prefer to use in all new projects, or the frequency with which SureTrak automatically saves your projects.

Some options you specify apply to all projects you open, whether they are new or existing projects. Others are project-specific.

Ideally, you should set default options before the start of a project; however, you can reset options at any time.

Setting Up Project Options

When you create a new project, define the project's default duration, duration style, and the default activity types in the Options dialog box. SureTrak enables you to set default project options for all new projects even when no projects are open. To set project options, choose Tools, Options and click the Project tab.

To set options for all new projects, set the options when no project is open. To set options for a specific project, open the project before setting the options.

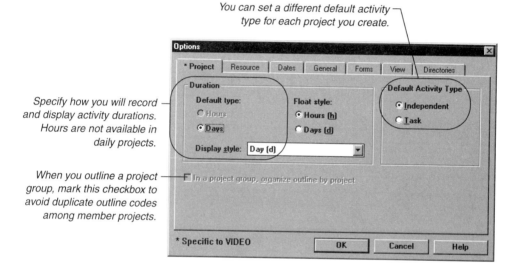

You can set a different default activity type for each project you create.

Specify how you will record and display activity durations. Hours are not available in daily projects.

When you outline a project group, mark this checkbox to avoid duplicate outline codes among member projects.

 Some options you specify in the Options dialog box apply only to the current project; others apply to all projects. When a tab or a section of a dialog is marked with an asterisk, the footnote indicates how SureTrak applies the option. If no projects are open, an asterisk indicates that it is specific to all new projects.

Defining duration default type and display style Each project has its own default duration and duration style settings. The default duration determines how SureTrak interprets a duration you type without specifying days or hours. For example, if you type 10, SureTrak assumes you mean 10 hours if you specify hours as the default duration.

For details on defining default activity duration, see *Setting Activity Defaults* later in the chapter.

The duration style determines how SureTrak displays durations. SureTrak can display durations as a combination of weeks, days, and hours, such as 2w4d3h. If you choose not to show weeks, this duration is 14d3h. SureTrak refers to the global calendar to determine how many days are in one workweek. If you choose hours, this duration is 115h.

Defining float style The float style determines how SureTrak displays total and free float amounts. SureTrak can show float in whole days or in hours.

Setting a project to day-long durations SureTrak always stores durations in hours, so you can switch back and forth between hours and days in a project at any time without losing precision. You're only controlling the default duration for display: if you choose hours, you can still specify a duration of 3d for 3 days; if you choose days, you can still specify an hourly duration such as 15h, but SureTrak rounds the duration to the nearest whole day, assuming 8 hours per day. For example, if you specify 30h, SureTrak rounds the duration to 4 days.

For more information about activity types, see the *Adding Activities* chapter.

Setting the default activity type If most of the activities you enter are task activities, change the default activity type from independent to task.

Setting Up Resource Options

When you create a new project, define the project's Autocost information along with other resource options in the Options dialog box.

To set up resource options Choose Tools, Options and click the Resource tab.

When a tab or a section of a dialog is marked with an asterisk, the footnote tells whether the option applies to all projects or only the current project.

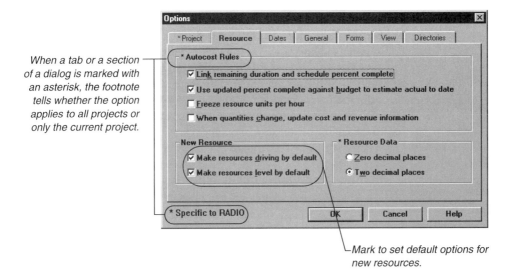

Mark to set default options for new resources.

Setting Autocost rules Autocost, SureTrak's automatic resource and cost statusing feature, is a shortcut for project statusing. For example, the first rule links remaining duration and percent complete so that SureTrak updates percent complete when you change an activity's remaining duration; or SureTrak updates the remaining duration when you revise the percent complete. The updated percent complete can, in turn, be used to automatically status resource and cost data. Set Autocost rules for all projects or set them individually for each project.

For detailed information about each Autocost rule, see the Updating Resources and Costs *chapter.*

To define a set of rules to apply to new projects, choose Tools, Options, then click the Resource tab before you open a project; to set up rules for a specific project, open the project and choose Tools, Options, then click the Resource tab. You should establish a standard set of rules at the beginning of a project and keep them consistent throughout its duration.

Displaying decimals in resource and cost data SureTrak enables you to show resource, cost, and revenue values to two decimal places or with no decimal places (rounded to whole values). You can use a different setting for each project.

After a project has started, if you switch from showing amounts with decimal places to showing amounts without decimal places, SureTrak rounds the amounts to the nearest whole number. If you subsequently change the option to show decimals again, the original accuracy is lost.

Configuring the Date Format

Configure SureTrak to accept your input and to display dates using any date format you choose. The configuration applies to the current project and you can change these options at any time. If you set options in the Dates tab before you open a project, the options become the default settings in all new projects.

To configure the date and time formats Choose Tools, Options, then click the Dates tab.

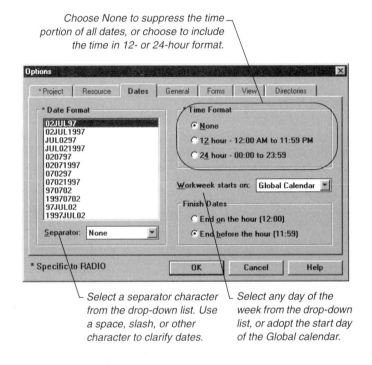

Choose None to suppress the time portion of all dates, or choose to include the time in 12- or 24-hour format.

Select a separator character from the drop-down list. Use a space, slash, or other character to clarify dates.

Select any day of the week from the drop-down list, or adopt the start day of the Global calendar.

Setting Activity Defaults

Defining the default activity duration When you add an activity, SureTrak assigns it a default duration that you can specify in the General tab of the Options dialog box. Although SureTrak can display durations in hours, days, weeks, or a combination of these units, specify the default duration in hours. For example, a default duration of 24 will apply a duration of 3 days to new activities as you add them. Depending on your setting in the Display Style field in the Project tab, SureTrak displays the 3 day duration as 24 hours or 3 days.

Choose Tools, Options and click the General tab to set these defaults.

SureTrak can display an 8-hour default duration using any of several display styles.

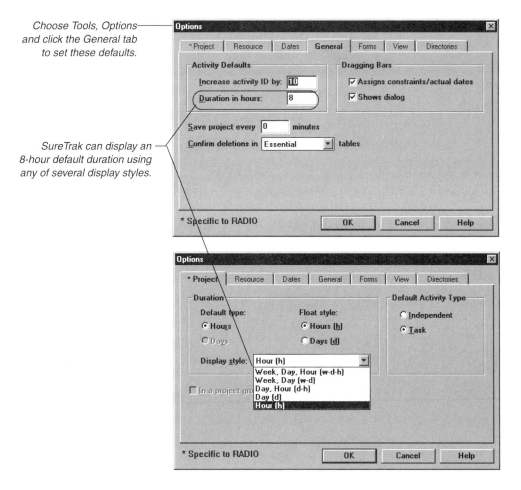

For information on defining the default duration type, see *Setting Up Project Options* earlier in this chapter.

Setting the automatic Activity ID Increment SureTrak assigns the ID number 1000 to the first activity you add, and increments each new Activity ID by the number you specify. If an activity with the next ID already exists, SureTrak skips to the next regular increment. Choose Tools, Options, then click the General tab.

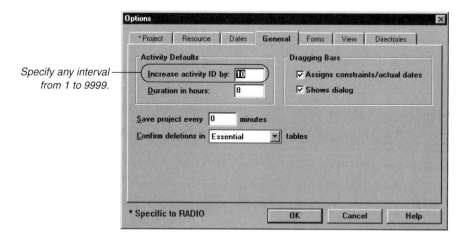

Specify any interval from 1 to 9999.

SureTrak follows the Activity ID pattern you establish. For example, if you number an activity 1040A and the increment value is 10, the next Activity IDs will be 1040A10, 1040A20, and so forth. Edit any new Activity ID and SureTrak picks up the new pattern for the next ID it provides.

Automatically Saving Projects

Minimize the possibility of lost work due to a power outage or other unforeseen shutdown by saving the project periodically. Specify the time interval and SureTrak saves the project automatically. Remember that SureTrak does not store your data permanently until you save it, either manually (by choosing File, Save) or automatically.

To specify when SureTrak saves projects Choose Tools, Options, then click the General tab.

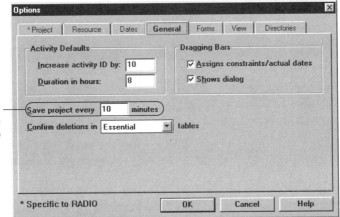

When set as shown, in the event of a power outage you can lose, at most, the last 10 minutes of data you entered.

Working with "What-If" Scenarios

While you try various "what-if" scenarios to optimize your schedule, turn off automatic save by specifying 0 in the Save Every __ Minutes field. With automatic save disabled, you can close (without saving) and reopen the project as often as you like without permanently affecting any data.

Confirming Deletions

Use caution when deleting data. Some data items, such as activity descriptions, do not affect other data and can easily be re-entered. Other deletions can affect calculations or can require significant work to replicate. SureTrak enables you to specify when you want to be prompted to confirm data deletions.

To specify confirmations when deleting data Choose Tools, Options to open the Options dialog box, then click the General tab.

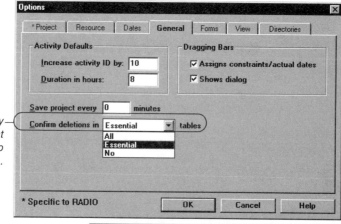

Select Essential to only confirm deletions of data that would be time-consuming to recreate. For example...

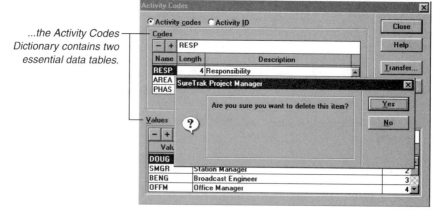

...the Activity Codes Dictionary contains two essential data tables.

Setting Constraints Options

SureTrak assigns constraints or actual dates when you drag an activity bar before or after the data date in the Bar chart view. You can have SureTrak not assign constraints or actual dates by clearing the Assign Constraints/ Actual Dates checkbox in the General tab of the Options dialog box.

Mark this checkbox to show a constraint or actual dates reminder message whenever you drag an activity bar.

For detailed information about assigning constraints or actual dates, see the *Creating and Fine-Tuning the Project Schedule* chapter.

Setting Activity Form Defaults

Using the Activity form is a convenient way to add project data, as all data fields are conveniently located and visible regardless of the layout you are using. SureTrak always opens the Activity form when you add an activity in the PERT view. You can control whether or not SureTrak opens the Activity form when adding activities in the Bar chart view.

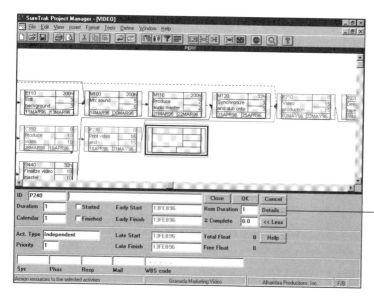

Click to display detail forms, such as Constraints, Dates, and Resources.

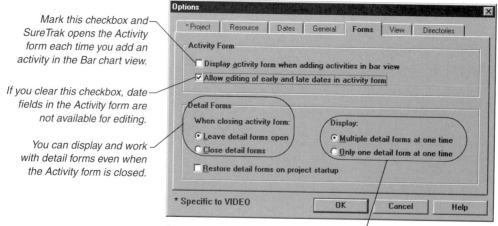

Mark this checkbox and SureTrak opens the Activity form each time you add an activity in the Bar chart view.

If you clear this checkbox, date fields in the Activity form are not available for editing.

You can display and work with detail forms even when the Activity form is closed.

To prevent hiding onscreen data, choose to display only one detail form at a time. Or, display multiple forms at once.

Setting the View Options

Options on the View tab control the appearance of activity codes in the Bar chart and PERT views as well as the display of other elements.

To configure the view options Choose Tools, Options to open the dialog box, then click the View tab.

Mark to include a thousands separator in numbers larger than three digits.

Mark to display the startup screen when you open SureTrak.

Clear to hide the status bar.

Choose whether to display activity codes as names or descriptions in the Activity columns, on bars, or in PERT activity boxes.

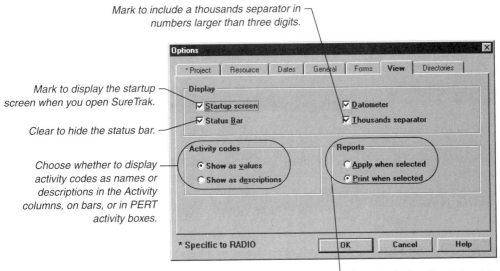

Control whether SureTrak prints or applies the selected report when you choose a report in the Run Reports menu or double-click a report in the Reports dialog box.

Configuring additional view options SureTrak's data displays are very flexible. For example, you can choose to show or hide the Datometer and status bar; show or hide thousands separators in numbers; and print or display defined reports when you select them. You can also choose to show activity codes as values or descriptions in the Bar chart and PERT views.

 If you add an activity code description column (choose Format, Columns) in the Bar chart and you choose to show activity codes as descriptions in the Options dialog box, the fields in the column are non-editable.

Defining User Information

Directory and user information options relate to all projects. In the Directories tab in the Options dialog box, users at each workstation can edit these settings to show their name and organizational affiliation. This information appears in the Help About SureTrak window only, and has no bearing on report headers or footers.

Setting default directories Configure SureTrak to find project files, layouts, and templates in any directory of your system. In a network environment, SureTrak stores these preferences separately for each workstation. You can change these paths at any time, and SureTrak uses the new settings immediately.

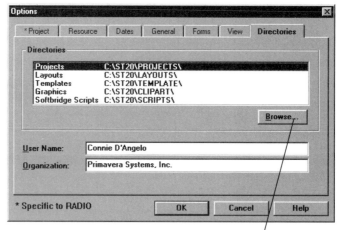

Click Browse to locate the appropriate drive,
directory, or to map to a network drive.

Customizing the Custom Tools Menu

SureTrak is delivered with custom tools that perform common functions: globally changing data, creating recurring activities, defining the default activity duration, and updating the data dictionary. You can use Basic scripts to define additional custom tools to perform SureTrak functions or start other programs from within SureTrak. Add your new tools to the Custom Tools menu.

To define a new custom tool Choose Tools, Basic Scripts; select the directory where your Basic scripts are stored and select the Basic executable titled ADDTOOL.SBX; then click Run. You can also change the hotkeys used to start tools; change the position of tools in the list; modify existing tools; or remove tools from the list.

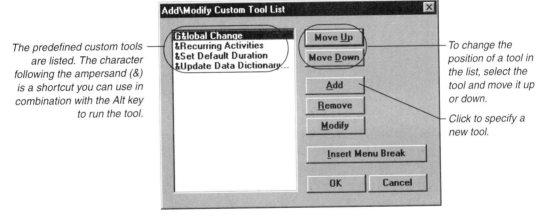

The predefined custom tools are listed. The character following the ampersand (&) is a shortcut you can use in combination with the Alt key to run the tool.

To change the position of a tool in the list, select the tool and move it up or down.

Click to specify a new tool.

A new custom tool can be an SBL script or executable, or a command to run any executable program on your system.

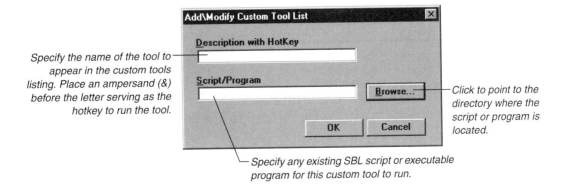

Specify the name of the tool to appear in the custom tools listing. Place an ampersand (&) before the letter serving as the hotkey to run the tool.

Click to point to the directory where the script or program is located.

Specify any existing SBL script or executable program for this custom tool to run.

Configuring Toolbars

The Bar chart view provides two toolbars: a main toolbar and an editing toolbar, while the PERT view has just the main toolbar. If you have a mouse, you can click the icons on the toolbars to perform most menu-driven tasks. You can open, save, and print projects; open dialog boxes; cut, copy, and paste activities; and find, select, collapse, and expand activities. For example, you can quickly create a new project by clicking the New Project icon, instead of choosing File, New.

To display or hide toolbars You can display one, both, or neither toolbar. Choose View, Toolbar or View, Editing Toolbar (Bar chart view only) to toggle the main or editing toolbar displays on or off.

To configure a toolbar Choose Tools, Customize, Toolbar to open the Toolbar dialog box, or Tools, Customize, Editing Toolbar to open the Editing Toolbar dialog box (Bar chart view only).

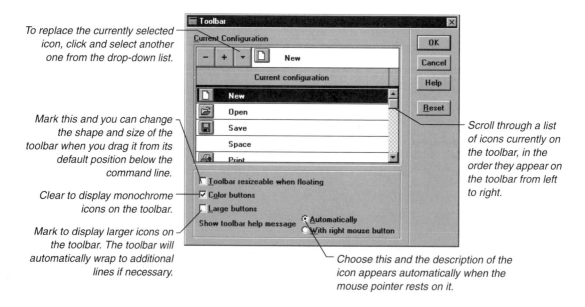

To replace the currently selected icon, click and select another one from the drop-down list.

Mark this and you can change the shape and size of the toolbar when you drag it from its default position below the command line.

Clear to display monochrome icons on the toolbar.

Mark to display larger icons on the toolbar. The toolbar will automatically wrap to additional lines if necessary.

Scroll through a list of icons currently on the toolbar, in the order they appear on the toolbar from left to right.

Choose this and the description of the icon appears automatically when the mouse pointer rests on it.

To move a toolbar around the layout Click any empty space on the toolbar (between icons or at the end of the row) and drag the toolbar to any area of the layout. Drag it to the left, right, top, or bottom edge of the layout and the toolbar jumps to that edge. Drag it anywhere in the middle of the screen and the toolbar becomes a rectangle of icons. If you mark the Toolbar Resizeable When Floating checkbox, you can resize and reshape the rectangle.

The editing toolbar appears below the main toolbar on the Bar chart view. Like the main toolbar, you can reposition it anywhere on the layout.

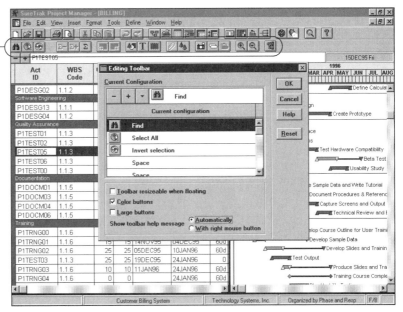

To insert an icon anywhere on the toolbar In the scrolling list of icons, select the icon before which you want to insert the new icon. Click ⊞ to insert a row for the new item; click ⊡ to view a drop-down list of available icons; click the new icon to select it and add it to the toolbar.

To remove an icon from a toolbar In the scrolling list of icons, select the icon and click ⊟.

To replace an icon on a toolbar In the scrolling list of icons, select the icon you want to replace. Click ⊡ to view the drop-down list of available icons and select the new icon.

To reset a toolbar to its default settings Click Reset.

Using the Status Bar

The status bar along the bottom of the SureTrak window contains messages from SureTrak, information about the currently highlighted activity, and information about the active project.

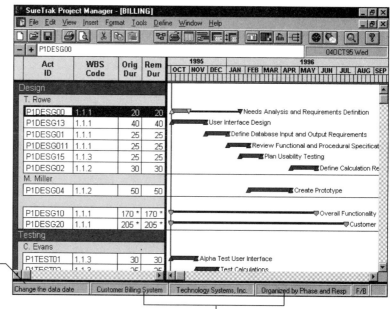

Messages from SureTrak about the current cursor function such as "Change the data date."

These three boxes display project data that you specify, such as the project title, company name, and layout description.

The fifth box indicates the scheduling setting: F/B indicates forward and backward passes, FWD indicates forward pass only, and OFF indicates no automatic scheduling.

The rightmost box on the status bar indicates the leveling setting: LEV indicates leveling is on, and a blank field indicates leveling is off.

To display or hide the status bar Choose Tools, Options, click the View tab, and mark the Status Bar checkbox.

To configure the status bar Double-click anywhere on the status bar to open the Status Bar dialog box, or choose Tools, Customize, Status Bar.

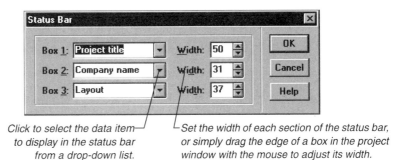

Click to select the data item to display in the status bar from a drop-down list.

Set the width of each section of the status bar, or simply drag the edge of a box in the project window with the mouse to adjust its width.

Choosing the Default Language

SureTrak makes working in a multilingual, international environment easier by enabling you to change the language in which SureTrak presents its output and printable onscreen text (excluding user-input text) and to access international date separators. This enables you to produce more easily understood reports for colleagues in other countries.

You can select a language in which SureTrak presents default text, such as Activity column titles, by using the Set Language feature. This feature enables users to use the same language for user-entered project data and SureTrak's own text. You cannot edit text translated into the selected language. You also cannot edit month names on the timescale and in columns, text for the Bar chart, PERT, or resource legends, or header and footer data items.

You can edit translated column-title text; however, edited text will not be translated again if you select a different language later.

To change the default text language setting Choose Tools, Customize, Set Language; select one of the many languages available; click OK.

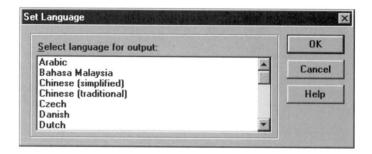

 Data you type into SureTrak are unaffected by the language selection.

Fonts for non-Latin characters Some languages use characters that are not in the standard English ANSI character set. To change the default-text language to one that contains non-Latin characters, use a localized version of Windows with fonts for that language. Without these special fonts, some text in SureTrak may be unrecognizable.

International date separators You can configure SureTrak to display dates using the format and separators you specify in the International Date Format setting in the Windows Control Panel.

1 In SureTrak, choose Tools, Options, and click the Dates tab.

2 Select Intl Settings from the Separators drop-down list.

3 Click OK.

SureTrak configures dates according to the current country and date format settings in the Windows Control Panel.

Using SureTrak's Language Features

You may need to share project information with other organizations around the world. For example, suppose you enter into a joint venture agreement with a German company to complete a project. You will occasionally need to print reports for both the German company and your own management. Using Set Language and report options, you can quickly meet both needs.

Use a Log Text field to enter the translation for the German activity descriptions; this enables you to display descriptions in both languages. Then, create separate reports (reports include layouts, filters, and page options) for the English report, the German report, and a combined English/German report, if necessary. Because Set Language controls the language in which header and footer text is displayed, you can customize

report output for each target audience.

Before printing the German report, apply the layout that contains the log text with the translated activity descriptions. Use Set Language to switch SureTrak's default text from English to German. To set the date display to the German format, specify Intl Settings in the Separator field in the Dates tab of the Options dialog box (choose Tools, Options); in the Windows Control Panel's Regional Settings dialog box, specify the country as Germany.

Before printing the English report, apply a layout that contains the regular Activity Description data item. Use Set Language to return the SureTrak default text to English. Configure the date display as you want it to appear.

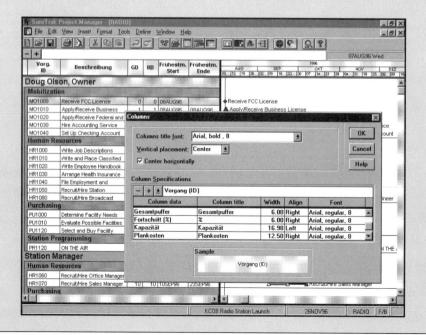

Choosing the Default Font

You can choose a default font for most text in your SureTrak project and change fonts for specific data items that you want to emphasize. Specify the font, font style, and point size of new text items. All new text you type uses these settings unless you specifically choose different settings for an item. For example, you can specify non-default font settings for the Activity column headings by defining them in the Columns dialog box.

To specify the default font Choose Tools, Customize, Default Font.

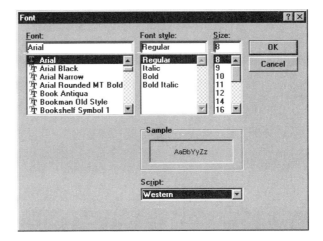

Creating and Printing Layouts and Reports

In this part: *Using SureTrak Layouts*

Creating SureTrak Reports

Publishing Reports on the World Wide Web

Printing Project Information

This part discusses the different ways you can use and customize layouts and reports in SureTrak to sharpen the content and appearance of your project presentations. A layout displays a set of activities that is defined by a filter. It also includes visual elements of the project, such as the format of activity bars, columns or activity boxes, and the organization of activities and screen colors. SureTrak reports are pre-formatted, yet flexible enough to be modified to meet your project requirements.

Use SureTrak's Web Publishing Wizard to guide you through the steps of publishing reports on a Web page that can be accessed by any project participant, local or remote, through an office network or the Internet.

This part also discusses how to create output using a printer or plotter supported by Windows.

Using SureTrak Layouts

Customizable layouts and reports offer you complete control over the appearance of onscreen displays and printed reports. You can use your customized layouts and reports with any of your projects, so you can spend more time managing projects instead of repeatedly preparing the same display or report.

This chapter discusses using and modifying SureTrak's default layouts, and creating your own.

What Are Layouts?

You can customize nearly any part of the SureTrak Bar chart and PERT views to show different aspects of a project. For example, you can format columns and bars to meet your specific needs. Select from a list of schedule, resource, cost, and coding items to tailor activity information. Modify the size, endpoints, colors, and schedule dates on bars in the Bar chart and activities in PERT. Organize project information by grouping activities by meaningful codes, such as department or responsibility.

When you customize the Bar chart or PERT view by modifying items such as columns, colors, shapes, fonts, activity selection, and by grouping, you are creating a layout. A layout is one view of project data. You can define an unlimited number of layouts for a project. For example, you can create a layout just for updating schedule data and another for analyzing resources and costs with your own set of color and font choices. Your managers may want to view only summary information, using the colors they specify. You can save layout specifications. Once you create and fine-tune them, you can use them again with any project.

SureTrak comes with a number of useful layouts. You can use these layouts, modify them, or invent your own.

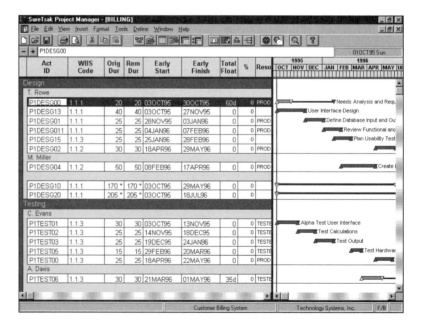

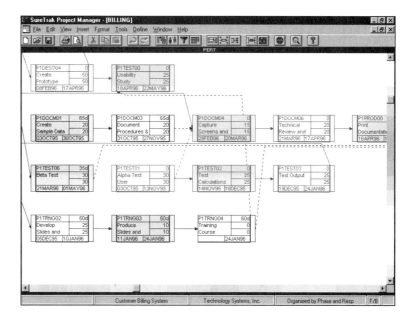

 SureTrak stores the layout created for each new project in a file that has the same name as the project, with a .LAY (layout) extension. To use one of your own layouts for this default layout instead of SureTrak's, create the layout and use Windows File Manager or Explorer to copy this .LAY file to the SureTrak program directory, then rename it TEMPLATE.LAY.

For information about reports, see the *Creating SureTrak Reports* chapter.

How layouts and reports relate Reports build on layouts by adding a filter and a set of page options. You can save and apply reports to any project. You can print a single report or a series of reports—an invaluable time-saver if you use the same kinds of reports several times during a project or from project to project.

For easy access to reports you use frequently, add them as menu items in the Run Reports menu.

A report and its layout control the content and layout of the current project window. When you change any part of the project window, SureTrak makes those same changes to the layout and report currently controlling the project window. This means that even when you print directly from the project window, without choosing a report, you're using a report.

Using SureTrak's template layout When you create a project, SureTrak creates a layout using template settings for the Activity columns, Bar chart, PERT view, Resource profile/table, project window colors, sight lines, row height, relationship lines, and organization. SureTrak applies any formatting changes you make to this starting layout, which has the same name as the project.

Using SureTrak's Predefined Layouts

In addition to the template layout that SureTrak creates when you add a new project, SureTrak includes a set of layouts which you can use for different project scenarios. For example, use the Outline layout when you want to outline a project. You can modify or delete these layouts, or create your own.

Use any layout with any project—if you create a layout for one project, you can apply that layout to any other project. Use the Layout Control dialog box to apply a layout other than the current one.

Predefined layouts The following table describes the layouts, in addition to the template layout, that are supplied with SureTrak.

SureTrak Layout	Description
2LEVEL	Activities organized by phase and responsibility
AREA	Activities organized by area
BUDGET	Budgeted costs
DAY	Activities organized by day
EARNED	Earned value: BCWP (percent complete x budgeted cost)
GANTT	Classic Gantt chart
HOUR	Activities organized by hour
HPGL	Formatted for HP/GL export
LEVEL	Early dates and leveled dates
LOG	Log text fields displayed in 10 columns
MONTH	Activities organized by month
OUTLINE	Activities organized by outline to five levels
PERT1	PERT Organized by Phase
PERT2	PERT logic review
PERT3	PERT cosmic view
PHAS	Activities organized by phase
PRED	Activities organized by predecessor
QUARTER	Activities organized by quarter
RECUR	Organized by Outline
RES1	Organized by resource, shows quantities
RES2	Organized by resource, shows costs

SureTrak Layout	Description
RES3	Organized by resource, shows revenues
RES4	Organized by resource, shows earned value
RESCOMP	Comparing Resource Assignments
RESP	Activities organized by responsibility
REVENUE	Revenues
SORT1	Activities sorted by early start and then total float
SORT2	Activities sorted by total float and then early start
SORT3	Activities sorted by late start and then total float
SORT4	Activities sorted by Activity ID
SUCC	Activities organized by successor
SUMMARY1	Activities summarized by responsibility (one bar per band)
SUMMARY2	Activities summarized by phase (one bar per band)
SUMMARY3	Activities summarized by area (one bar per band)
SUMMARY4	Activities summarized by responsibility and phase (one bar per band)
SUMMARY5	Activities summarized by area (individual bars)
SUMMARY6	Activities summarized by phase (individual bars)
SUMMARY7	Activities summarized by responsibility (individual bars)
SUMMARY8	Activities summarized by responsibility and phase (individual bars)
SUMMARY9	Activities summarized for entire project (individual bars)
TARGET	Current vs. target layout
TURN	Collect updating information for turnaround reports
UPDR	Organized by resource for updating
WBS	Activities organized by top four levels of WBS code
WEEK	Activities organized by week
YEAR	Activities organized by year

Working with Layouts

Layouts contain formatting specifications that you set up in several different dialog boxes. You can open these dialog boxes by using the icons on the toolbar or in the Layouts dialog box, or by using menu commands. Regardless of how you open the dialog boxes, SureTrak applies any changes you make to the current layout. When you change a layout, you must save the changes or SureTrak discards them.

For example, if you are using the SORT4 layout in the Bar chart view and you change the row height and screen colors, those changes become part of the SORT4 layout; the next time you apply the SORT4 layout to this or any other project, it will have the changed row height and screen colors.

Each layout has one description but includes a Bar chart aspect and a PERT aspect. You may want to create layouts that focus on either a Bar chart or PERT view and name them with meaningful descriptions, such as "Bar chart organized by RESP", or "PERT view showing WBS codes".

 If you add a new Bar chart layout, its PERT component is copied from the last applied layout; if you add a new PERT layout, its Bar chart component is copied from the last applied layout.

For more information about customizing layouts, see the *Customizing the Bar Chart View* and *Customizing the PERT View* chapters.

Layouts do not control the position of split bars, the presence of the Activity form or any detail forms, the locations of the toolbars, the presence of the page-break ruler, or the arrangement of multiple, open project windows. Layouts also do not control the presence of either toolbar, the status bar, Datometer, or legends. Control the toolbars from the View menu; to control the status bar and Datometer, choose Tools, Options, and click the View tab.

To open a layout Choose View, Layouts. The Layouts dialog box provides quick access to all aspects of the layout format. You can change a layout and apply the changes to the project window immediately, or change and save a layout without applying the changes to the current project window.

Double-click the layout you want to apply, or select the layout and click Apply.

Layouts open in the mode from which they were last saved: Bar chart or PERT view.

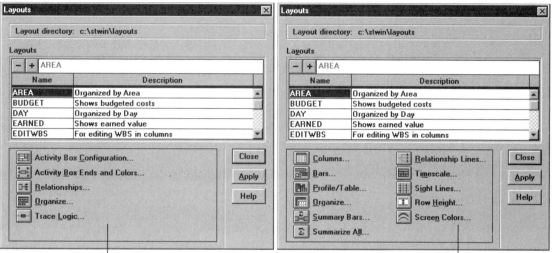

The icons available in the Layouts dialog box are different for the Bar chart and PERT views. The Bar chart Layouts dialog box contains icons for customizing the Bar chart view while the PERT Layouts dialog box displays icons for customizing the PERT view.

Saving changes to the current layout Choose File, Save to save any changes you have made to the project, including layout changes. If you make any change to the layout currently in use and then open another layout, SureTrak prompts you to save or abandon the changes to the current layout before opening the new layout.

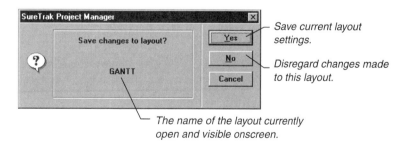

Save current layout settings.

Disregard changes made to this layout.

The name of the layout currently open and visible onscreen.

To create a new layout

1 Choose View, Layouts.

2 Select the layout you want to use as the basis for a new layout.

3 Click ⊞.

4 In the Name cell, type a name for the new layout and click ☑.

5 In the Description cell, type a description for the new layout, then click ☑.

6 Use the icons at the bottom of the Layouts dialog box to change any layout element.

7 Click Apply to apply the layout to the current project and close the Layouts dialog box, or click Close to close the Layouts dialog box and save the new layout without applying it.

To customize an existing layout

1 Choose View, Layouts.

2 Select a layout other than the current layout.

When you open the Layouts dialog box, the name of the current layout appears in parentheses.

3 In the bottom half of the dialog box, click the icon for the layout element you want to change.

Make any changes, then click OK to close the icon's dialog box.

4 Click Close to save the changes to the layout and close the Layouts dialog box without applying the changed layout.

Click Apply to save the changes to the layout, close the Layouts dialog box, and apply the new layout.

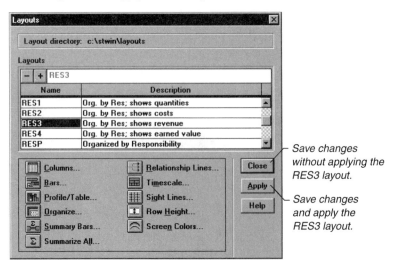

To delete a layout

1 Choose View, Layouts to open the Layouts dialog box.

2 Select the layout to delete and click ▣.

   If you delete the current layout, SureTrak prompts you to verify the deletion.

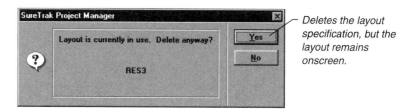

   Deletes the layout specification, but the layout remains onscreen.

3 Click Close.

Working With Read-Only Layouts

If you are working with a project that has a Read-Only layout applied, you can save any changes you've made to the layout under a different name. This feature prevents overwriting shared layouts on a network or accidentally altering individual layouts.

When you try to save a project while using a Read-Only layout, SureTrak displays a message asking whether you want to save the layout under a different name.

Choose Don't Save Changes To The Layout to save only the project and its data; any changes made to the layout will be lost.

Choose Save The Layout to a Different Name and type a new name for the layout to save the project data and the old layout under their original names, and the changed layout under the new name, with Read-Write accessibility.

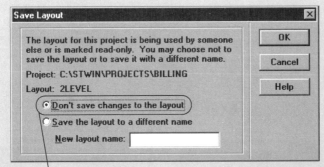

The default setting discards your changes to the layout. To save your changes, choose to save the layout using a different name; type a name using up to eight characters.

For details about assigning Read-Only access at the network or the system level, see your network administrator.

Using Color Schemes in Layouts

Color is an important component of every layout. Use colors to emphasize and differentiate elements of your layout. You can control background and text colors of a Bar chart's visual elements, including the Activity columns and column titles, selected-row highlights, timescales, Bar chart, Resource profile and table, the Progress Spotlight, activity bars and endpoints, grouping bands, and sight lines in the specific dialog boxes of the Format menu that control their display. In PERT views, you can control the colors of activity boxes, borders, text, connectors, relationship lines, and grouping bands.

Bar chart color schemes To assure a consistent use of colors in all of your SureTrak projects, use SureTrak color schemes. Define colors for all the fundamental Bar chart layout elements; select any of the predefined color schemes, or add and define your own. If you prefer, you can use your current Windows color scheme. Choose Format, Screen Colors to open the Screen Colors dialog box.

Add a new color scheme, or select one you don't use and delete it from the list.

Scroll through the alphabetical listing of available color schemes.

Right-click in any cell and select a color from the Colors palette. You can even define custom colors.

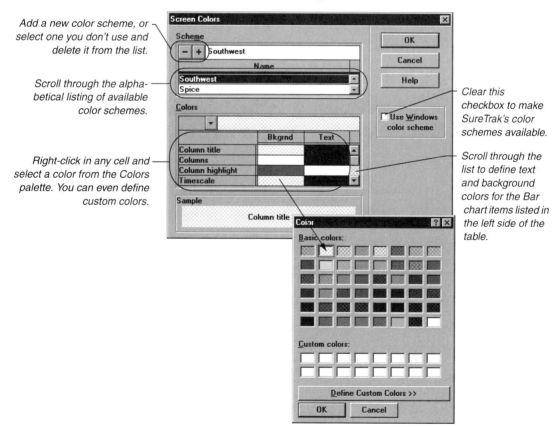

Clear this checkbox to make SureTrak's color schemes available.

Scroll through the list to define text and background colors for the Bar chart items listed in the left side of the table.

You can change a color scheme at any time, and the changes affect all projects using the scheme. You can create many color schemes and save them. Perhaps you want to use one set of colors for working with the project on your computer, another set when printing, or another when working with a laptop's monitor.

 Text colors must be solid colors supported by your video display. If you select a color for text that isn't a solid color, Windows uses the solid color closest to the color you selected. See your Windows user's guide for more information about how solid and nonsolid colors work with your video display.

To change the box ends and colors for all existing activities, choose Edit, Select All and then specify the colors you want to use.

PERT color schemes To specify the colors SureTrak uses for activity boxes in the PERT view, choose Format, Activity Box Ends and Colors. One specification applies to all selected activities, while another applies to activities yet to be created.

Click a tab to set specifications for existing selected activities, or for new activities.

Other elements of the PERT view can be customized in their relevant dialog boxes. For more information, see the *Customizing the PERT View* chapter.

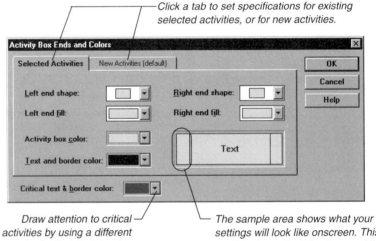

Draw attention to critical activities by using a different color for their text, border, and relationship lines.

The sample area shows what your settings will look like onscreen. This section shows the fill pattern and the shape for the left end area.

Creating SureTrak Reports

SureTrak provides specifications for over 40 commonly used reports, which you can use or adapt for any project.

Build reports by adding filters and page setup specifications to layouts. You can save and apply reports to any project. You can print a single report or a series of reports—an invaluable time-saver if you use the same kinds of reports several times during a project, or use the same reports in many projects.

For easy access to reports you use frequently, you can add them to the Run Report menu.

Reports SureTrak Provides

SureTrak includes several reports you can use with any project; they are listed in the Reports menu when you first install SureTrak. You can choose up to 20 reports—those supplied by SureTrak or those you create—to appear in the Run Report menu. Some reports are tabular, containing only information from the Activity columns; others combine the tabular information of the Activity columns with the graphical display of the Bar chart while others are specific to the PERT view. Some reports also include the Resource profile or Resource table. You can run reports not listed in the menu from the Reports dialog box.

The following report specifications come with SureTrak:

Report Name	Description
BUD1	Budgeted costs
BUD2	Revenues
BUD3	Earned value
BUD4	Positive net earnings
BUD5	Negative net earnings
GNT1	Classic Gantt chart
GNT2	Classic Gantt chart sorted by early start
GNT3	Classic Gantt chart sorted by total float
GNT4	Classic Gantt chart sorted by late start
GNT5	Classic Gantt chart sorted by ID
LST1	Daily to-do list
LST2	Weekly to-do list
LST3	Monthly to-do list
ORG1	Activities organized by responsibility
ORG2	Activities organized by area
ORG3	Activities organized by phase
ORG4	Activities organized by phase and responsibility
ORG5	Activities organized by predecessor
ORG6	Activities organized by successor

Report Name	Description
PRT1	PERT view
PRT2	PERT logic review
RES1	Activities organized by resources
RES2	Resource profile
RES3	Resource table
RES4	Resource costs
RES5	Resource revenue
RES6	Earned value
SCH1	Project schedule by early start
SCH2	Project schedule by total float
SCH3	Project schedule by late start
SCH4	Project schedule by Activity ID
SUM1	Activities summarized by responsibility
SUM2	Activities summarized by phase
SUM3	Activities summarized by area
SUM4	Activities summarized by phase and responsibility
SUM5	Timescaled logic diagram by area
SUM6	Timescaled logic diagram by phase
SUM7	Timescaled logic diagram by responsibility
SUM8	Timescaled logic diagram by phase and responsibility
SUM9	Project timescaled logic diagram
UPD1	Target comparison
UPD2	Update turnaround

To display reports in the Run Report menu Choose Tools, Reports. If you include a report in the Run Reports menu, you can print it simply by choosing it from the menu.

Double-click to toggle between Yes and No.
Specify Yes to have the report appear in the menu.

ID	Description	View	Layout	Filter	Series	Menu
	(RADIO1)	Current	RADIO1	All		No
BUD1	Budgeted costs	Current	BUDGET	All		Yes
BUD2	Revenues	Current	REVENUE	All		No
BUD3	Earned value	Current	EARNED	All		No
BUD4	Pos. net earnings	Current	REVENUE	NET+		No
BUD5	Neg. net earnings	Current	REVENUE	NET-		No
GNT1	Classic Gantt	Current	GANTT	All	A	No

Close
Help
Transfer...
Apply

Click Close to close the dialog box without changing the onscreen display, or click Apply to make the current layout use the selected report specification.

Layout Control...   Print...
Filter...   Run Series...
Page Setup...

Click any of these icons to open the corresponding dialog box.

Previewing a Report

To see the format and layout of a printed report without actually printing it, apply the report to the project window and view it in Print Preview.

To preview a report

1 Choose Tools, Reports to open the Reports dialog box and select the report you want to preview.

2 Click Apply.

   SureTrak applies the report to the project window and closes the dialog box.

For more information about using Print Preview, see the *Printing Project Information* chapter.

3 Choose File, Print Preview to switch to Print Preview mode.

4 Adjust the appearance of the report using the icons at the top of the Print Preview display.

5 Choose File, Project Window to return to the normal display, or choose File, Print to print the report.

To print several reports consecutively, see *Creating a Series of Reports* later in this chapter.

When you change the project window, you are also changing any layout and report you are using. For example, if you are using the SORT4 layout and change the row height and screen colors, those changes become part of the SORT4 layout and appear the next time you apply that layout to any project. Because the current report includes the current layout, changes to the layout also become part of the report.

You can make any change to a layout permanent. If you change a report in a way that affects the current layout, SureTrak prompts you to save or discard the changes to the layout when you close the project or open another layout.

Printing a Report

After creating and fine-tuning your project, you'll want to communicate project information to others. You can print any of SureTrak's reports or create your own.

To print a report from the Reports menu

1 Choose Tools, Run Report to open the Reports menu.

2 Select the report you want to print.

SureTrak opens the Print dialog box.

3 Specify the print range, print quality, and number of copies, and indicate whether you want to print to a file.

4 Click OK.

 If SureTrak does not list a report on the menu, or if you want to make changes to a report format, you can print it from the Reports dialog box.

To print a report from the Reports dialog box

1 Choose Tools, Reports to open the Reports dialog box.

2 Select the report you want to print.

3 Change any report element (layout, filter, or page options) by clicking the appropriate icon at the bottom of the dialog box.

For details about the Print dialog box, see the *Printing Project Information* chapter.

4 Click the Print icon to open the Print dialog box. Specify the printer, print range, print quality, copies, and other printing information.

5 Click OK.

Creating a Series of Reports

To save time, you can print one or more series of reports without loading each report individually. Define up to 26 series of reports; identify any report with a letter indicating the series it is a member of.

To create a series of reports

1 Choose Tools, Reports to open the Reports dialog box.

Decide which reports you want to include in the series.

2 In the Series column for each report, type the letter identifying the series (if any) to associate the report with.

3 Click Close.

 A report can belong to only one series. To make a report a member of more than one series, duplicate the report specification and assign a copy of it to each series. To duplicate a report, select a report and add a new specification; the new specification is a duplicate of the one currently selected.

To print one or several series of reports

1 Choose Tools, Run Report Series to open the Report Series dialog box.

Before printing a series of reports, check your printer or plotter to make sure enough paper is loaded to complete the printing task.

2 In the Series section, select the letters of the series you want to run.

To select more than one series to print, press Ctrl and click the letter for each series to include.

3 Click OK to open the Print dialog box; specify the printer, print range, print quality, copies, and other printing information.

4 Click OK.

Creating a Custom Report

The report specifications delivered with SureTrak cover a variety of commonly used reporting requirements. However, for the unique requirements of your project, you can create your own report specifications.

If you modify a layout or filter used in a report, the report automatically uses the modified layout or filter.

Use the Reports dialog box to define report specifications or to modify a predefined SureTrak report specification to match your reporting needs. A report specification consists of a layout, filter, and a set of page options. You can also specify whether the report is part of a series, and whether to include it in the Run Report menu. You can use the same layouts and filters for several reports.

To create a custom report Choose Tools, Reports.

1 Select a report that resembles the one you want to create, and click to add a new report.

2 Assign the report an ID of up to four characters, then click ☑.

3 Right-click in the View, Layout, and Filter columns to specify the view, layout, and filter on which to base the report. The view options are Current, Bar chart, and PERT.

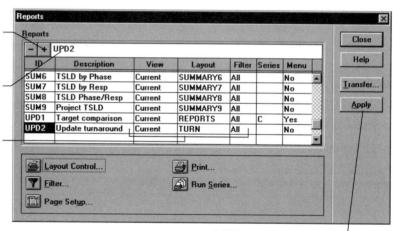

4 Click to apply the report's view, layout, and filter.

Double-click in the Menu column to toggle between Yes and No, determining whether the new report appears in the Run Reports menu.

For more information about the Page Setup dialog box, see the Printing Project Information *chapter.*

Click the Page Setup icon and specify the parts of the screen to print, the timespan and scale of the report, and the headers and footers. These page settings affect only printing and print preview; they do not affect the onscreen layout.

Customizing the Printed Report Page

When you click the Page Setup icon at the bottom of the Reports dialog box, SureTrak opens the Page Setup dialog box. Changes to these settings apply to the printed report only—not to the current project window.

Use the Page Setup dialog box to control the elements of the project window SureTrak prints. The elements differ for the Bar chart and PERT views.

Headers and footers can include a title; legends for the Bar chart, Resource profile, or PERT view; a logo, comments, revision boxes, and page numbers.

Use these elements to tailor and enhance the appearance of the printed report.

For details about the Page Setup dialog boxes, see the *Printing Project Information* chapter.

In the Bar chart view, include any of these elements in the report.

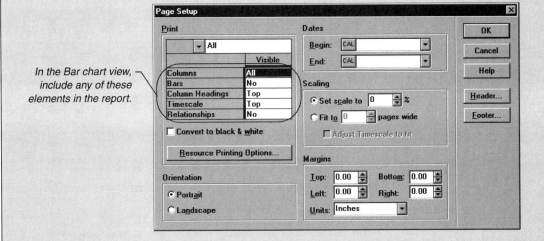

In the PERT view, choose to print the full layout or the Trace Logic view.

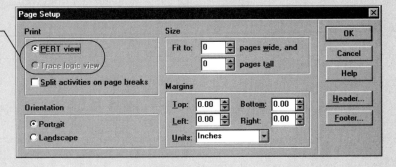

Transferring Reports from Other Projects

If you create reports in another SureTrak project that you want to use in the current project, you can transfer them. Choose to overwrite all reports in the current project with those of the project from which you're transferring reports, or update the current set of reports by adding reports with different names and replacing those with the same names.

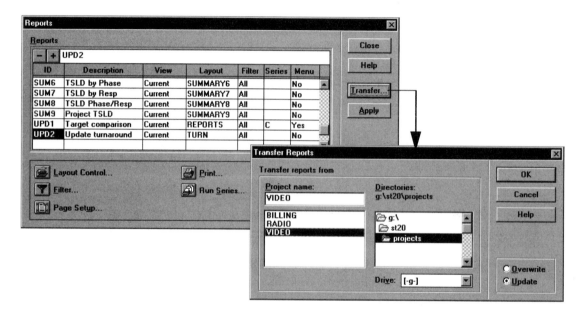

To transfer reports from other SureTrak projects

1 Choose Tools, Reports then click Transfer.

2 Specify the drive and directory of the project from which you want to transfer reports.

3 Select the name of the project from which you want to transfer reports.

   If the project you are looking for does not appear in the list below the Project Name field, make sure the drive and directory are correct.

4 Choose Overwrite or Update.

   Choosing Overwrite deletes all existing reports in the current project. Choosing Update adds only those reports whose names differ from those in the current project, and overwrites those having identical names. Reports in the current project with unique names are unaffected if you choose Update.

5 Click OK to confirm your decision to transfer reports.

6 SureTrak also asks whether you want to transfer filters with the reports. Click Yes to transfer filters.

You can customize any report by changing the layout, filter, or page options attached to it, or by creating new layouts and filters. In the Reports dialog box, click Layout or Filter to open the appropriate dialog box. When you make changes in the Layouts and Filter dialog boxes, you change the characteristics of the layout or filter wherever SureTrak uses them, with this or any other project.

Creating a Microsoft Excel Pivot Table Report

SureTrak enables you to transfer and present project information in a cross-tab report. Use the SureTrak Pivot Table Wizard to select project data items and insert them in an Excel pivot table. A pivot table enables you to move a worksheet's column and row headings around the main data to show different views for data analysis. It also enables you to quickly summarize a large amount of data using a customized structure and set of calculations.

SureTrak helps you create an Excel pivot table with the SureTrak Pivot Table Wizard. To create a pivot table, you specify the activity and resource data you want to include and how you want to organize it by choosing the fields you want to appear in the pivot table, and specifying whether the fields are column, row, page, or table data. SureTrak also enables you to break down a project's resource usage into rows, columns, or pages.

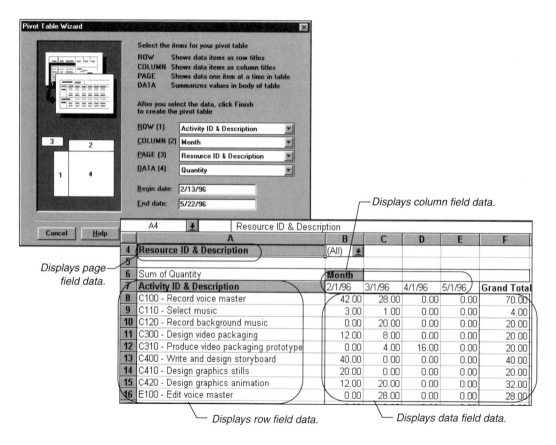

To create a pivot table using the Pivot Table Wizard Specify the data you want as column and row headings. Also specify the data you want summarized in the pivot table. When you specify a data item as a row, its values become the row headings. When you specify a data item as a column, its values become the column headings. If you specify a field as a page, you can view the field items one at a time on a single page.

1 Choose Tools, Wizards, Pivot Table Wizard. If you do not have a project open, the Pivot Table Wizard displays the Open Project dialog box. Select the project you want to open, then click OK.

2 In the Row, Column, and Page fields, select the data you want to display in the pivot table.

3 In the Data field, select the data item you want to display. If you select time-phased data in the Row, Column, or Page field, choose to display resource data, including budgeted cost for work schedule (BCWS), earned value, revenue, budget, net, costs, or quantity in the pivot table.

For more information about creating pivot tables using the Pivot Table Wizard, see the online help.

4 If you selected time-phased data in the Row, Column, or Page field, specify the date range in which the data should appear in the Begin Date and End Date fields.

5 Click Finish. The Wizard inserts the project information in an Excel pivot table. Depending on the size and complexity of your project, this operation may take a few minutes.

Publishing Reports on the World Wide Web

SureTrak's Web Publishing feature enables you to publish project information on the World Wide Web or on an office intranet for others to access.

Use the Primavera Web Publishing Wizard to guide you through the process of creating Web pages that contain the project information you specify. Once the pages are complete, you can transfer them to the Internet or place them on your intranet server. You can then access the information using any Web browser, such as Netscape Navigator.

This chapter describes how to create and revise documents for use on the World Wide Web.

Overview

Since most companies run multiple projects simultaneously, coordination is the key to achieving overall corporate objectives. Each project shares resources with other projects, its activities depend on the accomplishment of activities in other projects, and its information must be available to and shared by participants and management.

To facilitate communicating project data within a company with offices local or worldwide, you can create SureTrak reports in HyperText Markup Language (HTML) format using the Primavera Web Publishing Wizard, then place them on a central server—your office network, or the Internet.

By publishing project information on a central server, you can maintain a single copy of project reports, which administrators, management, or individual project managers can access at any time. Using the World Wide Web to disseminate information also supplies the most current project information to remote managers.

Creating a structure of HTML documents Primavera's Web Publishing Wizard creates a hierarchical structure of HTML pages based on the projects and reports you specify. These pages contain hypertext links, or jumps, to the other pages in the structure, enabling you to move between projects and reports and from page to page within a report.

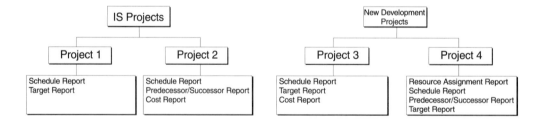

You need only set up the structure once, and then as the projects progress, use the Wizard to add new reports, remove outdated reports, or update existing ones with the latest data.

The first HTML page lists the project categories that have been defined, such as Development Projects, Construction Projects, Information System Projects, and so forth. Choose a category to display the list of projects, and overview information about each project it contains. Choose a project from this list to see the reports that are available. Choose a report to display an HTML page containing that information.

Viewing an HTML structure HTML is a platform-independent language, which means that pages do not have to be viewed using the same type of computer that generated them. Once a project manager has created an HTML structure, anyone can use an Internet browser to review HTML documents, whether they are downloaded from the World Wide Web or an office intranet.

A Cost Report Viewed Using a Web Browser

Using the Primavera Web Publishing Wizard The Wizard helps you designate document categories, choose projects from which to create Web documents, and choose reports to apply to the projects.

 If you did not install the Primavera Web Publishing Wizard when you installed SureTrak, the Web Publishing Wizard command on the Tools menu will be disabled. You can install the Primavera Web Publishing Wizard at any time by running the Setup program again and selecting the Primavera Web Wizard option.

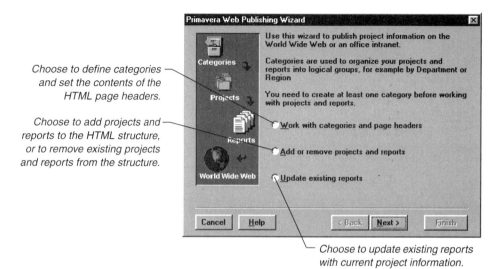

Choose to define categories and set the contents of the HTML page headers.

Choose to add projects and reports to the HTML structure, or to remove existing projects and reports from the structure.

Choose to update existing reports with current project information.

To create and maintain HTML reports using the Primavera Web Publishing Wizard

1 Define the structure of the projects by establishing categories for your projects.

2 Add projects to the categories.

3 Add reports for each project; define the reports based on a template to disseminate the information for that project.

4 Transfer the HTML documents to a central server.

5 Update the data contained in the reports at regular intervals.

6 Add new reports to projects as they are needed and remove old reports.

7 Transfer the updated HTML structure to the central server.

Defining Categories

Categories are containers used to organize projects into meaningful groups. Establish the categories you require and assign projects to them. If the structure of your Web documents changes later, you can rename categories or reassign projects to different categories.

Choose Tools, Wizards, Web Publishing Wizard to start the Wizard. Move forward through the steps using the Next button, or go back to change an entry using the Back button.

Choose to define categories for your HTML structure.

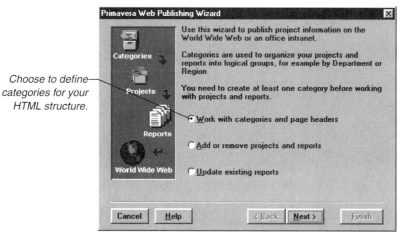

Type or browse the path to the directory where you want to store the HTML files the Wizard creates. This directory can be on your local hard drive or on a network drive, but it must remain constant for the entire document structure.

 If more than one person will be working with the HTML documents, you should place these files on a network server to facilitate access to the documents.

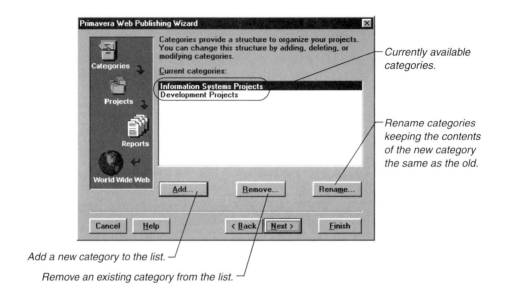

Currently available categories.

Rename categories keeping the contents of the new category the same as the old.

Add a new category to the list.

Remove an existing category from the list.

■ If you are creating a new document structure, add the categories that will be necessary to group the projects in the new structure.

■ If the existing categories no longer define the overall project structure adequately, or if you decide that a project belongs in a different organizational structure, you can add new categories to the structure.

■ Rename a category if the label does not accurately reflect the projects that it includes. When you rename a category, all projects associated with the old category are now associated with the new category. Reassign projects that no longer fit in the new category.

 Removing a category also removes the HTML documents for any projects and reports that are associated with the category.

When you finish defining categories, click Continue and the Wizard adds the categories to the document structure, then you can immediately define projects and reports for the categories. To examine the document structure before transferring it to a central server, mark the Open The Reports And Other Documents In Your Web Browser checkbox before you click Finish. To add the categories and exit the Wizard, click Finish.

 The names for all files and references in your document structure are in uppercase letters. The category page for the document structure is always PRMINDEX.HTM.

Defining Header Information

You can customize your document structure by adding information to the header of each Web page you generate. The header information you designate remains consistent throughout the document structure. Any header information you add is optional. If you do not want to display header information, clear the default settings in the fields and click Next.

Choose this option to define header information for your HTML structure.

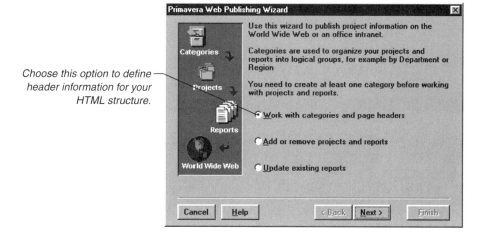

Header information can contain the company name, a link to a Web page, and a graphic logo file in .GIF or JPEG (.JPG) format.

Type the complete Universal Resource Locator (URL), or Web address, of the Web page you want to link to, including the HyperText Transfer Protocol (HTTP) designation.

Type the name of your company, using up to 48 characters.

Type or browse the path to the graphic file you want to attach to the HTML header.

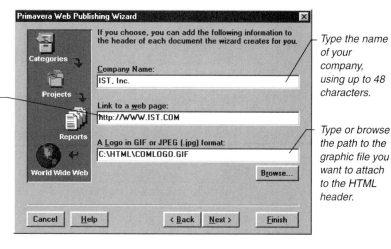

Defining Projects and Reports

If you have not defined categories for your document structure, see *Defining Categories* earlier in this chapter.

The Primavera Web Publishing Wizard helps you create a structure of HTML documents based on the projects and reports you define. Using the Wizard enables you to keep and manage only one set of documents that others on your team can access using standard Web browsers.

To start the Primavera Web Publishing Wizard Choose Tools, Wizards, Web Publishing Wizard, or click Continue in the final step of defining categories. Move forward through the steps using the Next button, or return to a previous step using the Back button.

Adding project Web pages Select the projects and reports that will form the basis of the HTML structure, or that you want to add to an existing structure.

Choose this option to add a new project and define reports for an existing project.

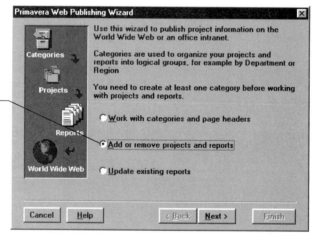

Type or browse the path to the directory where you want to store the HTML files the Wizard creates. This directory can be on your local hard drive or on a network drive, but it must remain constant for the entire document structure.

 If more than one person will be working with the HTML documents, place these files on a network server to facilitate access to the documents.

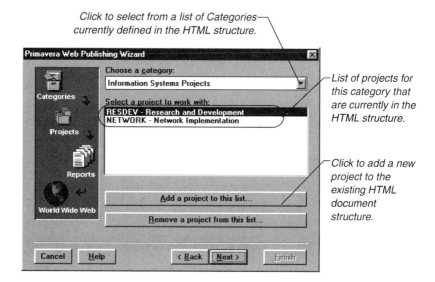

*Click to select from a list of Categories—
currently defined in the HTML structure.*

*List of projects for
this category that
are currently in the
HTML structure.*

*Click to add a new
project to the
existing HTML
document
structure.*

Projects in the hierarchical structure of HTML pages are grouped into
categories, such as Development Projects or Information System Projects.
You must define categories before you can add projects or reports.

Defining reports for projects After you add a project to the HTML
structure, define reports for the project to disseminate the project information. Define a set of reports and add those reports to the list. The
Primavera Web Publishing Wizard includes five basic report templates:

- Classic Schedule Report, showing basic activity information
  including, Activity ID, Activity Description, Remaining Duration,
  Percent Complete, Early Start, Early Finish, Late Start, Late Finish,
  and Total Float.

- Cost Report, showing activity cost information including, Activity
  ID, Activity Description, Remaining Duration, Percent Complete,
  Budgeted Cost, Cost To Date, Cost To Complete, Cost At
  Completion, and Completion Variance Cost.

- Pred/Succ Report, showing activity predecessors and successors
  including, Predecessor ID, Predecessor Description, Relationship
  Type, Relationship Lag, Early Start, Early Finish, Total Float,
  Activity ID, Activity Description, Remaining Duration, Early Start,
  Early Finish, Total Float, Successor ID, Successor Description,
  Relationship Type, Relationship Lag, Early Start, Early Finish, and
  Total Float.

■ Resource Assignment Report, showing resource assignments for each activity including, Activity ID, Activity Description, Remaining Duration, Percent Complete, Resource Description, Driving, Units, Budgeted Quantity, Quantity To Date, Quantity To Complete, and Quantity At Completion.

■ Target Comparison Report, showing current activity dates compared with target dates including, Activity ID, Activity Description, Original Duration, Remaining Duration, Percent Complete, Early Start, Target Start, Early Finish, Target Finish, and Finish Variance.

You can create a report in the project you selected that contains specific activities by selecting one of the five template reports included with the Primavera Web Publishing Wizard and applying a filter from the project.

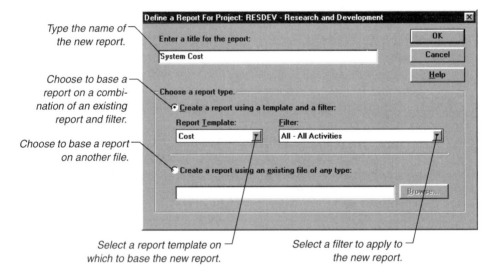

Type the name of the new report.

Choose to base a report on a combination of an existing report and filter.

Choose to base a report on another file.

Select a report template on which to base the new report.

Select a filter to apply to the new report.

After you define the projects and reports that you want to add, click Finish and the Wizard creates the HTML documents. All filenames for these documents are in uppercase letters. Once you create the structure, transfer it to your server.

If you want to examine the document structure before transferring it to a central server, mark the Open The Reports And Other Documents In Your Web Browser checkbox before you click Finish. The Primavera Web Publishing Wizard opens the PRMINDEX.HTM file with your browser, enabling you to inspect the document structure.

Reports containing many activities can cause problems with your browser; for this reason, Primavera recommends that you use filters to reduce larger reports into smaller sections.

For more information about file transfer protocol, see *Transfer Files to the Internet* in the Web Wizard Help.

Transferring pages to the World Wide Web If you intend to place your HTML documents on the World Wide Web, you will need to transfer them to your server using File Transfer Protocol (FTP). FTP programs are usually available from your Internet provider, or you can download them from their companies' Web sites.

Transfer the entire document structure the first time you create it. When you update the document structure you only need to transfer the updated pages; however, when adding a new report or project to a document structure, the index pages for the category or project will be regenerated by the Wizard and must also be transferred.

Basing a Report on Another File

In addition to using the reports provided with the Primavera Web Publishing Wizard, you can base a report on any other type of file. For example, a report can be a .GIF format picture of a construction site, or the schematics for a new circuit board. To base a report on another file type, choose Create A Report Using An Existing File Of Any Type and type or browse the path to the file.

If you choose to base the report on a file type that is not supported by HTML, you will need to specify a file association (helper application) on your Web browser in order to view the file. For example, if you add a .PDF (Portable Document Format) file for viewing the layout of a project, define Acrobat Reader as your helper application.

Removing Projects and Reports

As projects progress, you may find that certain projects or reports are no longer required in your document structure. You can remove these projects and reports from the document structure.

To remove a project Choose Add Or Remove Projects And Reports and type or browse the location of the HTML files.

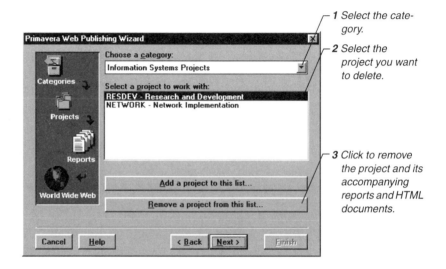

1 Select the category.

2 Select the project you want to delete.

3 Click to remove the project and its accompanying reports and HTML documents.

 Removing a project also removes the HTML documents for any reports that are associated with the project.

To remove a report Choose Add Or Remove Projects And Reports and type or browse the location of the HTML files. Select the category and project containing the report(s) you want to remove, then click Next.

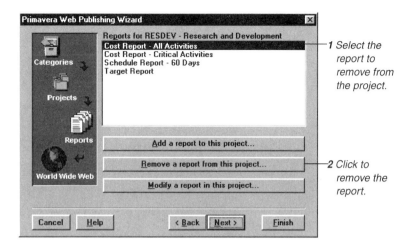

1 *Select the
report to
remove from
the project.*

2 *Click to
remove the
report.*

For details about transferring
HTML pages to the World
Wide Web, see *Defining
Projects and Reports* earlier
in this chapter.

After you specify the projects and reports that you want to remove, click
Finish and the Wizard creates the HTML documents. If you want to
examine the updated document structure before transferring it to a central
server, mark the Open The Reports And Other Documents In Your Web
Browser checkbox before you click Finish. The Primavera Web
Publishing Wizard opens the PRMINDEX.HTM file with your browser,
allowing you to inspect the document structure.

Once you modify the structure, transfer it to your server.

 *Removing a project or report from the HTML structure does
not affect the original project data—it only affects the data
within the document structure.*

Updating Reports

Once you create a structure of HTML documents, the Primavera Web Publishing Wizard enables you to update the reports in those documents to reflect the changing status of your project.

Choose this option to update the reports in an existing HTML structure.

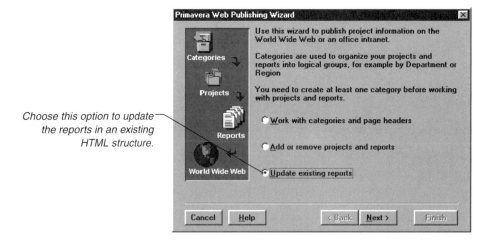

Type or browse the path to the directory where the HTML files are stored. This directory can be on your local hard drive or on a network drive.

You can update all template-based reports. To update a report based on another file type, you must delete the original report and re-define the report using the newer file.

Select the category containing the
project you want to work with.

Select the project containing the
reports you want to modify.

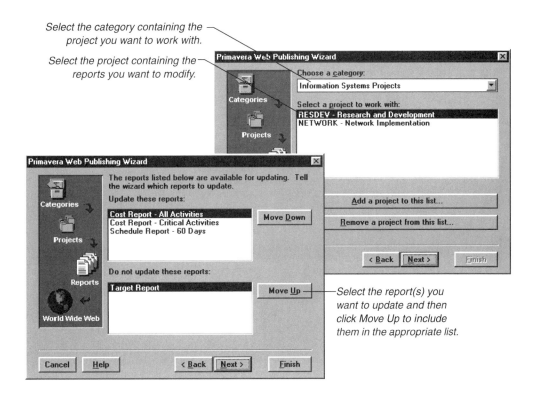

Select the report(s) you
want to update and then
click Move Up to include
them in the appropriate list.

For details about transferring HTML pages to a central server, see *Defining Projects and Reports* earlier in this chapter.

After you select the projects and reports that you want to update, click Finish and the Wizard updates the selected reports with the latest data from your project. If you want to examine the updated document structure before transferring it to a central server, mark the Open The Reports And Other Documents In Your Web Browser checkbox before you click Finish. The Primavera Web Publishing Wizard opens the PRMINDEX.HTM file with your browser, enabling you to inspect the document structure.

Once the reports are updated, transfer the latest structure to your server.

Printing Project Information

When you are ready to print a layout, SureTrak provides options for customizing the printed output. From the Bar chart view, you can print a combination of the Activity columns, Bar chart, Resource profile, and Resource table, or you can print any of these elements individually. From the PERT view, you can print the entire layout or the Trace Logic view.

Printing the Current Project

You can print the current project layout at any time; everything except printer-dependent color variations appears on the printed output as it does onscreen.

Choose File, Print to print the layout using the current project window and print settings. Use the Print dialog box to select a printer, define the range of pages to print, specify the number of copies of each page to print, and indicate whether to print to a file or directly to a printer.

For information about creating and printing reports, see the *Creating SureTrak Reports* chapter.

An alternative to printing the project window display is to print a report. A report provides a way of setting up a printout—a filter, layout, and page options—and saving those printout settings for use again later.

Before printing from SureTrak, first use the Microsoft Windows Control Panel to install a printer. If you are using other Windows applications, you probably have already done this.

To print the current project Choose File, Print. Specify the print range and number of copies, and indicate whether you want to print to a file. Click OK.

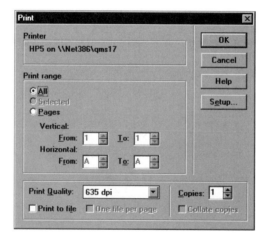

Numbering pages SureTrak numbers pages horizontally and vertically, assigning numbers to rows of pages, and letters to columns of pages. For example, the first page is 1A; the page to its right is 1B; the page below 1A is 2A.

To select specific noncontiguous pages for printing, display the project in Print Preview.

For more information, see *Using Print Preview* later in this chapter.

When you print, you can specify that you want to print all pages, for example, 1A through 3C; or part of the range of pages, such as 2A through 3C, the last two rows. Use the Print Range section of the Print dialog box to specify the pages to print. SureTrak prints an entire row of pages before printing the next row.

To print a range of pages Choose File, Print to open the Print dialog box. In the Print Range section, choose Pages. In the Horizontal From field, specify the column letter of the first page you want to print; in the Horizontal To field, specify the column letter of the last page you want to print. In the Vertical From field, specify the row number of the first page you want to print; in the Vertical To field, specify the column number of the last page you want to print. Click OK.

Printing to a file You can save a "printed" copy of the project as a disk file if you want to print it later or at another location. SureTrak creates the file for the currently selected printer; select the printer to which this file will eventually be printed before you perform this operation.

For example, if you select a Hewlett-Packard plotter, SureTrak creates an HP-GL (Hewlett-Packard Graphics Language) file. If you select a PostScript printer, SureTrak creates a PostScript file—regardless of whether this printer is actually connected to your computer or network. (The printer driver, however, must be installed on your computer.)

When you print to a file, you specify the name of that file. To store all pages in one file, clear the One File Per Page checkbox. To store each page in a separate file, mark the One File Per Page checkbox; each resulting file matches the filename you specify, plus an extension that designates the page number. For example, if you name the print file TEST, the files for separate pages will be named TEST.001, TEST.002, TEST.003, TEST.004, and so forth. Pages are numbered sequentially, across an entire row of pages before beginning the next row.

To print to a file

1 Choose File, Print to open the Print dialog box.

2 Mark the Print to File checkbox.

3 Specify whether you want a separate file for each page.

4 Click OK to open the Print to File dialog box.

5 Specify a filename, directory, and drive. Do not specify a filename extension.

6 Click OK.

Formatting Bar Chart View Page Settings

You can control the appearance of a printed project by changing margins, page headers, and page footers, as well as the items in the layout. When viewing and printing the Bar chart view, these include the Activity columns, activity bars, timescale, relationships, and Resource profile and table. Use the Page Setup dialog box to control the general appearance of the printed project.

For more information about reports, see the Creating SureTrak Reports *chapter.*

Control more specific aspects, such as bar colors and shapes, by changing the layout or creating a report. To specify other print options, such as the paper size or printer, use the Print Setup dialog box.

To format the Bar chart page settings Choose File, Page Setup.

SureTrak includes activities whose bars fall within the range of dates you specify. To further limit the activities that appear, apply a filter.

Mark to preview or print without the use of color or grayscale tones.

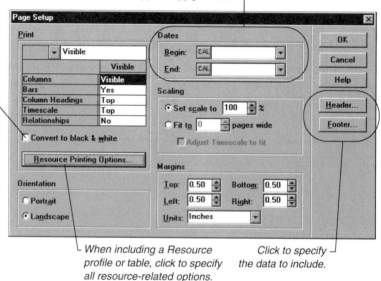

When including a Resource profile or table, click to specify all resource-related options.

Click to specify the data to include.

To print the Activity columns organized by activity data, outline, or work breakdown structure, first organize the layout.

You can print any combination of the project window elements: Activity columns, Bar chart, Resource profile or table. If you choose to print only the Activity columns, the printed report looks like a spreadsheet. Or you can print only the Bar chart, with or without a Resource table or profile. The items you choose to print have no effect on the layout; conversely, what you display in the layout has no effect on the elements you can print, unless you choose to print only visible Activity columns.

For information on organizing layouts, see the *Using SureTrak Layouts* chapter.

To print all, visible, or no Activity columns Right-click in the Columns cell in the Visible column and select All, Visible, or None from the drop-down list. Select All to print all Activity columns; Visible to print only those columns that currently appear in the project window to the left of the vertical split bar; or None to suppress all Activity columns on the printout.

To show or hide the Bar chart on a printout Double-click in the Bars cell in the Visible column to toggle between Yes and No.

Use the Columns dialog box to specify the Activity column titles to include, their alignment, and font size.

To position the Activity column titles Right-click in the Column Headings cell in the Visible column, and select Top, Bottom, Both, or None for the placement of the Activity column titles. If you select Both, SureTrak prints the titles at the top and bottom of each page.

To position the timescale Right-click the Timescale cell in the Visible column, and select Top, Bottom, Both, or None for the placement of the timescale. If you select Both, SureTrak prints the timescale at the top and bottom of each page that contains a Bar chart or a Resource profile or table.

For more information about setting up column titles, see the *Customizing the Bar Chart View* chapter.

Control the timescale's scope and minimum increment in the Timescale dialog box if you want these changes to affect the project window as well; or use the Begin and End Dates in the Page Setup dialog box if you want the changes to affect only the printed project.

To show or hide relationship lines in a printout Double-click in the Relationships cell in the Visible column to toggle between Yes and No. Select No to hide relationships on the printed layout, or Yes to print relationships.

Choose Format, Relationship Lines to open the Format Relationships Lines dialog box where you can specify the relationships that appear in the layout, and differentiate between critical, driving, and nondriving relationships by specifying the line types and colors used to represent them.

For information about headers and footers, see *Formatting Headers and Footers* later in this chapter.

To print a draft or to a single-color printer To see how your printout will look without the colors you formatted for it, or to print a draft of your project quickly, mark the Convert to Black and White checkbox.

Converting to black and white temporarily converts all sight lines, relationship lines, bar borders, and text to black; and all fill colors to white. Clear this checkbox to switch back to color or grayscaled printing, depending on the printer driver you selected.

Specifying the size Specify the number of horizontal pages to print in the Fit To ___ Pages Wide field, or specify a scaling factor (up to 400%) and SureTrak calculates the number of pages needed to scale the image. If you scale the image, a scaling factor greater than 100% zooms in, and a factor less than 100% zooms out. Use Print Preview to see the effect. When specifying the number of horizontal pages, the default setting of 0 pages automatically matches the zoom level of the onscreen display. Use Print Preview to see how many sheets SureTrak proposes; specify more or fewer pages and SureTrak scales the image accordingly.

 If you enter both a scale percentage and a number of horizontal pages, SureTrak ignores the scale percentage and calculates the scale based on the specified number of horizontal pages.

For more information about specifying date ranges, see *Defining the Date Range for Printing* later in this chapter.

If the range of dates specified in the Dates section of the Page Setup dialog box is too long to print using the current timescale density and the specified number of horizontal sheets, SureTrak can adjust the overall scale of the image or adjust the timescale density to force the dates to fit. Mark the Adjust Timescale To Fit checkbox to use this feature.

Printing Resource/Cost profiles If your Bar chart view includes a Resource/cost profile, you can print it together with the Bar chart and Activity columns. Click Resource Printing Options to open the Resource dialog box.

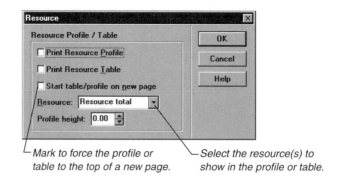

└ *Mark to force the profile or table to the top of a new page.*

└ *Select the resource(s) to show in the profile or table.*

Specify the profile height using the unit of measure you specified in the Units field in the Page Setup dialog box. The default setting (0) scales the profile to fit at the bottom of the last row of pages. If there are just a few bars on the page, and the profile is disproportionately tall, specify a smaller size for the profile. If the profile will not fit at the bottom of the last row of pages, SureTrak creates a new row of pages and prints the profile by itself.

Defining the Date Range for Printing

The settings of the Begin and End Date fields in the Bar chart view's Page Setup dialog box determine the portion of the Bar chart that SureTrak prints, and the timespan for the Resource profile or table. By default, SureTrak uses the Begin and End Dates from the Timescale dialog box. Specify different dates in the Page Setup dialog box if you want the timespan of the printed Bar chart to differ from the onscreen timespan.

For more information about filtering activities, see the Selecting Activities by Filter *chapter.*

SureTrak includes columnar information for all activities, including those for which bars are not printed because they are outside the timespan defined by the Begin and End dates in the Page Setup dialog box. To limit the activities to those occurring within a specific timespan for both the Activity columns and the Bar chart, use a filter.

You can use rolling dates rather than exact calendar dates. Rolling dates are relative dates based on the project start, finish, or data date.

To print the Bar chart for the two weeks before and after the data date

1 With the Bar chart view displayed, choose File, Page Setup.

2 In the Dates section, click Cal in the Begin Date field and select Data Date + from the drop-down list of rolling date formats.

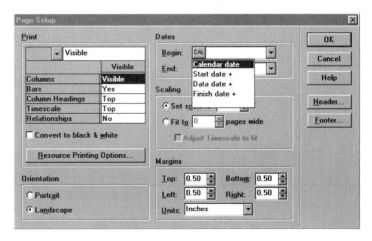

3 Type -14 in the date field, indicating that the printout should begin 14 days, or two weeks, prior to the data date.

4 Repeat steps 2 and 3 in the End Date field, specifying +14 for the end of the timeframe.

Formatting PERT View Page Settings

You can control the appearance of the printed PERT layout by changing margins, page headers, and page footers. Use the Page Setup dialog box to control the general appearance of the printed layout.

For details on layouts and reports, see the Using SureTrak Layouts and Creating SureTrak Reports chapters.

Control more specific aspects, such as activity box colors and shapes, by changing the layout or creating a report. To specify other print options, such as the paper size or printer, use the Print Setup dialog box.

When printing the PERT view, specify whether to print the full PERT view or to print the Trace Logic view. For any other kind of control over which activities appear in the layout, apply a filter.

To print the PERT view Choose View, PERT, then choose File, Page Setup. In the Print area, choose to print the PERT or Trace Logic view.

The default setting, 0, produces an image onscreen at 100% zoom. Specify a smaller number of pages than SureTrak proposes to compress the image to fit the allotted number of pages.

When marked, activity boxes will straddle pages; when cleared, activities that straddle page breaks are moved to the page below or to the right.

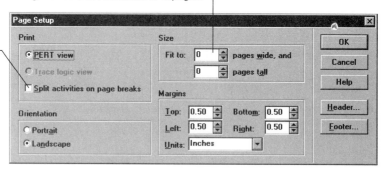

Specifying the size Control the size of the printed output by specifying the number of horizontal or vertical pages. Use Print Preview to see how many pages SureTrak proposes. If you specify a smaller number of horizontal pages, SureTrak scales the printout to fit that number of pages, and uses as many vertical pages (rows of pages) as necessary for that scale. Use the default settings of 0 pages vertically and horizontally and SureTrak provides a best fit.

Choose File, Print Preview to see the effects of your changes, or, if already in Print Preview mode, click OK.

Formatting Headers and Footers

Headers and footers are optional ways to add descriptive information to your printouts. Headers and footers can appear at the top or bottom of the first, last, none, or all pages of a printout. You determine the content of a header or footer, including items such as the project title, important dates, comments, Bar chart or PERT legend, Resource profile legend, a drawing, or even a company logo. You can define one header and one footer for each report you create.

For direct access to the Header and Footer dialog boxes, include the Header and Footer icons in a toolbar.

You can divide each header or footer into as many as six sections, numbered one through six. Use as many of these sections as you want; SureTrak controls their spacing across the page. Specify the information to include in each section by clicking the numbered section and then clicking the appropriate icon. SureTrak presents the appropriate options depending on whether you are viewing the Bar chart or the PERT layout.

To format a header or footer Choose File, Page Setup and click Header or Footer.

Select the numbered section where you want to place the information.

Print the header/footer on the first, last, all, or none of the pages.

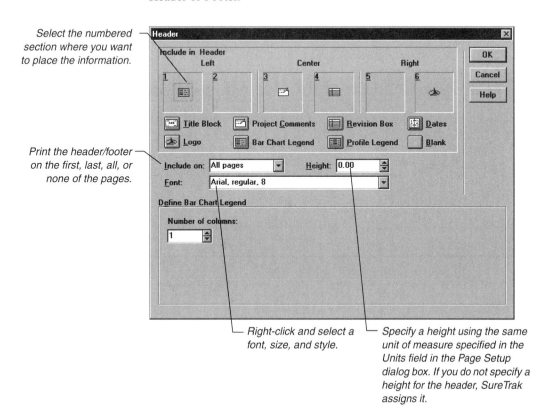

Right-click and select a font, size, and style.

Specify a height using the same unit of measure specified in the Units field in the Page Setup dialog box. If you do not specify a height for the header, SureTrak assigns it.

To preview the printout with headers and footers, choose File, Print Preview.

Choose the element you want to place in the header or footer by clicking its icon in the dialog box. Set up as many header and footer elements as you want. Click OK.

To delete a section of the header or footer Select the section of the header or footer from which you want to remove an element; then click the Blank icon. Setting a section to Blank does not insert a blank space in that section; it removes the element previously defined for the section, allocating the available space to the remaining sections.

Customizing the Title Block

Use the bottom part of the Header or Footer dialog box to customize its elements: the title block, project comments, revision box, dates block, logo, Bar chart legend, PERT legend, and Resource profile legend. For example, if the currently selected header or footer element is the title block, use the Define Title Block section to specify its content.

You can include any or all elements listed in the title block section.

The title block can include information defined elsewhere in your project, such as a revision number. You can also enter up to 48 characters of text. You can define separate title blocks for the header and footer.

The title block is divided into three sections, all of which fit into the numbered header or footer section you selected. Insert information into these three sections of the title block based on whether you want items in each section to be left-justified, centered, or right-justified.

To define the title block Choose File, Page Setup and click Header or Footer.

Select a numbered section of the header or footer.

Click the Title Block icon.

Click and select from a drop-down list of options to include in the title block. You can put text in any or all three fields.

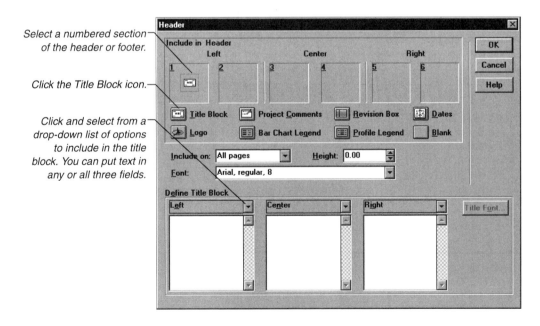

Select Page Number *and* Page Count *from the drop-down list to display information in the format* Page X of Y *in the title block.*

In the Define Title Block section, the field you select determines the justification of the text within the section, not within the entire header or footer. Selecting the Left or Right fields positions the title block flush left or flush right, respectively, in the section. Selecting Center centers the title block in the section.

Customizing the title block font Click Title Font in the Header or Footer dialog box to change the font for any of the three sections of the title block. For example, to print the Project Title in a large font in the middle (centered-text) title block, select the Center field and click Title Font. Select the font, style, and size from the Fonts dialog box.

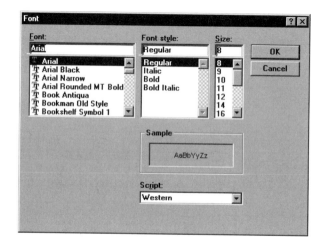

Customizing the Revision Box

You can create a revision box in the header or footer to make notes about any approvals related to your project. The revision box can be blank with space for handwritten notes, or you can type revision notations directly in the revision box in the Header or Footer dialog box.

To include a blank revision box in the header or footer Choose File, Page Setup and click Header or Footer. Select a numbered section of the header or footer. Click the Revision Box icon. Click OK.

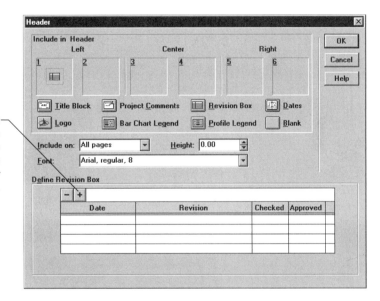

Click to add rows. You can also select a date from the pop-up calendar for the Date cell and enter text for other cells.

To customize the revision box

1 Choose File, Page Setup and click Header or Footer.

2 Select the section of the header or footer in which you have inserted the revision box.

3 In the Define Revision Box section, click any empty cell to add the first row of the revision box.

4 To specify a date, right-click in the date field and select a date from the pop-up calendar.

5 Add other revision information by clicking in the Revision, Checked, or Approved cells and typing any appropriate text.

6 Add more rows to the revision box by repeating steps four through six, or click OK.

Customizing the Dates Block

Use the dates block to show any or several of the project's dates: start date, finish date, data date, must finish date, target finish date, or printout production (run) date. You can include any of these dates in the title block, or put them in the date-block area of the header or footer. You can also include other kinds of information, such as project title, in the date block.

Company name	Olson Media Enterprises
Layout	RADIO
Start date	08AUG96
Finish date	26NOV96
Run date	03JAN97
Page number	1A
© Primavera Systems, Inc.	

To set up the dates block

1   Choose File, Page Setup to open the Page Setup dialog box.

2   In the Page Setup dialog box, click Header or Footer.

3   Select the section of the header or footer in which you want to put the date block.

4   Click the Dates icon.

5   Right-click in the first Data Item cell, and select a data item from the drop-down list. Add up to six rows of information in the dates block.

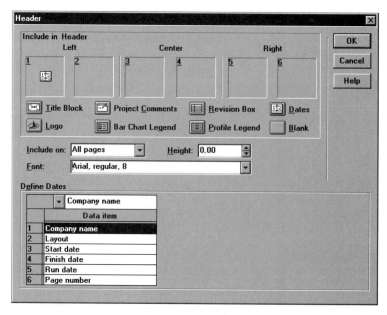

Creating Logos, Graphics, and Legends

To include a company logo or other symbol in the header or footer, click the Logo icon. Right-click the Type field and select from an extensive list of files types including bitmaps (.BMP) and Windows metafiles (.WMF). At the bottom of the Header or Footer dialog box, specify the file name, file type, and location of the symbol or logo you want to use.

To select a logo or other picture

1 Choose File, Page Setup to open the Page Setup dialog box then click Header or Footer.

2 Select the section of the header or footer in which you want to put a graphic.

3 Click the Logo icon.

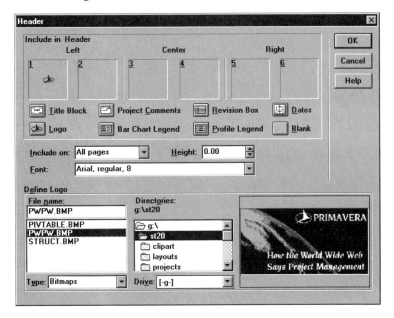

4 In the bottom portion of the dialog box, change the drive and/or directory to the location of the graphic, if necessary.

5 In the Type field, specify whether you are selecting a bitmap (.BMP), Primavera Draw file (.PMT), metafile (.WMF), or other file type.

6 Select the file from the File Name list. Preview the graphic in the lower right corner of the dialog box.

7 Click OK.

To print a legend If you print the Bar chart, PERT view, or the Resource profile, you can include the corresponding legend in the header or footer. Legends identify the color, bar style, and line types for various bars, activity boxes, endpoints, histograms, and curves.

Use the bottom portion of the dialog box to specify legend formatting. For example, if you have several bars and endpoints, you may want to divide the legend into two or three columns.

1 Choose File, Page Setup to open the Page Setup dialog box.

2 In the Page Setup dialog box, click Header or Footer.

3 Select the section (numbered 1–6) of the header or footer in which you want to put the Resource profile legend or the Bar chart legend.

4 Click the Bar Chart Legend or Profile Legend icon for the Bar chart view, or the PERT Legend icon for the PERT view.

When defining a Bar chart legend, these are the available objects. Different objects are available for PERT legends.

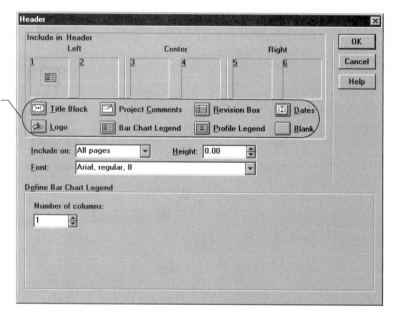

5 For the Bar chart or Resource Profile legend, indicate how many columns SureTrak should divide the legend into in the Number of Columns field.

6 Click OK.

Using Print Preview

Print Preview is a quick and convenient way to view the current layout, page breaks, margins, header and footer, as well as check the number of pages that SureTrak will print. You can also adjust the appearance of the project while in Print Preview.

Print Preview shows miniature versions of the pages in your printout as they will print. You can see one page at a time, several rows and columns of pages, or zoom in for a closeup of part of a page. Although you cannot change project data (activities and resources) in this view, you can change the layout. For example, perhaps a small change to row height or timescale density will fit the project more aesthetically on the size of page on which you are printing.

If you change the layout while in Print Preview, the changes remain when you return to the project window. If several projects are open that use the same layout, when you modify that layout in one project—whether in Print Preview or the project window—that layout changes for all open projects.

 To add or delete activities, change activity or resource information, specify new relationships among activities, or insert page breaks, you must return from Print Preview to the project window.

Navigating the Print Preview pages The preview window initially displays the first page of the printout. The current page number and the total number of pages appear at the left end of the status bar, at the bottom of the window. SureTrak labels pages horizontally and vertically, assigning numbers to rows of pages, and letters to columns of pages. The first page is 1A. If the printout contains only one row of pages, they are numbered 1A, 1B, 1C, and so on. If the printout contains only one column of pages, they are numbered 1A, 2A, 3A, and so on.

To move from page to page in Print Preview Click the Page Left ◀, Page Right ▶, Page Up ▲, and Page Down ▼ buttons to move from page to page. If no page exists to the right, left, above, or below, the corresponding button is unavailable.

To view one page at a time in Print Preview Choose View, Single Page to display one page at a time.

To view multiple pages at once in Print Preview Choose View, Entire Document, to display several pages at once and see a "bird's-eye view" of your project.

To switch view from many pages to one specific page While viewing multiple pages in Print Preview, click any page to view it in single-page mode. Choose View, Entire Document to return to the multi-page view.

To print from Print Preview Print from Print Preview as you would print from the project window. You can print all pages or a range of pages. You can also select several noncontiguous pages while in Print Preview.

To print the current page

1 Choose File, Print Preview to display the project in Print Preview.

2 Use the Page Left, Page Right, Page Up, and Page Down buttons to locate the page you want to print.

3 Choose File, Page Setup. In the Print section of the Page Setup dialog box, specify the items to include in the printout. Click OK.

4 Choose File, Print to open the Print dialog box.

5 In the Print Range section of the Print dialog box, choose Current. Set up other printing information as described in the Printing the Current Project section earlier in this chapter.

6 Click OK.

To print selected pages

1 Choose File, Print Preview to display the project in Print Preview.

2 Use the Page Left, Page Right, Page Up, and Page Down icons to locate the page you want to print.

3 Choose File, Page Setup. In the Print section of the Page Setup dialog box, specify the items to include in the printout. Click OK.

4 Choose File, Print to open the Print dialog box.

5 In the Print Range section of the Print dialog box, choose Pages. Specify the desired pages and set up other printing information as described in the Printing the Current Project section of this chapter.

6 Click OK.

Setting Up Zoom Levels

Use SureTrak's zoom features for a closeup or a "bird's-eye" view of portions of the project window. You can also use zoom features in Print Preview.

Zoom in or out incrementally. To zoom out, choose View, Zoom Out; to zoom in, choose View, Zoom In. In Print Preview you can zoom out by clicking the right mouse button, and zoom in by clicking the left.

To set an exact zoom level, choose View, Zoom. Choose one of the zoom percentages listed, or choose Custom and specify a magnification percentage between 25 and 400.

The Scale to Fit option automatically zooms to the magnification that fits one page to the project window. Using Scale to Fit is equivalent to clicking the View Single Page icon in Print Preview.

Copying Part of the Project Window

You can copy any visible area of the project window and insert it in any application that accepts bitmaps or metafile graphics. This feature is useful if you are preparing a report in a word processing document and want to use parts of the project as illustrations. When you copy part of the project window, you are taking a "snapshot" of it. The copied excerpt does not reflect subsequent changes to the project.

To copy a picture

1 Scroll around the project window until the information you want to copy is visible.

2 Choose Edit, Copy Picture; the mouse pointer changes to a camera and crosshairs.

3 Position the crosshairs in the upper left corner of the area you want to copy.

4 Drag the mouse down and to the right, enclosing the area you want to copy within a boundary box drawn with a dotted line.

5 When the boundary box encloses the area of the project window you want to copy, release the mouse button. The boundary box disappears and SureTrak places the copied image on the Clipboard.

Pasting information The image remains on the Clipboard until you clear the Clipboard, cut or copy another piece of information to the Clipboard, or exit Windows. You can paste the information as many times as you want while it remains on the Clipboard.

To paste the image into another application Open the application into which you want to paste the SureTrak project image. Position the cursor at the location you want to insert the SureTrak picture. Paste the picture using Paste commands appropriate for the application to which you are pasting. For Microsoft Windows 3.x- and Windows 95-compliant applications, press Ctrl+V.

Controlling Page Breaks

When you print a project, SureTrak automatically divides the output into pages. You can preview where these page breaks will fall before you print. In the Bar chart view, you can insert "hard" page breaks between activities or activity groups. In the PERT view, you can start new pages based on activity groups.

To display page breaks in the Bar chart view You can display page break indicators on page-break rulers at the top and left edges of the layout. With the Bar chart view displayed, choose View, Page Breaks.

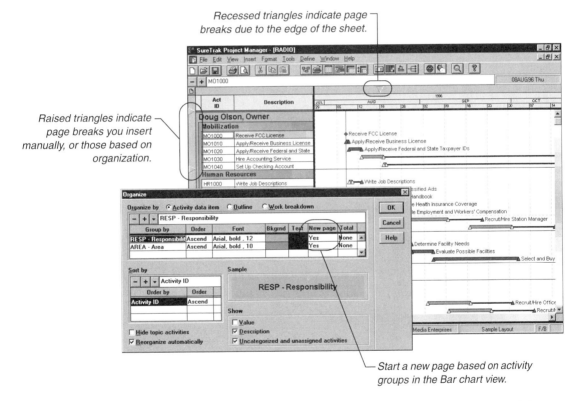

Recessed triangles indicate page breaks due to the edge of the sheet.

Raised triangles indicate page breaks you insert manually, or those based on organization.

Start a new page based on activity groups in the Bar chart view.

In the Bar chart view, to delete a "hard" page break, select the activity below the page break and choose Insert, Delete Page Break; to clear all "hard" page breaks, choose Insert, Clear All Page Breaks; to recalculate all automatic page breaks, choose Insert, Repaginate.

To insert a page break at a specific location

1 Choose View, Page Breaks.

2 Select the activity you want to print at the top of the next page.

For details on inserting page breaks based on groups of activities, see the *Organizing and Summarizing Activities* chapter.

3 Choose Insert, Page Break. SureTrak displays a raised triangle on the page-break ruler in the left margin, just above the selected activity.

Drag the page break up or down to adjust its location.

 Control horizontal page breaks in the Bar chart view by adjusting the timescale density, column widths, or the beginning and ending dates of the printout.

To display page breaks in the PERT view

When using the PERT view, choose File, Print Preview and SureTrak calculates the exact location of each page break. Return to the PERT view, then choose View, Page Breaks to toggle page break indicators on or off. Page break indicators, which appear onscreen as thick, black, vertical and horizontal lines, appear where page breaks will fall in printed output. Use page break indicators as an aid in precise placement of activities that would otherwise straddle page borders. For example, if one or two activities fall on a page by themselves, you can manually drag those activities to an open area on the previous page.

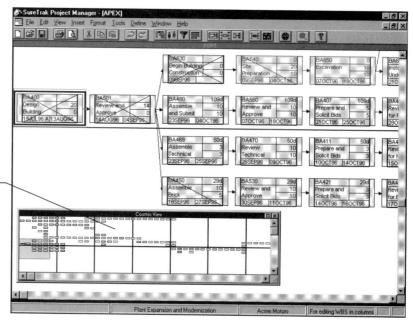

Choose View, Cosmic View to see a bird's eye perspective of the network, including the locations of all page breaks and their relationships to the activity boxes.

Selecting a Printer

To select a printer, choose File, Print Setup. When you print from SureTrak, you can use the default printer or change to another printer or plotter installed in Windows for your computer. Control some aspects of printing from the Print Setup dialog box: choose Portrait (long edge vertical) or Landscape (long edge horizontal) orientation, and specify the paper size and source.

The printers listed in this dialog box are those installed on your computer through the Microsoft Windows Control Panel. If the printer you want to use does not appear on the list, use Control Panel to install the printer.

For details on advanced print options, refer to your Windows documentation.

You can access advanced printer setup options by clicking Options in the Print Setup dialog box. Available options depend on the type of printer you are using.

To use the default printer Choose File, Print Setup to open the Print Setup dialog box; choose Default Printer; click OK.

To use a specific (non-default) printer Choose File, Print Setup to open the Print Setup dialog box. Choose Specific Printer. Then click ▼ and select from a drop-down list of available printers. Click OK.

 If you use a color printer, SureTrak automatically selects printer colors that most closely match the colors displayed onscreen.

Changing page orientation You can set the paper orientation in the Page Setup dialog box, and the paper orientation, size, and source in the Print Setup dialog box. When you open a project, SureTrak remembers its previous page orientation and applies it to the entire printout.

Choose File, Print Setup or File, Page Setup. Choose Portrait (long edge vertical) or Landscape (long edge horizontal) orientation; click OK.

 You need not specify page orientation in both the Print Setup and Page Setup dialog boxes. Changing page orientation in one dialog box changes it in the other.

To select a paper size and source Use the Paper Size and Source fields to select any paper size your printer supports. When you specify a paper size or source, that information applies to the entire printout.

1 Choose File, Print Setup to open the Print Setup dialog box.

2 Click ▾ in the Paper Size field and select a paper size from the drop-down list.

3 Click ▾ in the Paper Source field and select a source from the drop-down list.

4 Click OK.

If the Options button is available, additional options for print quality are available, depending on the type of printer. For example, if you select a Hewlett-Packard LaserJet III, three options are available for print quality: High, Medium, and Low. If you select a PostScript printer, only one option may be available: 300 dpi. Click ▾ in the Print Quality field and select an option from the drop-down list.

Index

Symbols

PRIMAVERA LICENSE AGREEMENT

This is a legal agreement between you, the end user, and Primavera Systems, Inc. By using the software you are agreeing to be bound by the terms of this agreement. If you do not agree to the terms of this agreement, promptly return the software and the accompanying items (including printed materials and containers) to the place you obtained them for a full refund.

1. GRANT OF LICENSE. Primavera grants to you A NON-EXCLUSIVE right to use one copy of the enclosed Primavera software program ("the SOFTWARE") in OBJECT CODE FORM on a single terminal connected to a single computer (i.e., with a single CPU), or on a LICENSED COMPUTER NETWORK. A computer network is any combination of two or more terminals that are electronically linked and capable of sharing the use of a single software program. A LICENSED COMPUTER NETWORK is a computer network for which you have purchased one copy of Primavera SOFTWARE for each user of the SOFTWARE on the network.

2. COPYRIGHT. The SOFTWARE (including any images, "applets", photographs, animation, video, audio, music, and text incorporated into the SOFTWARE) is owned by Primavera or its suppliers and is protected by United States copyright laws and international treaty provisions. THE SOFTWARE IS LICENSED, AND NOT SOLD. Therefore, you must treat the SOFTWARE like any other copyrighted material (e.g., a book or musical recording) except that you may either (a) make one copy of the SOFTWARE solely for backup or archival purposes, or (b) transfer the SOFTWARE to a single hard disk, provided that you keep the original solely for backup or archival purposes. You may not copy the written materials accompanying the SOFTWARE.

3. OTHER RESTRICTIONS. You may not rent or lease the SOFTWARE, but you may transfer the SOFTWARE and accompanying materials on a permanent basis, provided that you retain no copies and the recipient agrees to the terms of this Agreement. You may not reverse-engineer, decompile, or disassemble the software.

LIMITED WARRANTY

LIMITED WARRANTY. Primavera warrants that (a) the SOFTWARE will perform substantially in accordance with the accompanying materials for a period of 90 days from the date of receipt; and (b) any hardware accompanying the software will be free of defects in materials and workmanship under normal use and service for a period of one year from the date of receipt. Any implied warranties on the SOFTWARE and hardware are limited to 90 days and one year respectively. Some states do not allow limitations on duration of an implied warranty, so the above limitation may not apply to you.

CUSTOMER REMEDIES. Primavera's entire liability and your exclusive remedy shall be, at Primavera's option, either (a) return of the price paid or (b) repair or replacement of the SOFTWARE or hardware that does not meet Primavera's Limited Warranty and which is returned to Primavera with a copy of your receipt. This Limited Warranty is void if failure of the SOFTWARE or HARDWARE has resulted from accident, abuse, or misapplication. Any replacement SOFTWARE will be warranted for the remainder of the original warranty period or 30 days, whichever is longer. **OUTSIDE THE UNITED STATES, THESE REMEDIES ARE NOT AVAILABLE WITHOUT PROOF THAT YOU ACQUIRED THIS COPY OF THE SOFTWARE FROM AN AUTHORIZED SOURCE.**
NO OTHER WARRANTIES. Primavera disclaims all other warranties, either expressed or implied, including but not limited to implied warranties of merchantability and fitness for a particular purpose, with respect to the SOFTWARE, the accompanying written materials and any accompanying hardware. This limited warranty gives you specific legal rights. You may have others, which vary from state to state.

(continued on next page)

PRIMAVERA LICENSE AGREEMENT *(continued)*

LIMITATION OF LIABILITY. In no event shall Primavera or its suppliers be liable for indirect, special, incidental, economic, consequential or punitive damages whatsoever, regardless of the nature of the claim, (including, without limitation, damages for loss of business profits, business interruption, loss of business information, liabilities to third parties arising from any source, or other pecuniary loss) arising out of the use or inability to use this Primavera product, even if Primavera has been advised of the possibility of such damages. In no event shall Primavera's liability exceed the amount paid by you for the SOFTWARE. Because some states do not allow the exclusion or limitation of liability for consequential or incidental damages, the above limitation may not apply to you.

U.S. GOVERNMENT RESTRICTED RIGHTS

The SOFTWARE, documentation and any accompanying hardware are provided with RESTRICTED RIGHTS. Use, duplication, or disclosure by the Government is subject to the restrictions set forth in subparagraph (c)(1)(ii) of The Rights in Technical Data and Computer Software clause at DFARS 252.227-7013 or subparagraphs (c)(1) and (2) of the Commercial Computer Software-Restricted Rights 48 CFR 52.227-19, and our GSA contract, as applicable. Contractor/manufacturer is Primavera Systems, Inc., Two Bala Plaza, Bala Cynwyd, PA 19004.

TERM. This license is effective upon your completion of registration of the SOFTWARE with Primavera, and shall continue until terminated. You may terminate this license by returning the SOFTWARE, the accompanying written materials and all copies thereof to Primavera. Primavera may terminate this license upon the breach by you of any provision contained in this license. Upon such termination by Primavera, you agree to return the Software, the accompanying written materials and all copies thereof to Primavera.

THIS LICENSE AGREEMENT REPRESENTS THE ENTIRE AGREEMENT BETWEEN YOU AND PRIMAVERA CONCERNING THE SOFTWARE, AND IT SUPERSEDES ANY PRIOR PROPOSAL, REPRESENTATION, OR UNDERSTANDING BETWEEN THE PARTIES.

This Agreement is governed by the substantive laws of the Commonwealth of Pennsylvania. If this product was purchased outside the United States, then local law may apply.